Speaking of Economics

Based on themes emerging from his popular *Conversations with Economists* (1983), Arjo Klamer once again distinguishes himself from other academic economists by writing about the profession – and its foibles – in plain English. How is it that a discipline that so permeates daily life is at once "soft" and scientific, powerful and ignored, noble and disdained? Here is an attempt to make sense of all that. Whether you are a student, academician, journalist, practicing economist, or interested outsider, *Speaking of Economics* will get you interested in a conversation about economics.

Economists disagree so fundamentally that conversation becomes impossible: students of the most prestigious graduate schools emerge with significantly different views; mathematical equations become more real than the everyday world. And, after all these years, the Nobel Prize-worthy profession cannot tell us, say, how a 1 percent increase in the price of electricity will affect the utility industry. How can this be a science? Here, an economist reconciles all of this with an intimacy and readability rarely seen in books concerning economics – *without* eschewing academic methodology. We come away with the sense that, despite its strangeness and pitfalls, economics *is* scientific and powerful and noble.

Arjo Klamer is Professor of Cultural Economics at Erasmus University in Rotterdam, the Netherlands, and dean of the Academia Vitae.

Economics as social theory
Series edited by Tony Lawson
University of Cambridge

Social theory is experiencing something of a revival within economics. Critical analyses of the particular nature of the subject matter of social studies and of the types of method, categories and modes of explanation that can legitimately be endorsed for the scientific study of social objects are re-emerging. Economists are again addressing such issues as the relationship between agency and structure, between economy and the rest of society, and between the enquirer and the object of enquiry. There is a renewed interest in elaborating basic categories such as causation, competition, culture, discrimination, evolution, money, need, order, organization, power, probability, process, rationality, technology, time, truth, uncertainty, value, etc.

The objective for this series is to facilitate this revival further. In contemporary economics the label "theory" has been appropriated by a group that confines itself to largely asocial, ahistorical, mathematical "modelling." Economics as Social Theory thus reclaims the "Theory" label, offering a platform for alternative rigorous, but broader and more critical conceptions of theorizing.

Other titles in this series include:

Economics and Language
Edited by Willie Henderson

Rationality, Institutions and Economic Methodology
Edited by Uskali Mäki, Bo Gustafsson and Christian Knudsen

New Directions in Economic Methodology
Edited by Roger Backhouse

Who Pays for the Kids?
Nancy Folbre

Rules and Choice in Economics
Viktor Vanberg

Speaking of Economics
How to get in the conversation

Arjo Klamer

Routledge
Taylor & Francis Group

LONDON AND NEW YORK

First published 2007
by Routledge
2 Park Square, Milton Park, Abingdon, Oxon OX14 4RN

Simultaneously published in the USA and Canada
by Routledge
270 Madison Ave, New York, NY 10016

Reprinted 2007

Routledge is an imprint of the Taylor & Francis Group, an informa
business

Typeset in Times New Roman by
Prepress Projects Ltd, Perth
Printed and bound in Great Britain by
Antony Rowe Ltd, Chippenham, Wiltshire

British Library Cataloguing in Publication Data
A catalogue record for this book is available from the British Library

Library of Congress Cataloging in Publication Data
Klamer, Arjo.
  Speaking of economics: how to get in the conversation/Arjo Klamer.
  p. cm.
  Includes bibliographical references and index.
  ISBN 0-415-39510-0 (hb) – ISBN 0-415-39511-9 (pb) 1. Economics. I.
  Title.
  HB71.K53 2006
  330–dc22

ISBN 978-0-415-39510-6 (hbk)
ISBN 978-0-415-39511-3 (pbk)
ISBN 978-0-203-96448-4 (ebk)

For Marijke and Deirdre

Contents

x   *Contents*

Illustrations

Figures

Tables

Exordium

Getting into the conversation

Nothing Gold Can Stay

Nature's first green is gold,
Her hardest hue to hold.
Her early leaf's a flower;
But only so an hour.
Then leaf subsides to leaf.
So Eden sank to grief,
So dawn goes down to day.
Nothing gold can stay.
Robert Frost, 1923

The towers – boasting grand conference hotels with grand entrances – loom large amidst the urban wasteland of the American metropolis. At street level, people pour out of taxis. The lines to register for the conference lengthen. Lobbies and lounges quickly congest. The guest count exceeds 6,000, all of them economists. Six thousand economists in one place make for a lot of noise, most of it emanating from small and huddled groups. Now and then two people greet each other loudly, enthusiastically. Many stand alone, looking pensive or intimidated – or are they just alone? The talk – heavy now in bars and lounges – fades out long before the next morning when the proceedings start. Sessions take place in small meeting rooms and large ballrooms. People hurry through hallways and outrun escalators. At the elevators, well-dressed (younger) men and women anxiously await the next carriage. They are en route to their interviews in the suites occupied by representatives of universities, colleges, or international organizations looking for new colleagues. In a large hall publishers display their wares. Welcome to the world of economists.

When so viewed, their world must seem somewhat odd. What are they all doing so far away from home, clustered together in a few large hotels? The interviewing of job candidates makes sense. It is, after all, efficient to have all employers and applicants in one place, something that resembles a real market with buyers and sellers – and what we expect from economists. The publishers' displays make sense as well, since they are making money from the economists. But what to make of the conference proceedings? Outsiders will wonder what is going on. The sessions usually have only a few people in attendance. The majority of participants are presenters of papers, their discussants, and a chair. One presenter after another holds a monologue followed by a monologue by one of the discussants. Maybe a few people will have questions. Most are stilted affairs. What is the point, the outsider will ask? Who is getting anything out of these somewhat autistic exchanges? The proceedings in the large ballrooms are no different except for having more people in the audience. The livelier, more animated conversations in the corridors and lobbies are usually not about economics or the economy. Talk about the Fed's latest move, the grand government deficits, the imminent financial crisis, or the enduring poverty gap is rare. It is, rather, gossip and chatter. "[The former Chicago star] is *where*? And did *what*?" Economists apparently prefer to talk about each other and themselves.

Later in the afternoon the hotel suites and smaller ballrooms fill up with people for some reception or another. Economic departments throw them for alumni; publishers to court authors. The refreshments are quite nice. In the evening, the nearby restaurants and cafés fill up with groups of less than flashy-looking people. They are, after all, economists, some still bearing their conference badges. At night they sleep as economists do. (Economists do not make a very exuberant, creative, musical, or, for that matter, erotic crowd.)

Journalists in search of a story are at a loss. Little of what is being discussed in the sessions bears on actual and real-world topics. Economists now talk mostly mathematics (so it seems) – hardly compelling story matter. The journalists, then, are left to write about that – the aloofness of economists, the sorry state of economics, the lack of answers to the provocative questions of the day.

The adventurous will stumble into sessions of alternative groups. Here are the feminist economists; there, the economic methodologists. They will come across the institutionalists, the Christian economics group, the cultural economists, the evolutionary economists, the Austrian economists, the urban economists, the statisticians, the development economists, the financial economists, the Marxists, the post-Keynesians, rhetorical economists, and so on. All appear to form worlds in and of themselves. Outsiders will have difficulties grasping that they are all of one academic field. Hearing all the different voices, they will also wonder who is telling the truth. These are, after all, self-proclaimed scientists. So what about the truth? Or do all these economists tell different versions of it? Someone, please, explain what to make of all this.

I am writing this book to make sense of economists and their world. To show that such a conference is really what economics is about. Yes, it is about the chatter as much as it is about the models, the math, the econometrics, the theories, and the ideas that come from the enormous aggregate of literature that economists generate. Knowing about economics requires the bookwork *and* the mingling with economists.

This book is the result of my finding out what it is that economists do, what makes the science of economics tick. The main point: *think of economics in terms of a conversation, or, better yet, a bunch of conversations.* That may seem odd, but will be much less so after you have read a little further. Things – lots of things – will logically follow (and change) if you start from this main point – like the importance of academic culture, rhetoric, the getting and giving of attention, the subsidiary role of truth as a criterion, the changes of the conversation over time, and the divergences within (and the gap between) what academics do and say and what people do and say in their everyday lives. It all is going to make sense.

I have written with all kinds of people in mind, such as:

- *Students of economics.* I started this book when I began teaching 1,000 or so first-year economics students at the University of Maastricht about the science of economics. I wanted to show you students what it takes to get into the conversation of economists. It is not enough to do the problem sets, to get good grades, and be on good terms with the teacher. A great deal more is at stake. Even if you decide that the conversation of economists is not yours, you will have learned something about what it takes to get into the conversation of your choosing.
- *Practicing economists.* Since you are a teacher, researcher, or policy advisor, you are already in the conversation. You undoubtedly know a great deal about it, probably more than I. But my impression is that not all of you make the effort to seriously reflect on your world. You may, without giving it much thought, "hear voices in the air and distill their frenzy from some [methodological] scribbler a few years back" – in which case I am in for a serious challenge. You may be attached to a different picture of our world, believe that what you do is serious science and get irritated with an equation-less, model-barren book like this. You may even say that this is not economics, not science (surely), and I am therefore not your colleague.

  But even as I wonder whether we have much to say to each other, I wish you would consider the argument, whether it somehow makes sense. You may identify with some of the descriptions of your world and find others at odds with your own experiences. You must agree that it takes a great deal to get into the conversation as well as continuous effort to stay in it, be noticed, and get appreciation for hard work. If you wonder where you stand in the world of economists, let me pose a personal question: Whose applause are you seeking?

  The answer will be revealing. You read more about the implications in the following pages.
- *Well-known economists.* You are one of a small group who work for a reputable university, get cited a lot, and travel the world to attend conferences. You are in the thick of the conversation. I have talked with some of you in the course of my career – see for the record the *Conversations with Economists* (Klamer 1983), the interviews in the *Journal of Economic Perspectives*, and some videos. Most of you have outspoken opinions on what the science of economics is all about, but, truth be told, they are not as fleshed out and developed as the opinions that you hold on theorizing and modeling the economy. I hope

you are not offended by this. It is also in conversation with you that I have developed this perspective on your science. Consider this an invitation to continue, and possibly alter, in a modest way, the conversations.

- *Methodologists and philosophers of science.* I have had you on my mind all the time. After all, I have been quite involved in your conversation. With some of you I appear to have a major disagreement about the best way to depict and characterize the science of economics. Please consider the following as an attempt to further the argumentation. It is a plea to look beyond the propositions of the science and consider the conversations as such (or discursive practices, if you prefer). Please accept this as an exercise in what Alan Janik calls practical philosophy, that is, an attempt to see how economists cope with the complex world of science. Uskali, I already grant you that this argument betrays a realist stance but it wants to be more than that, as I hope you, too, will be able to see. And Mark, pointing at the prominent importance of attention does not necessarily imply that it is foremost on my mind.

  I would not mind having your attention though.
- *Fellow rhetoricians, discursive analysts, and practical philosophers.* This book is obviously meant to be in conversation with you. Need I say more?
- *Austrians, institutionalists, (pomo) Marxists, feminists, and other heterodoxists.* You all will benefit, I think, from the idea that economics is made up of a bunch of conversations. I know you will wish I had been more critical of orthodox economics and more supportive of your approaches, that I had been more explicit about how power works in the profession and gender influences the practice. Please add such arguments. As to the critical edge of this book, maybe my age makes me less willing to be critical in a negative sense. This is meant as a constructive proposal and is, as such, quite critical, at least so I think.
- *Future generations of economists and philosophers.* I am seriously considering the possibility that this book will be a dud, that few economists of this generation will pay it serious attention. The reason could be that it calls for a change of metaphor in the conversation about economics, and people do not make such a change easily. So my hope is vested in the coming generations of economists who are less wedded to one metaphor or another and are willing therefore to entertain a metaphor that really makes sense of what they are getting involved in. Who knows, the current students may already be receptive.
- *Other academics.* The walls that separate the disciplines continue to be thick, all the buzz about interdisciplinary and multidisciplinary work notwithstanding. If it is not our interests and our subjects that separate us, it is that we are in quite different conversations, at least that is what this book points out. Many of those who have read drafts of the book's chapters pointed out that a similar analysis would apply to other disciplines such as your own. They may well be right. The reason I focused so much on the conversations of economists is that I know those better than any other. I would be very pleased, of course,

if this does not prevent us from having a sensible conversation about science and academia. Might it be that this way of looking at our worlds stimulates other priorities? Does it make us realize that multi- and interdisciplinary work amounts to anything only if it leads to sustainable conversations?

You guessed my answers. What are yours?

- *Journalists.* I have talked with quite a few of you and know what frustrations you often experience when you are trying to get a story out of what economists are doing and to explain their ideas in layman's terms. I have learned from your experiences and observations and hope that you recognize them in the following account. Who knows, it all may make a little more sense.

- *Interested outsiders.* You are the non-economists who, professionally or otherwise, are interested in what economists are doing but do not desire to be part of their conversation. You may be an editor of economics books, a manager, a politician in need of economic advice, or just someone interested in economics. Parts of this book are not meant for you as they are about what it takes to get into and stay in the conversation of economists – which you are not interested in. But the overall message is intended to help you to make sense of what it is that economists are doing and why the science that seems to be so strange at first, so contrary to what you would expect, is not so strange after all – *if* you use the proper metaphor to make sense of it. It will also clarify why you may easily feel excluded and not taken seriously by insiders. It is not because economists are necessarily arrogant or exclusionary (although they can be); the nature of their conversations, as you will find out, is the problem.

- *Involved by circumstance.* You are not particularly interested in economics or its practitioners. This book has little to offer you. But suppose you are married to, or befriended by, an economist. You may come to understand that he or she is less weird than you thought, or understand why your partner or friend is often so preoccupied and worries so much about faculty standing or the profession at large. You may be able to appreciate him or her better for learning that it is a tough world. And here is another reason: ever been made to feel stupid in the presence of economists for knowing so little about the economy? Or thought that economists are stupid with their theories that neither predict nor have concrete results? Read on – especially Chapter 8 – and you will realize that no one here is stupid. You and they just live in different worlds or, better put, are in different conversations.

- *The author.* The protocol of the conversation is that we exclude ourselves from the proceedings. Science is about the world out there, and not about us. This book will show that much of what economists do is indeed about themselves and that that is neither strange nor bad. In order to be in a scientific conversation you had better have the right passions, and those you will not have if you do not involve yourself, your own story, in some way or another. Accordingly, a great deal of this book involves me. I have not tried to exclude myself from the story. The point is not to tell you so much about myself but rather to stimulate you, the reader, to figure out where and how you fit in.

Do I qualify as an economist? The question pops up now and then: "Are you an economist really?" I am in the sense that I have a PhD in economics, occupy the chair of cultural economics, write on the cultural dimensions of economies, and do now and then comment on economic affairs via the various news media. But I am not an economist who talks in terms of models, games, complex systems, and the like. I have in the past, and I am well trained in, for example, econometrics. I'd say that I am not in those conversations. Economics is rich, though, and comprises a bunch of conversations; in some I feel quite at home. So, yes, I consider myself an economist, even if here I am writing *about* economists.

The book is personal. (Show me one that is not.) I had to write it. I carried it in me for more than twenty years. It is about time I put my thoughts down on paper. Even if no one pays any attention to them, the book has satisfied my hunger to make sense of the world I am part of.

Being conversational

The style is – what shall I say? – conversational. One reason I try to write simply is to make as much sense as possible. Another is that it underscores the message that economics is a conversation, or better, a bunch of conversations. We are actually in conversation with each other, no matter how we write. Even so, this style is somewhat unusual – non-academic, some would complain. Then again, Plato reported about the thinking of Socrates in the form of dialogues, and Lakatos did something similar in his *Proofs and Refutations* (1976). They pushed the conversational style further than I do here.

The conversational style is also an attempt to draw you in. Even though a book like this makes sense only if you are willing to step away from the daily practice of economics, I suggest we do not distance ourselves too much. I prefer to be as close as possible to the lifeworld of economists, as hermeneutics would put it, that is, the world as you experience it. I hope it works better than the systematic accounts found in so much methodological writing.

Once you become aware of the conversational character of your lifeworld you may begin to look differently at other things in other worlds, like things economically. That is usually what happens when you switch the metaphor. If you ask what follows – the inevitable question when you are partially seduced – the clue lies within. But before getting to that, let us see what evolves in the subsequent pages. We start with the motivational part, with everything that makes economics appear strange, if not weird. After that you will have to read on. At least, so I hope.

Acknowledgments
In conversation with

It is a cliché that no author writes a book on his or her own. Authors are in a conversation with others, and their book has meaning only because of that conversation. A book like this also comes about in numerous conversations, more than I will ever be able to recall. I have appropriated ideas and insights at will. Sometimes I have been able to acknowledge their source, but more often I am unable to trace the origin. After I had been writing quite a bit about attention, and was quite content with myself for having that insight, Olav Velthuis, then still a graduate student, coyly pointed out that he had implanted the seed in my brain in a conversation we had. I had completely forgotten about that particular conversation. Then again, I noticed how others have appropriated ideas that came up in conversations with me without any acknowledgment. So it goes. Authorship is an invention anyway. The conversation comes first.

I do want to acknowledge some of my conversation partners over time. There are too many to list exhaustively. I hope that those who look for their name will find it, and that others can get an idea in which conversational context to place the making of this book. Maybe I go a little too far in listing all these conversations but I am thinking of those who limit their reading of the book to this part.

Joop Klant was the first to show me that you can seriously reflect on what economists do. I was still a student at the time and felt encouraged when he took me seriously as well. As my academic father he inspired me to do it differently from the way he had done it. Too bad he is no longer among us as I surely would have liked to have convinced him. With Wim Driehuis I experienced what it is to practice the craft of economics, and in particular the building of large-scale econometric models. I continue to draw on that experience. Neil de Marchi drew me into real conversations that were not only about economics, Keynes, and all that, but also about personal stuff. Ever since I have taken it for granted that it is possible to combine the academic and the personal, although I have to admit that it does not happen too easily in the academic world. He also helped me to cross from the prudent academics of the Dutch to the more heroic academics of the Americans. At Duke I ran into Martin Bronfenbrenner, Roy Weintraub, Bob Tower, Craufurd Goodwin, and so many other serious and honest economists. Roy Weintraub, in particular, taught me how to change my Dutch (read German) style of writing into the pointed and argumentative way you tend to write in English; above all he made me stand up for my own position. He has immersed himself in the nitty-gritty of the way economists have constructed general equilibrium theory. I suspect that he will find my account too sweeping. We'll see.

Most important of all were the students at Duke: Janet Seiz, Robert Fisher, and Rod Maddock in particular, and Janet most of all. I have not talked so intensely with someone about economics and everything else as I have with her. In our endless conversations I found out not only what I wanted to think but also how to put it in proper English. Neil de Marchi and I organized a seminar on methodology in which Bruce Caldwell also participated. Early on Saturday mornings we had special sessions with students in other disciplines. I still remember those discussions. It was my first experience of talking across disciplines. And don't let me forget my first students, who taught me how strange economics sounds when you hear it for the first time. Anne Pitcher's passion was inspiring, and Linda (whose last name I have forgotten) showed me how to write a final exam with citations only. And then there was the disciple of Ayn Rand – with my bad memory for names I have forgotten hers entirely – who gave me a really hard time and forced me to reconsider a few of my fixed beliefs.

The result of all those conversations was a methodological thesis about rational expectations economics in which I suggested that economists argue on various levels of discourse. I actually thought that I could turn that thesis into this book. How wrong I was. The first to show me that so much more was at stake were Allan Janik and Alasdair MacIntyre, who were at Wellesley College when I arrived there to teach. They pointed me to a literature that I did not know about. Wellesley proved to be a stimulating intellectual environment, good for conversations about economics and other disciplines. I learned a great deal from Michèle Grimaud, a French scholar, who taught me how to read a text seriously. (Years later he responded with style to my questions about how he was doing: "Very well, apart from the fact that I am dying." A year later he was dead.) With him, Owen Flanagan, a philosopher, Marilyn Sides, an English scholar, and Marty Brody, a composer, I discussed great texts. Those were the times I came alive intellectually. As Wellesley is a good liberal arts college, its economists had an open mind and proved to be an important source for my methodological inquiry. Chip Case, Jim Grant, Rod Morrison, Julie Matthei, Bruce Norton, Len Nichols, David Lindauer, Sandy Baum, Carolyn Shaw Bell, and others were good to talk with. And so were students, such as Susan MacDonald (who is still doing my editing), Denise Goldfarb, Paula DeMasio, and Kim, who introduced me to the subject of modernism in a paper that she wrote for a class of mine.

The book that I subsequently did write instead of this one got me to talk with well-known economists. The title, *Conversations with Economists*, still seems appropriate. I cannot claim to be in conversation with them, but it felt as if I was at the time. Let me make an exception for Rob Clower. I wanted to interview him for a sequel. We were sitting in a revolving restaurant and he was talking about how he went into economics when his father died from a stroke. He suddenly began to sweat profusely; I thought he was hyperventilating but it turned out to be a stroke.

Later, after he recovered somewhat, we continued our conversation, but I never did that sequel and the interview was not published. That was too bad as he surely provides a fascinating and most critical perspective on economics. He is one of the rare characters in the profession.

This was also the time that I made new intellectual friends. They happen to span the political spectrum with Don Lavoie, the Austrian economist, somewhat to the right, Jack Amariglio, the postmodern Marxist, somewhat on the left, and Phil Mirowski somewhere in the middle. The conversation with Don ceased when he passed away, much too early. Conversations with these people keep me honest. The same could be said for conversations with outsiders such as Barend van Heusden, a literary scholar, and various philosophers whose company I seek now and then.

Around the same time I became involved in the conversation of economic methodologists: Bruce Caldwell, Wade Hands, Mark Blaug, Uskali Maki, Warren Samuels, and many others. For a while they were my intellectual community. I wonder now what they will think of this book. Uskali, my colleague at Erasmus, will probably find some inconsistencies. And Mark Blaug, if he is in a good mood, will strongly object.

Most important, however, proved to be the contact with the economic historian and Chicago economist to boot, Donald McCloskey. Weintraub had shown me McCloskey's paper on rhetoric just when I was about to finish my thesis. After reading it I was almost convinced to give up on my thesis as it said it all and so much better. When I met him for the first time – it was on a snowy ride from an airport in Vermont to Middlebury College – we got into a conversation about art, economics, rhetoric, and a great deal more. That conversation continues. In the meantime we organized a conference, and together with Robert Solow, we decided to write a textbook (about to be finished, finally). I moved to her university in Iowa while she changed gender and took a part-time position at my current university; one of my daughters shares her new name, Deirdre. I owe much to her, and to her gentle art of writing and brilliant art of conversation. I dedicate this book to her.

With Dave Colander I wrote a book on the profession, *The Making of an Economist*. He continues to be an important source about where the profession stands. In Iowa I came up against other economists, but the outstanding experience was the POROI seminars, in which I learned rhetoric and a great deal more. The interdisciplinary setting proved to be most inspiring once again. I even learned about deconstructive accounting and Victorian poetry.

With a position at George Washington University I landed in the square mile with the highest concentration of economists anywhere in the world. The IMF, the World Bank, the Federal Reserve, and the Treasury are all there. It must have gone to my head somehow. Colleagues like Bob Goldfarb, Joe Cordes, Bryan Boulier, Tony Yezer, Bradley, Stephen Smith, and Bob Dunn, as well as (graduate) students such as Tim Leonard, Jennifer Meehan (both of whom co-authored articles that formed the basis of chapters in this book), were good for a great deal of conversation. Nothing autistic in that department. Will I ever experience as much collegiality as I did there?

Once back in Holland I began to learn from people outside the economic conversation. In numerous symposia, lectures, and debates, I learned what it takes not to be an economist. I began to talk more with journalists (although I had started that conversation already with David Warsh in Boston), politicians, and other "normal" people. They undoubtedly influenced my perspective on the world I came from. With Harry van Dalen I wrote on Dutch economists and got to think about the role of attention. The collaboration is smooth and stimulating, so we are continuing it. My current position is in the department of art and culture. I am ambiguous about being outside an economics department. I miss the constant presence of economists around me but enjoy the company of people who are into the sociology and history of the arts – Ton Bevers, Suzanne Jansen, Berend Jan Langenberg, Wouter de Nooy, and others. They may be surprised to read what I have been working on the last few years, as it is not directly focused on the economics of the arts. Erik Pruijmboom has known all along, but then he was my attentive and most reliable assistant who, with his structure and organization, compensated for my lack of structure. Ticia Herold has taken it on herself to protect me from my tendency to do too much at the one time.

My most important source is the weekly seminar on cultural economics. Every Friday people from various disciplines gather in my room to discuss a text for an hour and a half. Wilfred Dolfsma, Olav Velthuis, Irene van Staveren, Barbara Krug, Hans Abbing, David Kombrink, P.W. Zuidhof, Rick Dolphijn, Anna Mignosa, Susana Graca, Willem van Schinkel, Swalomir Magala, Almut Krauss, Simon Goudsmit, Gjalt de Graaf, Bregje van Eekelen, Bregje van Woensel, Onno Bouwmeester, Sophie Schweiker, and many others play a greater role in my intellectual life than they may realize. The same is true of Jos de Beus, a political scientist, and Harmen Verbruggen, an environmental economist, with whom I run every Sunday, mainly to be in a conversation about everything and nothing. They have become important sparring partners. Since I finished the book the conversations have taken another turn because of the new university I am trying to set up, the Academia Vitae, for the sake of – you've guessed it – academic conversations that matter to life. I can only hope that this book will matter in those conversations.

The academic conversation tends to be quite global. I am thinking of the conversations I am having with David Throsby (Australia), Bruno Frey (Switzerland), Francesco Louca (Portugal), Michael Hutter (Germany), and Kazuko Goto (Japan). The conversations with Bruno Frey have been especially important because some of our interests overlap so clearly although I could never match his many other interests. I discussed this work in seminars and conferences everywhere – too numerous to mention here.

This conversation of mine draws on personal resources as well. My father (a preacher who really had no idea what I was doing but admired it anyway), my mother, brother (who got me to do *Conversations*) and sisters, children (Renee, Lucas, Anna, and Rosa), girlfriends, and friends. They all have affected me in some way or another. They will understand that I am not getting specific. I make an exception for one, my partner in life.

She has probably been the toughest conversation partner for me, at least when it comes to economics. She keeps saying that she is practically minded and that all this academic talk seems to her a lot of idle and rather inflated chatter. When I talk about my stuff, like this book, she will say something like, "What's your point?" or "I don't get it" or "Why is this relevant?" And when I try to be to the point and say something about the importance of attention and conversation, she will roll her eyes and exclaim: "Wow, that's news to me. Listen, psychologists talk about nothing else. People need attention? Where have you been?" Frankly, all I can do in that situation is laugh at first. Then I realize that I love her for her directness and for being different, and subsequently look forward to the upcoming seminar that makes sense of what I am writing. Yet it is she who encourages me to write the way I do, simply and as directly as I can. If you like it, please thank her. I like it this way so I dedicate the book to her as well.

The writing took place in intermittent phases, in places away from the hustle and bustle of the daily life of a Dutch professor and a father of four. I began in a Tudor house in eastern Massachusetts, with thanks to Elias Khalil, and continued in various places in Holland, especially in the house of Louk Hulsman, a professor emeritus at Erasmus University (who taught me a few wise lessons as well), and finished in Catania, Sicily, where the people are hospitable and the food is excellent. You will see that Italy and its people get an important supporting role in the story that is about to unfold. Each time I sent my drafts to Susan MacDonald, who turned it into the prose that it is now. I am most grateful for her dedication and effort.

The norm prescribes me to exonerate all these people from any fault or error in this book. That is obvious. But they share a responsibility and are somehow part of the conversation that this book intends to be.

But we are not only in conversations with people. A major part of the conversation takes place by means of reading and interacting with texts, with articles, books, newspapers, and journals. The custom is to bring the reader into the literature that I have drawn from by means of many citations. Alasdair MacIntyre once told me that he left out the citations because the writing should make clear what his sources were. I kept a few citations here and there just to be polite and to be helpful. At the end of each chapter I reveal my most important sources and references that the reader may use to explore the argument further.

1 The strangeness of the discipline

Big + important = normal?

Taking up the discipline of economics appears to be a perfectly normal thing to do. What else could it be? Many thousands join its ranks every year. New recruits find out that a profusion of economists makes up an apparently powerful discipline that easily prevails in academic status over other social sciences such as sociology, psychology, and anthropology. They will find out that economics is the only social science to have its own Nobel Prize, and learn that economists are well represented in government, occupy high-ranking offices such as cabinet ministers and presidents, and assume powerful positions as chief executive officers (CEOs) and chief financial officers (CFOs) of major corporations. Economists are also regularly featured as experts in the media. With such size and regard, it must be perfectly normal. Or so it seems.

Economics appears to be a vital discipline, too, because it promises to help understand important things: Why do some countries' economies work better than others? How do we cure unemployment and world poverty? How does money work? Jan Tinbergen, a Dutch economist who won the first Nobel Prize for econometrics, was my economic hero. He devoted his work to the causes of social justice and world peace. Tinbergen was not only an idealist, but also a serious scientist. As a young man, I set out to do the same. What reward, what benefit, could be greater than having the ability to show politicians the economic means by which they could work toward greater justice for all?

Even without such high-mindedness, economics demands attention because of its permeation of daily life. It is a major part of any country's daily newspapers and dictates the goings-on of politicians. If we are not told to worry about a lack of economic growth, we are warned of inflation. Government deficits, recessions, wage increases, productivity figures, degrees of consumer confidence – these are always in the news, and affect our ordinary, day-to-day lives.

There is no escape from economics. It confronts all of us, all the time, whether we want to see it or not. The artist who professes to loathe anything about that niggling thing called "money" has to figure out how to stay alive. Vincent van Gogh relied on the generosity of family; other artists apply for grants. Both are economic decisions. When artists chat among themselves about the best place to find the finest brushes, they are practicing economics. Nurses working in a public hospital about to be privatized are confronted by economics, however far from the fray they feel. Parents regularly ascribe an economic value to chores done by their children. There is, simply, no escaping it.

And yet people are good at escaping economists and ignoring their economics.

Suspicion and derision in everyday life

I learned at first hand that economists are considered less than likeable company. Get introduced as an economist in a social gathering and conversation dims. "How interesting," someone says politely. Sensing the discomfort, I add quickly that I'm also involved in philosophy. "Ah." A flicker of approval. With the momentarily captive audience, I tell them I study the world of the arts. "How interesting." Eyes light up! The economist is now talking about something with which they are socially comfortable – and in which they are interested.

It is strange that the economist – knowledgeable about a subject that commands commonplace activity, which fills newspapers daily, which can break the most powerful people on earth – is a socially unpopular companion. It is strange that so many routinely skip the economics articles in their newspapers and tune out when the economy is being discussed on television. It is strange to know how unknown most economists are. And while economists endeavor to be heard, their books, with few exceptions, have dismal sales. (I am not talking about "how to" business books – how to be a leader, how to have vision, how to make money out of nothing – general economics is not business economics.)

Economists experience worse than a mere lack of interest in their work. Dare to hold forth at a dinner party on the latest economic theory and more than boredom may ensue. The wife of a colleague once actually nodded off at the table while we were engaged in our econ babble – she was tired but I doubt she would have fallen asleep if we had been talking art. And the application of economics is more often ridiculed than intelligently considered. At one college faculty meeting, the item up for resolution was a shortage of parking spaces. An economist suggested auctioning them, a perfectly sensible solution in our world. English teachers, historians, scientists, *et al.* – some of them incredibly creative people – were appalled. The economist was astounded by his colleagues' economic naiveté.

Culturalists – people who care about art, literature, or anything else cultural – call economists "Philistines," "rationalists," and a host of other names that characterize them as less dimensional. They consider economics, and consequently economists, to be devoid of culture. After I assumed a chair in the Economics of Art and Culture at Rotterdam I was dared to try to understand the economics of artists' work. Some opinions of these efforts are not printable here.

Representation of the discipline is nearly non-existent in literature. Economists do not appear in novels, and economic themes are suppressed. There are exceptions

– Defoe's *Robinson Crusoe*, Dickens's *Hard Times*, Steinbeck's *Grapes of Wrath* and *In Dubious Battle*, and various novels by Sinclair Lewis – but they are just that, exceptions. The only economic historian in literature is the unspeakably boring husband of Ibsen's Hedda Gabler. The denial of economic themes in literature echoes the condemnation of money in religious writings and traditions, especially Christian. The New Testament tells how Jesus banished money exchangers from the temple, that "you cannot serve God and mammon" (Matthew 6:24), and that "it is easier for a camel to go through the eye of a needle than for a rich man to enter into the kingdom of God" (Matthew 16:26). Even though the Bible refers more to money than to, say, love, the references are never encouraging for those in love with money.

❖ ❖ ❖

Throughout the centuries, religious practice and the interpretation of religious texts have adapted somewhat to the intensification of commercial life. Calvin's reading of the Bible, for example, allowed for hard work as an economic norm, and arguably saw a blessing in amassing wealth. But, although quite a few religious leaders demonstrate deftness in the management of their financial affairs, churches generally keep the economic perspective of life at bay. This is strange considering how economics permeates daily life.

Suspicion and derision in political life

Self-assured economists can cope with the derision of culturalists and everyday people. It would be more fun to be respected and admired but, let's be honest, do dentists, accountants, engineers, and managers fare that much better? I would have thought that economics is more intellectually appealing than dentistry and accounting, and would lend itself to better conversation at the dinner table, but I have learned otherwise. I have not given up on economics sparking day-to-day lay conversations, but there is much to be understood before that happens.

How much more difficult it is to accept the suspicion and indifference that economists receive in politics. After all, a major portion of the economist's work is designed to affect policy, and the understanding of government systems is a cornerstone of economic thought. The disparagement of the input of economists is not necessarily visible. Economists are regularly called in to advise policymakers: the American president has a Council of Economic Advisors, European governments are backed by economic research institutions, and economists are prominent in central banks. Even so, economic advice is almost never implemented straight away, and it is often dismissed. Mockery is not uncommon. Exasperated with economists who intervened with the remark, "On the other hand, . . ." Harry Truman once exclaimed, "Give me a one-handed economist!"[1]

Academic economists complain about their limited roles in public debate. The widely acclaimed Paul Krugman expresses his frustration that the role of the economist who cares about policy can be dispiriting: one may spend years devising sophisticated theories or carefully testing ideas against the evidence, then find that politicians turn again and again to ideas that you thought had been discredited decades or even centuries ago, or make statements that are flatly contradicted by the facts.

(Krugman 1994: 292)

As an academic economist with experience in politics in the Joint Committee on Taxation, Alan Auerbach is well qualified to observe: (a) the "shorter time horizon" in Washington compared with academia, "with ideas being raised and discarded with more frequency than the occasional visits to Washington during my existence," (b) the important role of lawyers, and (c) the disproportionate amount of time spent on issues that affect specific taxpayers versus the broader issues that concern an academic economist (Auerbach 1992: 239). Stuart Eizenstat, who served as advisor to President Carter, complains that economists and politicians "too frequently are like ships passing in the night, neither understanding the needs of the other" (Eizenstat 1992: 71).

❖   ❖   ❖

Even allowing that these observations are only partially true, they make for a puzzling phenomenon. Economics is a discipline that boasts of its lofty reign as the queen of social sciences, draws a million undergraduates to its introductory courses at American colleges every year (of whom 30,000 choose it as their major), and counts 130,000 practitioners in the US alone. PhDs number 17,500, with many serving as presidents (Mexico), cabinet ministers, business leaders, and International Monetary Fund (IMF) and World Bank bureaucrats. Each year, a member of this community is awarded a Nobel Prize, lending the discipline scientific authenticity. Yet its authority in political debate is tainted by suspicion and its policy decision-making questioned.

The strangeness of the subject

People often don't get it – what we are talking about, that is. "These economists don't know what they're talking about," a businessperson will blithely say. They consider our way of talking strange. And they do not get the point, or the practicality, of what we are doing. "If they're so smart, why aren't they rich?" is the archetypically American question that appears to silence virtually all economists (considering their modest cars and homes). A businessman whose daughter I once courted thought very little of her prospects with me. With my head in the clouds the way it was, I would certainly not keep her in the manner to which she was accustomed. (How correct he was.) At the same time I was puzzled that, although this man had been very successful, he could not make much sense of the economy. Beyond a few commonplace fragments of knowledge, he was quite inarticulate. The science of economics had no meaning to this man of practice. So what does it mean?

When I tell first-year students that economics is not about money or the making of it, they become restive. When I tell them they are not going to learn anything practical, the evaporation of their enthusiasm is palpable. They do ask the inevitable question: What, then, is economics good for? My answer is strangely vague; at this point it must be. I offer them something about a way of thinking – the economic way of thinking; that they will gain a perspective that may help them make sense of the economy. This buys back a tiny bit of their interest, but not much. Only when I hit them with a production possibility curve do they settle down to work. Students are always attentive to territories that look like they might reappear on exams.

When students hear the definition of economics – the study of choice and allocation of scarce resources – they are too disconnected from it (or overwhelmed by it) to raise objections. In expecting to learn about the economy and to make sense of articles in the economic pages, talk about choice and allocation of resources strikes them as somewhat daft. They want to understand how businesspeople behave, why economies go up and down, how economies grow, and how money works. What does that have to do with the allocation of scarce resources? And choices – businesspeople have choices we all are more or less familiar with, but to have "choice" define the subject of economics . . .? That can't be right.

If students manage to attain and maintain a critical stance while going through their courses of economics, they will notice how scarce references to the real economy are. Professors may offer a generous amount of "real-world" economics in the beginning because it is effective in piquing the interest of the students and luring them into the economic world. But it is possible – in some schools more than others, and with some professors more than others – to ascend through one course of economics after another, learn about models, equations, and concepts, and struggle with increasingly complex problem sets without ever discussing economic institutions. The further into the study of economics, the more abstract the classes and the less relevant the real economy. Economics becomes more about itself than about the economy. Students learn more about the science of economics than the world of economics.[2]

In a survey among graduate students at the most prestigious schools in the US (Klamer and Colander 1987, 1990), we found that students considered a knowledge of math and problem-solving abilities far more important for their careers as economists than being knowledgeable about the economy.[3] Sixty-eight percent of those surveyed actually considered knowledge of the real economy unimportant. Think how weird this is. Here is a profession dedicated to the study of the economy, and the brightest graduates are tethered to the mathematical abstractions of choice and allocation of scarce resources. When something in the real economy is at stake, they don't know how to talk.

This is not the only strange feature that novices find in economics. The way we talk is strange as well. I keep telling my students that economics is like a foreign language to them. It has become easy for me to talk what I will call *econospeak*, but they should not be misled by that – it takes a great deal of practice. "Shifting the demand curve" is quite different from "movements along the curve," and economists speak about elasticities, rational choice, externalities, public goods, income multipliers, transaction costs, Nash equilibrium, and derived demand with as much ease as today's weather. They make inside jokes in econospeak to show off how good they are at it. I began to speak it comfortably only after teaching it. Like any foreign language, it takes practice, practice, and more practice.

You had better not practice econospeak with non-economists. The terms often call up unpleasant or wrong meanings and upset people. When I want to sort out a love affair and begin with the notions of utility functions, constraints, and rational choice, every economist would understand, and might even think highly of the argument, but my partner might consider it compelling evidence that the two of us make a bad match after all.

Strange is also how economists depict the market. After having said something about products, demand, supply and price, their teacher will take a few seconds (at most) to draw the picture in Figure 1.1. "This is a market," the professor says. "Don't be ridiculous," the students think. Where are the people screaming on the floor of the stock exchange? Where are farmers' markets in town? Whatever their images of "market," they do not conform to a diagram with four lines. The skeptics – and rightly so – protest. "Suspend your disbelief," the professor will say (a polite way of saying be quiet and listen). More and more stuff goes on the board and, as it looks mighty high on the exam index, this is no time to challenge it. The indoctrination is quick and insidious. Students become so intimate with these curves – ascribing a term to each point on the graph and giving meaning to the dynamics of each change in terms of "movements along the curve," "a shifting of the curve to the right," "the point of equilibrium," "an inelastic curve" – that, yes, it is accepted as a market. Why not? It's got prices and products and choices. By that time they will need an outsider, such as a parent, to remind them how weird and unrealistic the picture is. Some of us do try to have students continually

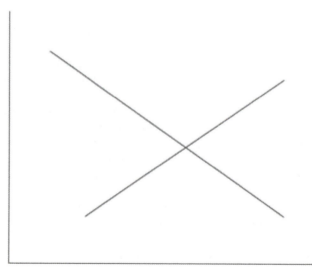

Figure 1.1 A market

consider the diagram in a critical (real-world) manner, but I doubt that the efforts are effective. The numeral has outdone the number.

Diagrams and their symbols lead the way to equations. Students thus next come to accept the following "market":

$$Q_s = f(P, Q_e, w/p, A, r, \varepsilon) + b \text{ and } Q_d = f(P, Y, Y_e, r, \varepsilon)$$

This is the mathematical representation of a market, one that economists treat quite a bit more seriously than the diagram of it (which actually serves only as an initiation ritual for first-year students, something like the Rutherford model of the atom for beginning physics students). A sound person may wonder how such an abstraction can capture the complexities of something like a market, but economists are quite comfortable with it.

After studying economics for some time, students will have learned to think in terms of models and a foundational rite of passage is complete. Quite a few economists cannot think without a model, and require it of anyone with an interesting economic insight. Once I tried to sell the utterly sensible idea that trading comes about because of differences in knowledge. My teacher's response was, "Interesting, but what is your model? Let's talk when you have a model." Modeling is the sine qua non of academic econospeak. Strangely, it is what economics is all about. Assuming that it is a science, that is.

The strangeness of the science

Not that economists care about all this abuse and miscomprehension. "There is something wrong here" does not resonate in academic hallways and at international conferences. For the most part, economists seem content with and even conceited about their discipline since they consider it superior to any other social science. They brush off criticism easily. When students and other outsiders complain that the theory of rational choice and the abstract models are unrealistic, economists will typically refer to the scientific character of their discipline. "Economics is a science and like any other science it proceeds by means of unrealistic assumptions and abstract models." And: "Scientists do not speak in comprehensible terms about the real world either." "This is a science, to be sure; if you seek our advice you will have to take our scientific analysis for granted unless you want to immerse yourself in our scientific inquiry." That should shut the critic up, shouldn't it?

But if economics is a science, it must be a rather strange science. Real scientists subject theories to empirical tests, reject those that fail and continue with the ones that are successful. Economists try to do the same, running regressions of theories that involve enormous sets of data. But while they do produce empirical results, it is impossible to pinpoint the series of empirical tests that prove a theory wrong and cause its rejection. Empirical evidence may favor one theory over another, but if an economist believes in her theory, she can – perhaps even innocently – work the data for evidence that suits her model better. No empirical evidence is decisive. There are no parallels in economics to the Morley experiments that proved Einstein's theory of relativity. If empirical research fails to falsify its theories, how scientific is economics?

The empirical failure of economics as a science goes further. Despite a vast amount of research, economists cannot provide a set of empirical results that is interchangeable, as physicists can. Economists cannot talk about a standard for the price elasticity of the demand for electricity. For all its importance and amount of time spent on the empirical testing of it, economists cannot state the impact on investment of a 1 percent change in the interest rate. As a textbook author, I find that I can demonstrate nothing more important about empirical research in economics than that economists do a great deal of it. Where, then, is all this effort in empirical research going?

The hallmark of "real" science is a reliable, reproducible, and predictable result, yet economists fail famously to predict what will happen in the real economy. They miss the onset of recessions and are often surprised by strong growth just after they predicted a slowdown. Economists are bad in predicting the future course of the dollar, or the interest rate. Don't ask them about the stock market because they wouldn't know. As a matter of fact, serious predicting has become a low priority. Some research institutes will still generate predictions for public consumption – usually on the basis of large econometric models – but the work is not taken seriously in academic circles. After so often proving to be obsolete and superfluous, the scientific heyday of large models, on which the hero of my youth Jan Tinbergen had vested all his hope, is over. Again strange, predicting the outside world is not a skill that graduate school teaches, yet it is what the outside world expects.

The persistent disagreements

The dubious status of economics as a science is partly due to unrelenting conflicts among economists. In a war among natural scientists about, say, cold fusion or relativity theory, crucial experiment is a lethal weapon. Economists have no such arms. They operate in feudal groups here and there, some more powerful than others by sheer size, but always vulnerable to some younger and stronger group that has plotted its advance successfully. Some of the stronger armies are very small but good at surviving forever (Marxists); the campaigns of some have lost scientific steam after gaining political clout (Laffer and fellow supply-siders); others are loud and boisterous and enthusiastic but short on ammunition (Nelson and Winter followers). Two, maybe three, dominate at one time. The larger the army and the longer it is able to fight (Keynesians, neoclassicists), the more memorable it is. Famous leaders are usually trained at elite schools. In economics, the armies fueling these endless feuds are known most familiarly as "schools of thought," and arguably the most famous academy is the University of Chicago. (MIT, Stanford, and some leafy places would argue.)

Imagine, then, how difficult it is to agree on who should be allowed to teach economics at these prestigious schools? The disagreements can be quite ugly: a number of the faculty members must agree, and their ideas of what to teach and what they consider scientific or right vary widely. Some can be downright adolescent about it. "We'll hire another Marxist over my dead body!" "What the f*** do we need another game theorist for?" "This guy is doing off the wall stuff. It's not even economics!" Strange, though: if economics were a real science, reason would prevail over this sort of bickering, wouldn't it?

A series of conversations with the major protagonists of various schools published in *Conversations with Economists* (Klamer 1983) revealed how these economists are thinking and what motivates them. They also brought out their differences. Robert Lucas, a major figure in neoclassical economics (who would later win a Nobel Prize), was serious and charming, and spoke emphatically about his way of doing science. "What would you do if you were on the Council of Economic Advisors?" I asked, as a logical follow-up to his theories and objections concerning government intervention. "Resign," he said, with dead seriousness. His students later related how he would simply dismiss east-coast Ivy League policy advisors who continually commuted to Washington. "Here in Chicago," he (allegedly) assured them, "we are serious about economics." In other words, advising policy-makers is not something that serious economists do.

The other economic camp made for quite a different story. James Tobin (an east-coast Ivy League policy advisor) had already won the Nobel Prize when I spoke with him. A true gentleman, he spoke softly about his life and his Keynesian approach to economics. With due respect, I worried after a time that the interview sounded so automatic, so "done" before, that it would add little to the book. Then I brought up Lucas's criticism. Tobin began to speak much louder and faster (on transcribing the tape I actually had to adjust the volume). He remained reasonable and gentlemanly but his voice betrayed his indignation toward Lucas and his camp, about how they were misleading sensible Keynesian economic thought. Bob Solow rubbed in the difference with his now quite famous remark:

> Suppose someone sits down where you are sitting right now and announces to me that he is Napoleon Bonaparte. The last thing I want to do with him is to get involved in a technical discussion of cavalry tactics at the battle of Austerlitz. If I do that, I'm getting tacitly drawn into the game that he is Napoleon. Now, Bob Lucas and Tom Sargent like nothing better than to get drawn into technical discussions, because then you have tacitly gone along with their fundamental assumptions; your attention is attracted away from the basic weakness of the whole story. Since I find that fundamental framework ludicrous, I respond by treating it as ludicrous – that is, by laughing at it – so as not to fall into the trap of taking it seriously and passing on to matters of technique.
>
> (Klamer 1983: 146)

How strange this is. How is it possible that very intelligent people in the same scientific discipline do not understand each other? Why do they dig deeper trenches rather than get together to resolve their differences? And the two examples above are about mainstream economics! Smaller schools of economics are further apart and communicate less. Siblings, even, may develop extremely different economic beliefs. The Americans Robert and David Gordon, the sons of a husband and wife team of economists, are well known in economic circles; one conventional, the other a Marxist. (David died in 1996 at the age of 51.) The two operated in completely different worlds. They read a different literature, related to different people, had exceedingly different views on the very economy in which they grew up together. However close they were as brothers, David told me that they "rarely talked economics" (Klamer 1983). They simply accepted it as not doable. How strange for a science, let alone brothers.

I was struck by these disagreements at the outset of my studies at the University of Amsterdam in the 1970s. The profession was then split among Keynesians, monetarists, and post-Keynesians. Post-Keynesians were favored at the university and monetarists were not; Keynesians were approaching the end of their reign. Milton Friedman, the leading monetarist, regularly had the academic door slammed in his face. One of our Keynesian professors of monetary theory actually refused to read a student's paper because it was about Friedman's ideas. "Hogwash," the professor called it. Our post-Keynesians, meanwhile, were discrediting his economics. We had exciting discussions, but I was puzzled. How can this possibly be a science?

❖   ❖   ❖

Economic tension does not always derive from a particular stance in theory, and, in fact, passions flare most when the discipline itself is at issue. Economists have vastly divergent perspectives on what constitutes the science of economics. The most devastating criticism an economist receives is that his or her work is not scientific. "What you are doing is not economics" is a powerful statement, and can destroy honest work. Primary research seems perfectly reasonable for modeling the real world but it is rarely taken seriously. For *Talking Prices: Symbolic Meanings of Prices on the Market for Contemporary Art* (2005), Olav Velthuis launched the development of his theory by asking people in the art market how they priced their paintings. How perfectly sensible! This type of approach, however, is likely to be rejected for being "unscientific" or "not economics." But it does very well under the label of socioeconomics.

The heavy emphasis on mathematical tools in contemporary econospeak strikes many an outsider as strange. Insiders insist on it as part of their scientific baggage. But do you really need to be a mathematician in order to be an economic scientist? If so, Adam Smith or John Maynard Keynes would no longer qualify for the job. They would be considered too wordy, too imprecise, too unscientific. They would have difficulty arguing with economists now even if their ideologies were identical. There are exceptions: Austrian economists, notably, take issue with theorizing with ever more complicated models. Deirdre McCloskey subscribes to the intuitive and verbal mode of reasoning characteristic of the so-called "Good Old" Chicago School (whose more prominent members include Ronald Coase,

George Stigler, Gary Becker, and Milton Friedman). When this Old Chicago gang was still in charge at Chicago, "lunchtime" economics focused on the real world. "How about that new government policy [which seemed to have had a real effect and in which, of course, they did not believe] . . ." would bring about a great discussion. The goal was to deal another blow to the myth that government intervention is good for the economy. Lunch with the "New" Chicago School (led by Robert Lucas) features more technical issues, such as computer programs or the effectiveness of new mathematical methods. Even though the political ideology is fundamentally the same, the style of argument has changed so completely that the Good Old Chicago economists, such as McCloskey, feel out of place on their own turf.

McCloskey has been a most outspoken critic of the New Chicago school, which she scornfully calls "Nouvelle" Chicago. She opposes the scientific engineering of Keynesian economics – the tinkering with models for the purpose of economic policy – and vehemently objects to what she calls blackboard economics. She sees Nouvelle Chicago's mathematical fiddling as math for math's sake. She points to flaws in all of economics, in which statistical significance is often mistaken for theoretical significance. At a seminar at the Tinbergen Institute she presented her critique of statistical significance, a bad use of statistics that appears to be dominant in the econometric literature (McCloskey and Ziliak 1996). This was the year after she changed gender. (Deirdre had been Donald McCloskey – how can you say economists are not interesting?) She had her audience by the balls, so to speak. One of the male economists sputtered somewhat in protest, but she was prepared and showed the flawed statistics in his own work. She ended her talk by standing in front of her audience, arms crossed the female way, bent over slightly and said slowly and emphatically, "Listen, you boys have been playing in the sandbox. Grow up!" Only in her current unmistakably female presence and former life as a male could she have gotten away with such a style of argument. Yet, attentive as the "boys" may have been to such stinging criticism, it has had little to no effect. McCloskey and Ziliak (2004) showed that since the publication of their earlier article the problem has only gotten worse.

Whatever, the criticisms have had little to no effect. If anything, mainstream economics is becoming more adamant about the use of sophisticated mathematics and statistics. That may be strange, depending from which perspective you look at it.

Economists are human, too

The vehemence of the disagreements is intensifying and the social context in which they are being aired is becoming less genteel. George Stigler (1911–91) was a Good Old Chicago economist who was as fluent with biting humor as Solow. Both were brilliantly, if cuttingly, entertaining. An MIT economist once presented a paper on efficiency wages at Chicago – how brave of the man, as Chicago is not inclined to entertain notions about imperfections in the labor market. The poor fellow started guilelessly by wondering whether he should stand or sit at the table to present. "With a paper like that," Stigler offered casually, "I'd do it *under* the table."

The passions that underlie such biting remarks are not always negative. Exclamations like Wow! Neat! Great! I love it! How exciting! are far removed from the image of the dispassionate and detached scientist but are not atypical of economic theorists.

Passionate as economists can be, they are also good for gossip. When economists confer, their conversations usually evolve along three stages. The first topic is other economists. Who got tenured, divorced, left the profession? Who got into a duel with another economist? The textbook advance was how much?! – These are the most important items and usually last for the social hour. (Imagine how many hours of non-economic conversation McCloskey's gender change caused.) What one is up to in economics comes second. Colleague-to-colleague talk. Mutual appraisal of each other's work. In this setting, do not stumble around. "She has no idea what she's doing . . ." will circulate quickly. For scientists, economists are unusually eager to share, eager to be considered. Rarely is a new theory kept secret. Like any other human, economists seek approval and are proud of their work. Only after these two areas are settled do economists talk about the economy. Even then, they do so rather timidly. Academic economists – who are quite eloquent in speaking about the economy in academia – are not inclined to real-world economic discourse in a social setting with their colleagues. Economists who work for, say, the Fed or the IMF, are less reticent, but, then again, continually writing and reading about events in the real economy is what they get paid for.

The fact that the gossip comes first verifies that economists are social beings. They experience marital anguish, celebrate births, seek professional approval, commiserate with failure, and applaud accomplishment. Parties are organized for Nobel Prize winners. Conferences are opportunities to share findings and get to know each other better. They are, quite simply, human. As such, they have inner circles and, especially in academia, judge each other implicitly by their university affiliations, the amount of respect given their particular school of thought, and what other academicians have to say about their work. Gossip may not seem to belong in science but in economics it is influential.

A strange lack of reflection

Given the amount of questioning we have just heaped on this science, isn't economics due for an overhaul? Not according to economists. They show a remarkable lack of interest in the history and foundations of their own discipline. Positions in the history of economic of thought are given less and less space in the curricula of prestigious universities. You may wonder how a social science can be divorced from its history without losing important knowledge. The presumption that only surviving fragments of work have value makes sense only if falsification of the bad ideas is definite. But it is not. Besides, you would expect that every self-respecting discipline honors its past, learns from mistakes, and benefits from knowing important thought rendered obsolete by time. Most economists do not even feign interest. Few young macroeconomists, for example, have read anything by the founders of their field, Knut Wicksell and J.M. Keynes.

Strange, too, is the marginalization of the methodology of economics. A few well-known economists have contributed to this field, most famously Milton Friedman with his *Essays in Positive Economics* (1953). Most practicing economists are content with Friedman's contribution and do not feel compelled to (nor are they made to) listen to current controversy in economic methodology. As a consequence, ignorance on methodological issues, especially among younger economists, is rife. They haughtily dismiss methodological writings for being unscientific while not having the faintest notion what they are. They tend to talk like the textbooks of nineteenth-century natural scientists, yet they make decisions in academia on grants, hires, and fires that stunt the growth of promising men and women in economics.

Puzzling, too, is the absence of serious studies on the impact of economics on its own behavior. Economists have studied every conceivable human activity but their own. One might logically conclude that those able to become "scientific" about the "rationality" of marriage and suicide might want to become scientific about the rationality of their own doings. Much academic research concludes with important policy implications yet I know of no academic research that traces the impact on policy decisions – at least none with the quality of a serious scientific study.[4] Economists cite Keynes's flippant remark that "[m]admen in authority, who hear voices in the air, are distilling their frenzy from some academic scribbler of a few years back" (Keynes 1936: 383) and thus absolve themselves from further self-examination. Thus, in the end, we have enormous effort, intelligent people, political ramifications, serious scientists – and yet the discipline hasn't a clue as to whether it makes a difference or not.

Why, then, economics?

Tireless young economists trying to get into the profession write papers that will not be published or, if published, not read, spend money traveling to conferences where they will not be heard, and sacrifice home and family to do it all. Go to a large conference such as the meetings of the American Economic Association (held just after New Year with 6,000 economists attending) and experience it for yourself. You find numerous sessions on the program and will find out that most of them take place in small rooms with only a few members in attendance. If you are lucky, your paper got on the program, and you need to be more than lucky to get some sensible comments from the discussant or the audience. More likely, you find yourself anonymous in the crowd attending some of the larger sessions where the famous economists hold forth. Some may ask why, why be an economist when the returns are so hard to detect? Indeed, I'm spending my time writing this book when, as we've discussed, the readership of a book on economics is more about hope than expectation. Whatever could be my motivation?

Perhaps it has everything to do with hope. If the unpopularity, the oddities of language, the dubious science, the dissimilarity of thought, the emotionalism, the gossip, the lack of reflection all make for the strangeness of the discipline of economics, they also compel me to hope to make sense of it. The contradictions encourage me to advance a framework that exonerates economics for its strangeness. To show, in fact, that it's not strange at all.

Further reading

There is a separate genre of writings dedicated to the science and practice of economics. They can be outright critical, apologetic, and laudatory. Quite a few Nobel Prize lectures and presidential addresses belong to this genre. I name a few:

*   R.H. Coase's *Essays on Economics and Economists* (University of Chicago Press, 1994).
*   David Colander's *Why Aren't Economists as Important as Garbagemen? Essays on the State of Economics* (M.E. Sharpe, 1991) and *The Lost Art of Economics: Essays on Economics and the Economics Profession* (Edgar Elgar, 2001).
*   George Stigler's *The Economist as Preacher and other Essays* (University of Chicago Press, 1982).
*   Benjamin Ward's *What's Wrong with Economics* (Basic Books, 1972).

Now and then economists write autobiographies. Reading them will help you to recognize how human economists are. Consider, for example:

*   John Stuart Mill's *Autobiography* (Cambridge University Press, 2004 [1873]).
*   Herbert Simon's *Models of My Life* (Basic Books, 1991).
*   Charles Kindleberger's *The Life of an Economist* (Basil Blackwell, 1991).
*   Milton and Rose D. Friedman's *Two Lucky People: Memoirs* (University of Chicago Press, 1998).

And for various other – and most interesting – reasons, read Deirdre McCloskey's *Crossing* (University of Chicago Press, 2000).

The survey results mentioned in this chapter can be found in *The Making of an Economist* (Westview Press, 1990), a book I wrote in collaboration with David Colander.

2 Economics is a conversation or, better, a bunch of conversations

Strange, continued

The strangeness of the science of economics and its practitioners, to be clear, is not necessarily economists' doing. Rather, the expectations with which people (like yourself?) approach economics and its practitioners are strange. To put it more bluntly, economics is not strange, but you who accuse it of being strange are strange in that you cannot (or will not) reconcile the image of the real economic scientist – bickering, gossiping, exuberant, obscure, and, yes, even interesting – with your own. But as any psychologist will tell you, people view the discipline through a personal framework of interests, concepts, and images. Most preconceived notions of what a science should be are not what people see in the science of economics. Most preconceived notions of what economists should be doing are not what they see in its practice. But these ideas come from them, from you perhaps, not from the scientific discipline itself.

If your notion of science is one of a steely discipline with lofty mathematical formulas and rigorous experiments that can definitively prove hypotheses wrong, economics is strange indeed. But then, is anything like your science? Might it be a fabrication of your own mind? Or some notion given you from sources you have never questioned? If your notion of scientists is one of reasonable and detached students of reality, economists must seem weird with their passions, discriminations, incriminations, and abuse. If you hold the opinion that that science is all about logic and fact, and hence about Truth, you are certainly in for a big surprise when you associate with economists.

The challenge that we face is to make sense of economists in such a way that it does justice to what they're doing. The objective here is to make sense of economists without going so far that you end up adopting the economist's mindset, thereby losing critical perspective. I want to make sense of them, without getting entangled in complicated philosophizing while still providing hooks for further inquiry.

A proposal and an image

Lemma: Economics is a conversation, or better, a bunch of conversations, and economists are economists because they are in conversation with other economists.

A game theorist is a game theorist because he is in conversation with other game theorists. An econometrician converses in the conversation of econometricians. Feminist economists have their own conversations, as do economic methodologists. And so on.

I want to have a conversation about this metaphor because that is what "economics is a conversation" is. It is not literally so, although I confess that, since working with this metaphor, I perceive economists having conversations all the time, whether they are formal or informal, scientific or literary, explicit or tacit. These conversations include small talk, which is important when trying to make sense of what economists do. Gossip serves critical functions, such as conveying opinions on other economists, on who and what are important. And, yes, conversation here includes the writing that economists are doing as well as the reading. It includes mathematical argumentation and all the talk that flows around it. Conversation is the regressions that economists run and the talk that they generate.

The point is that, if you want to be an economist, you must be in conversation with other economists, something that doesn't occur by mere desire. An economic conversation is not entered at will, like a conversation about the weather. It requires a range of skills, a mastery of econospeak, a diploma or two, a great deal of knowledge (in econospeak, "human capital"), and a good dose of self-confidence.

To elaborate on what a conversation is, let me recount an experience in Italy. I left my hotel room on the outskirts of Bologna at about two in the afternoon. After wandering down some small streets, I came upon the main square. It was quiet. I saw a few tourists, a bunch of pigeons. The Italians were relaxing, napping after one of their famous lunches, or had gone back to work. Wherever they were, it was not here; they had, for now, surrendered the square to pigeons and tourists like me. I strolled back to my room to write.

I decided to go back in the evening. Approaching via the little streets, I heard an ever-increasing noise. When I came within sight of the square I saw it had changed completely. I couldn't believe my eyes! The place that was so desolate a few hours ago was now teeming with people. Most were in clusters, talking. Here was a group of men arguing vehemently about, as far as I could tell, sports. A couple of guys were screaming at each other, making all sorts of gestures – as Italians are wont to do – and arguing as if their lives depended on it. I noted how much they talked with their hands. The women sat in separate groups, involved in their own conversations. A few groups were mixed. Some of the young women were involved in *fare le vasche,* strolling back and forth, pretending not to see the young guys hanging around the fountains – sometimes the keenest conversations are silent ones.

All these people were in conversation with each other. I wanted to join in, argue politics, offer my opinion on the Bologna soccer team. But, even apart from my bad Italian, I knew I couldn't. Each group had a history I was not privy to, referenced past conversations, called upon anecdotes that would have been lost on me. Even if I had managed to worm my way into one of the groups, I would have been immediately found out. I can't talk with my hands. With my northern temperament, I can't get worked up like they do. No matter what, I was not part of any conversations taking place in the square.

Getting into the conversation

I had a similar feeling when I went to my first economics conference, one on the history of economic thought. I knew quite a few of the economists there because I had read their stuff, and even understood what their papers were about. But I felt like an outsider. No one knew me, and I felt too shy to work my way into the huddles in the reception area. I felt even more like an outsider when I eavesdropped on their conversations: they talked about what other economists were doing, what happened at a previous conference, anecdotes.

I now know that they were gossiping, making small talk, a type of conversation graduate school did not prepare me for (gossip about teachers notwithstanding). The feeling of exclusion is even stronger for people without graduate training yet interested in economics. They do not know the names of the economists in the crowd, do not have a clue as to the content of the papers. If they try to mingle, the economists immediately find them out. Some elders may react politely, even sympathetically, but will squeeze such people out the conversation by some social method or another. Ignoring them appears to be the most effective way.

The circle opens more easily for those with a doctorate, if they identify themselves and their dissertation topic. Such information is necessary for initial placement in the conversation. I still recall how my self-confidence grew when Bob Coats, a well-known and highly respected historian of thought, was willing to engage me and talk seriously about my dissertation. Even so, it takes time to feel like one of them, to be in the conversation.

Being on the conference program – having the opportunity to talk about your work and get comments from other economists – is a necessary condition to be in the conversation, but not necessarily enough. At least you can tell yourself that someone has read your paper (or so you presume). People come up to you afterwards to request a copy of the paper and, if you're lucky, want to talk about it. Count on nothing happening apart from a few polite remarks. Congratulate yourself if someone strongly disagrees with you and causes a ruckus. That draws attention to your work. Unfortunately, such a confrontation rarely happens. The code of academic conversation at a conference is to be nice or say nothing.

I was helped a great deal when my book, *Conversations with Economists* (1983), did well. (Note that my predilection for the term conversation is at least that old.) After that I did not always need to introduce myself and was implicitly permitted to ask others who they were and what they were working on. I was in the conversation.

Having worked your way in does not mean that you are in the conversation of economists in general. I doubt that many economists can say they are. A Bob Solow, maybe, or a few others who are broadly oriented and well known. But even they will be uncomfortable if the conversation turns to some advanced econometrics or game theory. The life of an economist is an ongoing concern about being in the right conversation. Many different conversations are going on simultaneously. It requires work, usually very hard work, to stay in a conversation.

In the case of "hot" conversations, you have to arduously keep up. You must continually be invited to the good conferences and workshops; you must be able to present your papers at the right seminars, be cited, be in email contact with the other "hot" guys; in short, you must continue to be in the hot conversation. Unrecognized economists might elbow in, but will only be ignored if not on the program and not taken seriously they are – they will not be in the conversation. And if they want to present papers at prominent seminars they will simply be put off. The number of slots is limited, and the organizers select only people who are in the hot conversations. Some older, well-known economists (whom I shall kindly not name) have become frustrated as the stream of invitations dries up. They feel they are being left out. And they are.

The world of economics can be harsh. "You're only as good as your last paper," they say at Chicago. Someone once wrote a good paper on urban economics that drew her into the circle of urban economists. She switched to another topic of research and found herself quickly losing fluency in serious urban economic conversations. She read a current survey article and found that her contributions were no longer mentioned. She blamed herself, and wondered whether and how to get back in. She went with her best option: stick with the new research topic and work into a conversation where it counted for something.

Skeptic: Whatever does this have to do with science? You're a bunch of high-school snobs worried about being most cool, most popular, most talked about. I can't take this seriously.

Response: Not so quick. Be realistic. This is how science works. Keynes spoke of a beauty contest. Whatever your business happens to be, being in the conversation or not is darned serious. It determines whose work is prominent and which ideas will circulate. It also accounts for some of the strangeness of the discipline of economics as a science.

Probing the notion of conversation

I am using the concept "conversation" with emphasis and insistence. It denotes an interaction that is discrete. Once again, economics is a conversation, or rather a bunch of conversations. Economists walk in different schools and each school can be said to constitute a distinct conversation. The disadvantage of using "conversation" is its colloquial connotations. To avoid this, it might be better to speak of "discursive practices," the term that Foucault, Habermas, and so many others use. It has a more serious flavor about it, and therefore appears to better match the practice of a science. But, like Richard Rorty in *Philosophy and the Mirror of Nature* (1979), I prefer "conversation." It is the etymology of the word that I like.

The root of conversation means "turning together." Conversation denotes "intercourse," "manner of life," or "frequent abode in a place." Conversation has been used to connote the "action of living or dwelling in a place" and, more interestingly, the "action of associating with or having dealings with others." Among its definitions, the *Oxford English Dictionary* cites Thomas Shelton's "You know a man by the conversation he keeps." In this usage, conversation is a synonym for company, as in Wayne Booth's *The Company We Keep* (1988). Being in a conversation implies being in company with a certain group of people. At least that is what I intend it to mean. I also like the term conversation because it does not conjure up something hermetic; a conversation is fluid and if it is bounded the boundaries tend to be fuzzy.

Conversation also denotes "occupation or association with an object of study, in the sense of close acquaintance." Francis Bacon wrote of the "conversation in books." That meaning fits nicely as well – conversation refers not only to people's talking but also to their reading. I like to go into the libraries of the people I visit (provided they allow me). I learned a great deal about Deirdre McCloskey when I saw that she had Greek, Latin, and poetry books in front of her desk, and near her books of philosophy. Behind her were stacks of books on economic history; in an adjacent room were other economic books.[1] Her library is an exhibit of her plea for economists to join the human conversation, to be in conversation with the great books – especially poetry – so economists have that knowledge in common.[2]

The bookcase of John Hicks (the Nobel Prize-winning economist who was one the engineers of modern microeconomics) told another story. I visited him a few years before his death at his English countryside cottage. He was sitting in a red armchair in his study. The bookcase was mostly filled with old books (really old books, judging by their spines). The few new ones I noticed were from his own publisher, Oxford University Press. The bookcase betrayed the fact that he was not keeping up with the literature. Subsequent conversation affirmed it: this man was in a conversation that had ceased a few decades previously.

Later, in his living room, I recognized the Oxford don by his bookcases filled with history books, biographies, and poetry. How different the bookcases of contemporary economists look! They rarely have many books at all, unless they have some kind of hobby or are into heterodox economics. Journals fill the most space, with a few textbooks in between. Economists generally do not read books; they read journal articles. And that tells something about the conversations they are having.

Conversation can also mean "sexual intercourse." The final entry in the dictionary refers to the more colloquial meanings of conversation: "oral exchange of sentiments, observations, opinions, ideas." It can also mean a meeting or assembly. I will stress the earlier meanings of conversation – with the emphasis on its association with company, having dealings with, intercourse, and manner of life.

This metaphor versus others

"Economics is a conversation" is one conceivable metaphor to make sense of what economists do. In the context of McCloskey's rhetoric of economics, Habermas's communicative rationality, and Foucault's discourse or discursive strategies, the metaphor resonates well. The focus is on the language with which scientists cast theories, propose rhetorical devices, reconstruct facts,[3] and publicize papers.[4] An alteration in the conversation about science in general gave rise to this genre of metaphors, and it usually goes under the name the "linguistic turn." Of course, not everyone who engages in the conversations of science and economics has embraced the idea.

I expect resistance to the metaphor "economics is a conversation." It has, after all, some worthy competitors in the conventional arena. So let's look into them, compare and contrast "economics is a conversation" with the metaphors some readers may be determined to keep (which, of course, they are free to do).

Economics as "the body of accumulated knowledge"

The "body of accumulated knowledge" is the common picture of economics, from the way many economists talk about it. The metaphor focuses on the results of economic research. A massive amount of research is done, myriad hypotheses are generated, a slew of empirical findings are supposedly tested. According to this metaphor, all that counts are those hypotheses that survive the so-called empirical tests. They are the *results* and *findings* and constitute "the body of accumulated knowledge."

The metaphor is effective enough to be tremendously popular among practitioners. It justifies the selective reading of current articles, as they presumably contain the part of the body of accumulated knowledge that is worth preserving. Useless knowledge will have been discarded. Begone, history of economic thought! The metaphor is reassuring in that it conveys the sense that, as the science of economics advances, its accumulation of knowledge is ever more pure in truth and rightness.

The metaphor cannot be deemed flat wrong since any metaphor twists reality by comparing it with a thing that it is not. That is its nature. But the metaphor is flawed, and quite useless if used as a point of departure for further inquiry. Philosophers of science have been all over this metaphor. They long ago debunked it, crushed it to pieces and discarded it. (Apparently, the economics profession needs some time to catch up with philosophers.) Since trampling a metaphor to death was not convincing enough, philosophers stressed errors of the first and second orders: hypotheses added to the body of accumulated knowledge can be false (first order errors), and hypotheses discarded can be correct (second order errors). More importantly, as T.S. Kuhn (1970 [1962]) pointed out, entire bodies of knowledge can become obsolete in case of a paradigm shift. Pieces discarded long ago have to be retrieved to be in the conversation again. The metaphor does not do justice to the process by which science advances.

Moreover, the metaphor gets us nowhere in explaining the strange characteristics of economics. It does not allow for persistent disagreements and the existence of schools of disparate thought. And it has nothing to say about the strange relationship between the body of economic knowledge and its daily practice by politicians, businesspeople, and homemakers. In short, the metaphor is a sterile apparatus that does not work outside the conversation of economics. I suggest we drop it.

Economics as "logic and mirror"

Another way to picture the science of economics is as a logical structure of propositions, the logic, which mirrors the reality it intends to explain.[5] Until the linguistic phase of things came along, this metaphor prevailed in the philosophy of science. It calls for an analytical knife that cuts away all the fluff, all the social stuff, all the extraneous activities, reducing the product of economic scientists to a system of propositions, i.e., a theory or model.

The metaphors of logic and mirror have proven to be useful because they suggest, among other things, criteria for the discrimination between scientific and non-scientific statements. "Logic" calls for logical consistency within the model, the domain of deduction. "Mirror" calls for a correspondence between the model and reality, the domain of induction. It operates on two sides. By way of entry, induction leads to assumptions. By means of deduction, hypotheses are derived. The mirror side of the metaphor demands an inquiry into its correspondence with the real world. If we are willing to accept that the facts represent reality – a hazardous business in the case of economics and many other sciences – then an economic theory would be scientific if its predictions harmonized with the facts.

The metaphor looks simple enough and appears to be plausible. Alas, it too has serious shortcomings. Its contribution has been to motivate intensive inquiry about science in general and economics in particular, and has dictated the conversation about science in general and economics in particular until quite recently. It has caused endless debates: Is economics an empirical science or not? (The Austrian economists, for example, claim that it is not.) Can economic theories be proven empirically (the positivist hope) or can they only be falsified?[6] Do accurate predictions suffice as a test (Friedman 1953)? Or do the assumptions have to be realistic as well (Samuelson 1963, 1964)?

All sorts of problems have grown out of the metaphor.[7] Falsification of a proposition depends on three things: the quality of facts, the choice of statistical methods, and the auxiliary hypotheses used to render the empirical test possible. But economic facts are constructed (by surveys, for instance) and can be inaccurate. Econometric methods evolve continually, and may be inadequate or time sensitive. Add the auxiliary hypotheses that economists need in order to make their models testable, and you begin to realize that falsification can never be definite. That is also what the notorious Duhem–Quine thesis states: the falseness of auxiliary hypotheses (e.g., that such and such a survey correctly measures unemployment) may cause the hypothesis to fail when it is in fact true. Accordingly, inquiry on the basis of logic and mirror points only to some fundamental uncertainties in economics.

Economics as a "research program" or as "realism"

Even so, the methodologists among economists want to hold on to the metaphor and continue to view economic science as a series of logically connection propositions plus a series of empirical tests. This perspective has grown more sophisticated over the years. Philosophers of science such as Lakatos (1970) proposed that we consider entire research programs. Going on with a research program would be rational as long as it progressed both theoretically and empirically. This proposal generated a great deal of conversation. Among my fellow students, several produced Lakatosian reconstructions of research programs in economics.[8] (I intended to do the same but switched the metaphor halfway, so to speak, and started exploring economics as discourse.)

Realists like Uskali Maki insist on the criterion of correspondence: they want us to recognize and take seriously the ontological status of economic theories. Critical realists like Tony Lawson call for the same, but declare econometric work misleading and distorting. I like to be in conversation with them because they challenge my metaphor that economics is a conversation, especially that it can be extensive and precise.[9] Their conversation draws students who are attracted to its rigor and highly philosophical sophistication.

Apart from its singular emphasis on the logical properties of economic theories, the normative character of the methodological conversation gives me pause. As Rorty (1979) so sharply points out, its practitioners serve the discipline as philosopher-kings who, from lofty positions, judge which contributions qualify as science and which do not. They are quick to declare rules and principles to which scientific practitioners should adhere. They suggest that scientists choose among competing theories by applying methodological rules of their own making. The Lakatosians, for example, want us to believe that scientists are rational only when they stick to a research program that is progressive. Those scientists, then, who hold on to a degenerative research program (such as Marxism, said Lakatos) are deemed irrational.

Such ways of talking about economics encourage incriminations and condemnations. When Mark Blaug (1980) lamented, in an expression now famous, that economists "play with the net down" because they eschew falsification for their theories, he was admonishing scientists to stick to the rules that he, the philosopher, had figured out for them. Maki condemns those who do not stick absolutely and resolutely to the criteria of truth and consistency (in Maki (1995), for example). The scientist who relents in the face of some inconsistency, the scientist whose empirical research is not extensive and whose theories are not subjected to rigorous tests is, according to those wedded to logic and mirror, not a real scientist.

But why not defer to the practice of economics and take into account what the practitioners themselves are actually saying and doing? I'd much rather watch the game of economists and make sense of what they do than listen to philosopher-kings speaking *ex cathedra*. Yes, the metaphor of the conversation induces judgments too, but with more reason than presumptuousness.

Economics as "ideology"

A teacher of macroeconomics once confided to a student that the field was mere ideology, a posture of empirics and theories. As I was the student and he was my professor, the confession made a deep impression. The indictment resonated further because Marxist economists said the very same about what they called "orthodox economics." Within it, my Marxist friends saw an affirmation – if not an apology – for the capitalist mode of production with its alleged exploitation, its gross injustices, and its tendency toward crisis. Orthodox economists simply did not want to see the truth. Accordingly, orthodox economists practiced ideology, not science; Marxists practiced the real science of economics. Orthodox economists returned the favor, calling Marxist economics ideological and non-scientific. They alleged that Marxist economists were willing to twist the truth just to advance the cause of the revolution.

The metaphor never caught on with me. It might feel good to call a particular brand of economics an ideology – the implication is that if one is an ideologist, others are not. It ends conversation. What can I say, once another has declared everything I say is ideological? Do I admit to false consciousness, beg forgiveness? Nothing will work and I must return to the comfort of my own conversations, knowing that at least there I will be understood and taken seriously.

The metaphor, though, may account for the bickering and passionate disagreements among economists. It is consistent with empirical and predictive weaknesses of economics. If empirical tests do weed out good theories, bad ideologies would not survive for long. We would have found out a long time ago that neoclassical economics was only an apology for capitalism, and Marxism a false criticism of the same system. But, no, ideologies survive in the form of conversations. To make sense of that, we need to be more specific about the beliefs that inform a particular conversation, and we may need to understand how beliefs can change in light of what is happening. We also want to be alert to the interests an economic conversation serve, and how the conversation may affect other practices, such as political conversations and business conversations. Having acknowledged all that, I maintain that the metaphor of ideology is too static, too absolute, and therefore too hermetic to help the conversation about economics along.[10]

Economics as "a commodity traded in a market"

There are some who prefer to see science as an economy and, surprisingly, they are not only economists. And why not? Why not think of the market for economic ideas, and of economists pursuing some kind of maximum – be it truth, funds, or income – under certain constraints? Think of the costs and benefits of pursuing a research project, the tradeoff between fame and fortune that scientists may face, the market for attention with excess demand and limited supply, and so on. The list of applications goes on. Like everything else, science has an economic dimension, so why not push it?

Interestingly enough, economists have not been eager to push the metaphor that would account for their own behavior. That says something. Economists are not reluctant to discuss the most personal matters – sex, marriage, children – in economic terms, but when it comes to making sense of what they do as scientists, most jump to a different, more comfortable conversation – a different, more comfortable metaphor. That tells us that something is askew.

I am enough of an economist to acknowledge the economic dimension of what we do as scientists. The economics of funding, reputation, and income frames at least part of our conversations. A lack of funds may impede progress in a certain research program, and an availability of funds may be an incentive to pursue a particular research topic. The budget procedures of universities undoubtedly matter, as do the politics of research foundations.

But the metaphor has the wrong meanings for the experiences that people have when practicing science. Compare the practice of science with the practice of making love, relating to friends, performing religious duties, and engaging in the arts. Even if the market categories of price, supply, and demand were to apply in some way or another, they would distort and even violate the experiences that we have in such activities. They are sacred, not profane. There are practical problems, too, such as the definition of the product that has to be priced in the market for science. Economics cannot and would not produce distinct results that could be marketed. Economics matters, but its metaphor of the market does not matter enough to justify a framing in its terms.

Economics as a "social process"

The final alternative is the metaphor of the social process that began, more or less, with the work of Thomas Kuhn (although Robert K. Merton had preceded him). Students of science – as well as quite a few scientists – began to think of scientific activities in social terms. Instead of reducing all science to a matter of logic, they observed that scientists, including economists, travel in groups. As the groups are rarely in a unified physical setting, Diana Crane (1972) suggested that they form "invisible colleges." The metaphor strikingly changes the self-perception that comes with the first three metaphorical characterizations of economics as a science and has as one major effect the relativizing of the "science" in science. It accounts for the human factor that we noted as strange in the previous chapter – the role of status, the embarrassing competition for funds, attention, and recognition, and the role of conventions and social institutions such as scientific associations, faculties and the like. It is no wonder that some scientists take a liking to this metaphor. It tells them much about what they actually experience. But is also no wonder that many others detest it, because it deflates the aura of the science, and thus, the aura of the scientist.

The metaphor of social process has much in common with the metaphor of conversation because it is a possible focus for the study of conversations. Social process would help to explain some of the strange features of economics. But I submit there is more, such as the conversing. I prefer "conversation" because it draws attention to the linguistic aspects of what economists do. For example, conversations in texts can be read and interpreted. If we study the differences between their dynamics and bounded character, the differences among the struggles and confusions at their borders, we can learn more than that afforded by the social process of science. Then again, we need to weigh in the social to make sense of the conversing.

Back to the beginning: conversation

Those who know my earlier work may have expected the "economics as rhetoric" metaphor. Although I continue to believe that a great deal can be learned from studying the rhetoric of economics, I have grown somewhat wary of the way the metaphor works and the meanings it evokes.

The metaphor of rhetoric freed me from the grips of the body of accumulated knowledge and logic and mirror. It unearthed all sorts of valuable stuff, like economics' metaphors and narratives. But the metaphor's aggressiveness troubled me. To think of economics as rhetoric is to think of economists as rhetors in the occupation of persuasion – a characterization I am uncomfortable with. Economists are not on stage trying to change the minds of an audience. For that matter, do they have an audience? Colleagues will not be persuaded. Scientists do not want to be persuaded. They certainly do not want to be preached at. The metaphor stresses too much the gap that exists between the speaker and the audience. The gap makes you think of all the (rhetorical) devices that the speaker has to use to bridge it and reach his or her audience. Although I continue seeing the gap – how could you not when you are in the business of communicating ideas? – I do not want to overemphasize it.

Thus, I prefer the metaphor of conversation. Seeking conversational commonalities is not a persuasive process but rather an attempt to find the expressions for my ideas to be heard. Conversation stresses the cooperative, the sharing of ideas, the identification with others. At the same time, it points to the causes of difference, tension, and conflict because the conversation of one is not necessarily the conversation of another.

As McCloskey pointed out to me, "conversation" implies the combination of rhetoric – the art of speaking – with hermeneutics – the art of listening and reading. My proposal, therefore, is in line with a long tradition that she, I, and others want to honor.

I have also used "economics as discourse" in the past, but conversation is less formal and evokes notions of companionship and community. Like discourse, conversation connects with the linguistic turn the reflection on science took some decades ago, but, more than discourse, it evokes the social aspects of doing science. Conversation takes place not only with people, but also with traditions and literature. Reading Aristotle or Smith puts me in conversation with these great minds. Their words percolate in my mind and I see where they connect, subsume them in my frame. I can then try out these new conversations with colleagues and students. Conversation is precious, and ideas need company to make sense and develop.

The character of a scientific conversation

Knowing we need to be in a conversation to do what we want to do is one thing, knowing how conversations work is quite another. We do not need an extensive study to understand that conversations are complex beasts, and that one conversation is unlike another. So what makes conversations different? And what makes them work?

Conversations constrain what we are able to say. This is an important first point. Many to whom I have presented my case have the notion that conversation means "anything goes," the anarchistic slogan of the philosopher Paul Feyerabend presented as "anything but that!" The point of being in a conversation is being disciplined. There are certain criteria to meet and a variety of rules to comply with to be in the pertinent conversation. To be in conversation with my wife, I would do better to forget about the way I am conversing now. Being scientific, or pretending to be, would not work. Nor can I converse in this book the way I converse with my wife. The rhetoric and the hermeneutic are different.

Scientific conversations are particularly constraining because they are so highly disciplined – you have to work to be in one. So let us consider a few elements that are at play in a scientific conversation like economics.

Institutional constraints of the conversation

Whereas many conversations may take place anywhere and at any time, economic conversations are firmly ensconced in the academic setting. They were not always. Adam Smith was in the scientific conversation while being a customs officer; William Jevons was a civil servant; Karl Marx was in the scientific conversation through the generous support of his industrialist friend Engels; Einstein was a clerk in a patent office. Today, I cannot think of any prominent, active economist who is not a professor at a university. With the university come all kinds of institutions that facilitate but also constrain the economic conversation, among them the following.

Physical surroundings

While all universities exist in some sort of physical location with buildings, labs, computer rooms, a library, a gym, and cafeterias, some locations are more conducive to intellectual conversation than others. Quite a few universities are desolate places with stark and uninviting architecture that discourages the gathering of academics. Others, like Duke University (where I did my PhD) and Wellesley College (where I taught), are almost idyllic in their layouts and make it easy for an academic community to thrive. Urban universities are different from small-town universities in the sense that the urban setting makes it harder to contain the conversation and keep people from scattering. The University of Chicago in Hyde Park, MIT and Harvard University in Cambridge, Princeton University in Princeton, the colleges of Oxford University in Oxford – all have relatively secluded settings with distinctive architecture. This contributes to their intense academic environments which, in turn, may account for their prominent roles in the economic conversations. (Administrators take note!)

Economic constraints

To stay in the economic conversation you need to hold on to that university job. The chances of being in the economic conversation without a university affiliation are virtually nil. While your economic situation matters in general, it matters in particular to acquire funds to do research to be in the conversation the research brings about. Deans give rises only to reputable, and therefore highly desirable, university participants. If high income is the goal, the choices are tough. While consulting or writing a textbook may bring big money, it may also damage your standing in the scientific conversation because colleagues are suspicious of scientific work done for money. Pursue fast money, and you may find yourself simply locked out of the scientific conversation. I see it happening all the time. Respected colleagues give up conferences for their contractual work; others are barred because they "are no longer doing interesting work." It is my own struggle, too. Should I, for better money, conduct a study into the narrative of the Rotterdam harbor when it is time-consuming, takes me away from writing this book, and may not generate much for my portfolio of scientific contributions? A book like this will not encourage commercial parties to ask for my services nor will it make much money, but it may get me some seminar and conference invitations.

Scientific standards

To get or keep a job, you have to demonstrate that you are able and willing to adhere to the standards of the academic community. Most are implicit. There is no booklet stating what criteria you need to meet to be able to participate in an economic conversation. And it is not sufficient to know that you must be systematic, adhere to principles of logic, know the statistics, heed criteria for statistical significance, and so on. The more nebulous criteria matter more, like knowing the right literature, paying homage to authorities in your field, writing scientifically (meaning systematically; for example, using the scientific "we" instead of the "you" often seen in this book), and, most difficult of all, being interesting to the other participants. Undergraduate studies do not teach this. Only in pursuing a PhD, attending seminars and conferences, and talking a great deal with insiders do you find out what the standards are. As part of the ever-important university gatekeeping process, you later reference those standards when assessing the work of aspiring participants.

Technological constraints and possibilities

Once, long ago, economists communicated by means of books and pamphlets found in libraries. Towards the end of the nineteenth century – at the same time that newly formed academic departments began to constrain the economic conversation – journals became the mainstay of written communication. Instead of writing long monographs, economists' work began to appear in short papers. The length of the argument, therefore, became a serious constraint, and economists had to wrestle with "How do I say this in ten to twenty pages?"

The computer constitutes another important technological factor. When Jan Tinbergen did econometrics, he had only a mechanical calculator and needed assistants to do further calculations by hand. I had to learn to work with *ponskaarten* (known in the US as punch cards). Now that researchers have computers to do their computing, the quantity and complexity of empirical research done has increased. The computer has also increased our capacity to write. I wrote my dissertation on a $129 typewriter with lots of strikeouts and that white stuff to erase the many errors. I know colleagues who continue to write their drafts in longhand on yellow pads, but most of us are pounding the keys and filling our digital memories. Here is what Paul Samuelson, the old master at the craft of economics, has to say about the role of the computer:

> I ought to envy the new generation who have grown up with the computer, but I don't. None of them known to me sits idly at the console, improvising and experimenting in the way that a composer does at the piano. That ought to become increasingly possible. But up to now, in my observation, the computer is largely a black box into which researchers feed raw input and out of from which they draw various summarizing measures and simulations. Not having access to look around in the box, the investigator has less intuitive familiarity with the data than used to be the case in the bad old days.
>
> (Samuelson 1992: 245)

Are these the ruminations of an old man who has trouble of keeping up? Or is it wisdom? The arrival of digital technology is going to affect our practice of storing and retrieving our shared knowledge. The role of libraries will change, as will the role of journals. Email already has intensified the informal communication among the participants but it is hard to tell how it has changed the conversation as such. I know at least one colleague who does his most important work by means of email; he does not bother to publish in journals anymore (but, then, he has tenure).

Social constraints of the conversation

The practice of science revolves around people, groups, friendships, and communities. It is a social activity. You may want to believe that it is about logic, facts, and truth – and many scientists and philosophers of science will assist you in doing so – but you would be mistaken. Open your eyes and see the humans argue, calculate, measure, think, write, deliberate, and whatever else it takes beyond logic and facts to practice a science like economics. This means, for example, the following.

Scientific communities

Humans, said Aristotle, live in communities, and so do scientists. Despite the common belief, practicing science is no solitary affair. A good deal of work may be carried out alone, but the heart of it is to be in a conversation, and that means socializing, making friends, getting to know the right people, developing a network, and so on. Economists with any stature spend much of their time communicating and socializing with other economists. Those pursuing the Nobel Prize will make regular appearances in Swedish circles. Economists who cannot do this will be able to stay in the conversation only if they compensate with outstanding written work. Socially clever economists may do well even if their research is less remarkable in terms of quantity or quality.

Faculties, invisible networks, associations

The most immediate community is the faculty at the university that employs you. They are your direct colleagues; you will find yourself in regular conversation with them in the office, over lunch, and during seminars – if you are lucky. There's a good chance that no one on the faculty shares your specialty or, even if one does, the two of you don't get along. That doesn't necessarily set you back as far as your own conversation is concerned. The university may give you a pay check, and the faculty may form your direct community, but a scientist's significant community is the (often international) network of those who partake in his particular conversation, that "invisible college." PhD students need to learn this. Being loved by teachers is fine, doing well at teaching gives satisfaction, but the challenge for graduate students is to be noted by the important people in their field. Like them, you must do the drill: venture out, present at conferences, submit work to journals. Being ignored or unappreciated at your home base does not matter as long as you are noted and appreciated in the relevant network.

Membership of associations is a way of signaling your affiliation. Most associations do not screen, so you derive no distinction from such a membership. But the associations usually organize conferences where you find out what others are doing in your field and where you are possibly going to get noticed.

The game of getting and giving attention

Once in a conversation you need to recognize others in the conversation. Cite, cite well, and cite justly. Use footnotes to display your knowledge of the literature. Be aware that your readers will check whether you got the citations right, and certainly whether you have cited them. It is safer to be too generous with your citations than to be too skimpy. (This text isn't a good example – I'm cutting down on my citations for a change.) Being cited is a sign of getting attention for your work. For most of us it doesn't happen often. As a matter of fact, the distribution of attention in our world is highly skewed. A few of us get a great deal of attention and most get hardly any attention at all. It's a harsh world.

Scientific entrepreneurship

If you are not good enough to be on top of the game, or if you lack the energy to stay ahead of it, there is always the opportunity to distinguish yourself by getting grants, organizing conferences, and bringing groups of economists together. You become like a famous show host, inviting the stars to your place, setting up new associations, or starting a research institute – in other words, you become a scientific entrepreneur. To be effective, you need rhetorical skills to convince fellow economists to join in your ventures, and social skills to reason with university officials, research agencies, and the like.

Teaching

Conversations will be sustained only if they frequently receive new impulses. To that end we need to train people to join the conversation and take over, another reason economists are at universities. Think of graduate teaching as a community service and new recruits as our link to the future – a good reason for treating young scholars well. Undergraduates are another matter. Only a small percentage of them can be expected to aspire seriously to become part of the economic conversation. We need them for income but many of us have a hard time getting motivated for that kind of teaching. However little we may like it, the job needs to be done. Fortunately, some like the teaching of undergraduates (like myself) and are good at it (on that opinions vary). Rarely will undergraduate teachers be prominent in their scientific conversation, though – another tradeoff that faces the economist.

Scientific culture

Being "in" the world of economists or other scientists is unlike being "in" any other world. There is generally a clear sense of when it happens and a clear sense of being squeezed out. Inside that world you learn to appreciate a certain type of knowledge over others. You learn to value a clever argument, the mastery of a certain technique, scientific status and stardom; you learn to appreciate authority, know the right literature, and know the right people. People learn to adjust their expectations and aspirations of this world (and some of these lessons are painful) when going through graduate school, as David Colander and I noted in a joint study (Klamer and Colander 1987, 1990). Graduate school years are critical: it is then you must assimilate the culture of the world of economists and develop the habitus that allows you function in that world.

Part of the habitus is a community spirit: if you are asked to referee an article, you do so, even if you do not get pay or credit. You will be a discussant at conference panels, chair sessions, edit journals, organize conferences, and do whatever it takes to keep the conversation going. The community expects you to give freely, generously, and without complaint. Your papers are called contributions, as you are expected to share your findings, insights, and innovations freely with the community of scholars. Giving and sharing are as typically characteristic of the scientific culture as the mocking, gossiping, and power plays.

Scientific passions and emotions

Although the competition is tough, no one is expected to bash in the brains of an opponent. Rumors are that a Chinese scholar once punctuated a disagreement by hitting a colleague with his shoe, but such an event is unheard of in our culture. Get agitated, get angry, sneer occasionally, and make scathing remarks, but do not get too personal in public or your reputation will be harmed. (Getting personal in private is quite all right.) The general device is: control your emotions and be kind in your criticism, even if your own work is being challenged.

This may be difficult: scientific work is emotional. Reason without passion will not obtain. As Michael Polanyi points out, passions play a critical role in scientific work (Polanyi 1962 [1958]). He distinguished heuristic passions in particular, the emotions of intuition that tell us where to direct our research and let us know if we are on the right path. I feel them when I read something that puts me off or that confirms an idea that I am entertaining. Good scientists get tremendously excited now and then. When I select candidates for graduate school, I look for the right passions. They are ultimately more important for success than a good record or a clever research plan.

Borders

Each conversation is bounded. Anything does *not* go. Get too personal, too political, and you may find yourself shunned from the conversation. Misuse a term, use the wrong technique, or ask the wrong question and you may find yourself banned from the conversation. Nor is it always easy to know what will be considered "wrong." Because the borders that mark the conversation are so fuzzy, the "wrong" question may prove to be a breakthrough and become widely acclaimed. A controversial paper may shift the borders somewhat. Whatever the case, a solid scientific community carefully guards the borders of its conversation by screening or refereeing contributions to its journals, and by being highly selective and critical in the hiring and tenuring for its faculty.[11]

Border scrimmages are an essential part of the conversation process. When people challenge the status quo with their research, or try to change the topic, or even the entire conversation, they are trying to alter borders. The established participants will defend them by debunking the challenge as not being "economics" or, worse, being "unscientific." Tenure fights are often about the borders of the discipline. The question is whether the work of the candidate is sufficiently within the conversation or falls outside of it. Am I an economist or not? Some colleagues have passionately refused me that status because of the work I am doing now. It was a reason to be denied tenure at one place but given tenure at another. Borders matter, even if they are not clearly marked.

Disciplinary and rhetorical constraints of the conversation

Social and institutional constraints aside, a scientific conversation revolves around the writing, the talking, the measurement, the calculations, the experiments, and whatever else that collects in the bucket called "research." As scientists we have to produce papers, and that means we have to write. When we present our papers at a conference, we have to talk. Doing science involves a great deal of talk, much of it informal. It is impossible to participate without mastering the pertinent techniques, knowing the arguments, being familiar with the relevant literature, and knowing what others are doing. The rhetorical figures that mark the conversation must be well understood. Certain elements bind and constrain the economic conversation, among them the following.

Scientific research programs

A conversation usually has a certain direction and follows a certain heuristic. Subscribers to the neoclassical research program have to heed a hard core of assumptions (such as the behavioral assumption of constrained maximization), follow a certain positive heuristic (such as the search for the competitive equilibrium solution), and know which concepts, arguments, and methods are out of bounds (terminology borrowed from Lakatos 1970). They will not survey the subjects they are studying, will not consider their emotions or relations (that is psychology and sociology), and will leave out considerations of power and culture (again, not part of the economic argument). They will want to cast their contribution to the conversation in the right terms, with the right assumptions and the right methods, and follow the proper heuristics – all things learned in graduate school.

A spectrum of arguments

A variety of arguments exists to bolster a claim or thesis, and which is best to use may depend on the conversation. Each argument has its own requirements. For a theoretical argument in economics, it is usually the development of a model. Modeling is what economists do and what they are good at. Mastery of advanced mathematics is a must. Empirical arguments call for statistical techniques such as time series analyses and calibration. Econometrics is another field, and requires a conversation different from theoretical economics. When challenged, or when engaged in border disputes, a good command of methodological arguments is necessary, that is, statements about what is science and how it is done. When challenged from outside the world of science, by your mother for example, you will be able to articulate the scientific mission and the importance of seeking Truth. (Use this with politicians and businesspeople too. Don't use such arguments with colleagues – you do not want to be viewed as dishonest.)

Rhetorical devices and constraints

Once more, science is not a matter of logic and fact alone. The scientific conversation is fed by a certain imagination; it is kept alive and fluid with all kinds of meanings that the participants attribute to it. The resultant collaborative meanings find expression in the form of metaphors and narratives. To be in a conversation you have to connect with its key metaphors and know how to apply its narrative.

Foreign trade is a news staple. In politics and on the street, people tend to speak of it in terms of "us against them." "We need to protect our agriculture against the unfair competition of the *other* guys." "We need to be strong to go up against them." Such talk is reminiscent of warfare. Accordingly, we have devices of "protection" and even "retaliation," as if trade is a zero sum game in which, when *they* win, *we* lose.

In the economic conversation you quickly learn to drop the war metaphor and the narrative that comes with it. You learn to think in mechanical terms, as if the world economy is a system of markets moving toward equilibrium if left alone. The abstract metaphors that economists use make you forget about wars and winning or losing them. The narrative is about trade that is good for everybody, and the welfare loss due to protective measures.

The rhetoric of economics is different from anything the outside world is accustomed to. It matters in that it reshapes the way someone perceives the world, the way someone interprets a newspaper, and, indeed, the way someone lives a life. The metaphors and narratives of economics frame the thinking and talking of economists. Rhetoric is not a superficial thing; it is not enough to simply know it or to be able to con people with it. Graduate school is just one prerequisite for acquiring it. Rhetoric that has any power has great depth. In fact, assimilation of the rhetoric of the economic conversation sits so deeply that it estranges you from the outside world. People may not understand you, get angry or frustrated, give up – and you will not understand why. After all, you make perfect sense to your colleagues.

Economic PhDs pursuing government or business positions have to check some intellectual baggage at the front door. Their rhetoric would not work, and it would lose against the rhetoric of lawyers and accountants. Even within the university, economists have to restrain their conversations. Rational behavior and the pricing of human life do not fit in the mindsets of colleagues in, say, literature; the economist risks being branded unfeeling, asocial, and awkward. Some of my economic colleagues have yet to get that message.

Getting the right ethos

A beginning scholar cannot simply criticize dominant theory and proclaim his own alternative. Anyone who does will not be taken seriously. I made that error early on, and am now embarrassed by it. (The presumptuousness! How could I?) As any rhetorician will tell you, you need *ethos* to be heard. Ethos stands for "character" and indicates the status or authority that you have in a conversation.

Authority counts: when Robert Solow speaks, economists listen. He may make silly jokes, he may even make mistakes, but people pay attention. Given his status, his mistakes may be particularly interesting.

And knowing your topoi

Topoi are the common places to go to in discussions. There are lots of them and since they are, by definition, well known, you better know them to hold your own in the conversation. Think of them as shortcuts, things to say to move on. When challenged on the realism of an assumptions, the topos to go to is Milton Friedman's "the realism of assumptions does not matter." (You do not need to know much more than that. The point is that you are understood and can move on.) When the work of a critic comes up, you can score against him or her by going to the topos "that's not economics" or "that's not scientific." No need to elaborate. When politicians ignore your advice, it suffices to evoke the topos of "ignorant politicians." When asked about the practical usefulness of your abstract research, you may get away with the topos of "Who cares? As long as I get paid."

Be careful, though. The topoi that work in one conversation may not work in another. Your fellow economists may roar when you propose to think about a moral issue in terms of a constrained maximization problem. Non-economists may think you are out of your mind. You are actually out of your conversation.

So what?

My habit to so end a discussion stems from feelings that linger after most lectures and seminars: "It's fine and dandy what you've been saying, but what difference does it make? What does it all amount to?" A variant of this question is to ask for the "policy consequences." As I understand the question, it asks for the practical consequences of the argument or the interests that it serves. People want to know what the argument means for what people are doing.

An answer is that it can account for much of the strangeness of economics. The oddities of the previous chapter are now more understandable:

- *The bickering among economists and the persistent disagreements.* These occur because of differences in their conversations. I have not said much about those differences, but the notion of conversation along with the notion of rhetoric gets me there quite easily. Feminist economists are especially bristling in the mainstream because they persistently try to change its metaphors and narrative. The same applies to the Austrians. But even within the mainstream, disagreements exist because of different concepts of what constitutes good science.
- *The relevance of economics and the irrelevance of economists.* Even if it is easy to recognize the relevance of economics, economists may be seen as irrelevant because of their way of talking. Their rhetoric does not connect with that of non-economists. As a consequence, many of their insights and

results do not circulate as quickly and easily as they would wish, and their ethos in the public domain is limited.

- *The dubious scientific character of economics.* The science of economics is dubious when adhering to the metaphors of "the body of accumulated knowledge" and "the logic and the mirror." Adopt the metaphors of social process or, better, conversation and it makes more sense. Economics is scientific because economists operate within fine scientific institutions using honor-proven scientific standards. The scientific tenor of a conversation may be disturbing, but instead of focusing on its unscientific character, it might be better to simply acknowledge a desire to change it, or to participate in another conversation altogether. Discussion on what constitutes true science is fruitless anyway.

- *Econospeak.* Annoying as econospeak may be, recognize that any group intensely preoccupied with a certain subject matter tends to have its own internal language. Doctors do, computer scientists do, musicians do, so why not economists? An economist's language works in the lay sector no better than a physician's. They have to discipline themselves and apply the topoi and rhetoric of the conversation they want to affect. If you want to get into another's conversation, learn how to speak it.

- *Economists are humans, too.* Of course! Conversation is a human thing. The economic conversation is no different. So why wouldn't economists, at times, be emotional, exhibit anger, and mock others? Why would anyone expect economists to be wholly selfless, relentlessly objective, and all the other values that are ascribed to science? Economists, like everyone, are worried about income, reputation, and personal life.

- *The lack of reflection.* I have found it odd how little economists reflect on what they do, and also how much they resist a reflection in their own economic terms. It must be a characteristic of their conversation. Maybe there is no need for reflection since they feel secure about that conversation. I am still puzzled. Then again, given that you, the reader, are still with me, the desire for reflection must be there.

- *Obscure motivations.* The metaphor of the conversation will not immediately tell us why economists do what they do. Why do they keep publishing papers when nobody reads them? Why do they keep pushing the conversation when they have no clue as to whether it makes any difference? I wonder myself. Maybe being in the conversation is the reward.

Further reading

The metaphor of the conversation is not a hot topic in the literature. Richard Rorty uses it in his influential *Philosophy and the Mirror of Nature* (Princeton University Press, 1979), as does George Gadamer in *Truth and Method* (Crossroad Publishing, 1982). I also draw inspiration from writings such as "Me and My Shadow" by Jane Tompkins in *Gender and Theory: Dialogues on Feminist Criticism*, edited by Linda Kauffman (Basil Blackwell, 1989), in which she takes issue with the competition that debilitates so much scientific intercourse.

When you want to read more about discursive practices, you may want to start with the classics:

* Michel Foucault's *The Archeology of Knowledge and the Discourse on Language* (Pantheon Books, 1972).
* Jurgen Habermas's *On the Pragmatics of Communication* (MIT Press, 1998).
* Thomas S. Kuhn's *The Structure of Scientific Revolutions* (University of Chicago Press, 1970 [1962]). This is a classic. Here you find the introduction of the notion of "paradigm" into the discussion.
* Also interesting is Kuhn's *The Essential Tension* (University of Chicago Press, 1977).

To give you the notion of a research program, read Imre Lakatos in *The Methodology of Scientific Research Programmes Philosophical Papers*, Vol. I, edited by J. Worrall and G. Curie (Cambridge University Press, 1978).

To seriously challenge your conventional notions of a science, read Paul Feyerabend's *Against Method* (NLB, 1975).

The classic for the rhetoric, of course, is *The Rhetoric of Economics* (University of Wisconsin Press, 1983, 1998 [1985]) by Deirdre N. McCloskey.

For readings in the sociology of science, I suggest:

* Robert K. Merton in *The Sociology of Science: Theoretical and Empirical Investigations* edited by N.W. Storer (University of Chicago Press, 1973).
* Karin Knorr Cetina's *The Manufacture of Knowledge: An Essay on the Constructivist and Contextual Nature of Science* (Pergamon, 1981).
* Bruno Latour's *Science in Action* (Harvard University Press, 1987).

Sociological research into the world of economists is rather rare. See, for example, A.W. Coats's "The Sociology of Science: Its Application to Economics" in *The Sociology and Professionalization of Economics: British and American Economic Essays*, Vol. II, edited by A.W. Coats (Routledge, 1993).

For something quick on any of these topics (except for the topic of conversation), consult your library for *The Handbook of Economic Methodology*, edited by John B. Davids, D. Wade Hands, and Uskali Maki (Edward Elgar, 1998).

I also suggest reading Diana Crane's *Invisible Colleges: Diffusion of Knowledge in Scientific Communities* (University of Chicago Press, 1972).

3 What it takes to be an academic dog, or the culture of the academic conversation

Conversation and function

"You know the man by the conversation he keeps," Thomas Shelton wrote. Could we go even further and say that we *are* the conversation we keep? That the conversation makes us who we are? If you converse with me, I become a cultural economist, an academic, a teacher, a writer, a father, a Christian, and all the other things that are my talk. Rom Harré, a psychologist, notes that "conversation is to be thought of as creating a social world just as causality generates a physical one" (Harré 1983: 65). In depression, when conversation is impossible, the "self" and sense of things are lost. Indeed, how would we be able to make sense of the world outside a conversation?

The character Robinson Crusoe is about conversation. (We often refer to *Crusoe* in the economic conversation. The number of economists who have actually read the book notwithstanding, it has become a topos, inspiring "calculating man." No need to know more.) Defoe tossed Crusoe on an island for a couple of years, divorced him from his natural habitat, and after many years gave him contact with another human in the form of someone Crusoe rescues from the cooking pot. He and Friday shared little at first: no language, no literature; that is, no conversation. But under the pressure of the circumstances (and to make a living together), a new conversation developed, one of companionship.

Throughout all the years on the island, Crusoe did not have the luxury of his own conversation or mother tongue, and did not socialize with anyone of his own culture. Yet when Westerners finally arrived, he was immediately able to address them in Portuguese, Spanish, and English – the languages he commanded before the shipwreck. He also had grown personally, coming to terms with his father and God (in literary terms, this is a *bildungsroman*). Incredible? Well, yes, it is. In reality, the person whose story inspired Defoe had become wild by the time he was found, with no command of his native English and a fear of civilized people. He retreated, eventually, to a self-made cave somewhere in Scotland, unable to rejoin the human conversation.

We need to be in conversations to function in our human lives. We are always in various kinds of conversations, of course, but I want to focus on the conversation that makes people function as academic economists. It is not something out there, something to finger or to distinguish clearly. No one can say: *there* it is, *that* is what it takes to be part of it, and *this* is what it means to be in one – but I am going to try anyway.

Like the experience on the Italian square, observing people having conversations makes me wonder about them. My speculation about the economic conversation started with a book about Keynesian economics lent to me in my junior year of high school.[1] I had no clue as to what I was reading: economics was not a school course then. But I knew about money, had become intrigued by what money does in life, and thus wanted to understand it. I did not and could not discuss the book with friends because they hadn't a clue about it either. But I learned that there was something out there called economics, and it looked darned serious. Adam Smith could not have had this experience because there was no academic economic conversation in his time.

I then met Jan Tinbergen and was impressed with the man and his ideals. Solving the problems of the world by means of econometrics sounded like a good thing. I chose to study econometrics straight away, as is allowed in the Netherlands. What happened next is not terribly clear. I was not really conscious of the effects of my studies, or maybe I did not have the ability to reflect upon them. I waded through the courses along with everyone else, learned the linear algebra, the statistics, micro and macro, not knowing what it was all for, what I could do with it, or whether it added to my understanding of what money does. In fact, we hardly discussed the role of money in those early years. Tinbergen's ideals did not come up and I kept them to myself.

What did matter were the people I was with: the teachers and, especially, fellow students. I rather quickly found out that we were forming our own little world, with our own interests and our own jokes. I noticed this especially when I could not share my new experiences with old friends who were studying other subjects. At high school we at least read the same books; now the books were completely different and we had less to share. More importantly, the conversation of econometricians was not conducive to romance and intimacy, and I needed that too. The only chance I had was to lock out the world of econometricians from time to time, and seek out other conversations. Fraternities and the like were not an option then, so serious effort was required. I managed a student club, found companions in the artsy world, and remained close to my high-school friends.

As I struggled with the conversation that would make me an econometrician, I did not feel like one. I hadn't the sense of being on a mission, Tinbergen's econometric mission. A few of us tried to change the conversation in the econometrics program by having more economics inserted, but we failed miserably. You do not change the conversation without the proper ethos! I switched to economics, worked as an assistant on a large econometric model, was paid to measure the money stock of the Netherlands for a forty-year period, but still did not feel satisfied. The fit was not quite right. I found myself turning toward economic methodology, and continuing with it in the PhD program at Duke University.

I am not writing this to be personal but to show that, as a rule, one does not knock on the door of economic conversation and walk in. Economists stumble willy-nilly into it as many times as they do intentionally. Kenneth Boulding came to it by way of chemistry. John Hicks wanted to study history at first; Robert Lucas and Robert Solow had a similar interest but settled for economics. In the 1930s quite a few came from engineering or physics (such as Tinbergen and Koopmans). Nowadays, the natural sciences and mathematics prove to be good breeding grounds for economists. There are as many stories as there are economists, and most tell about people wandering in by chance, not knowing full well what awaits them. They stick to it because they want to, or, as too many economists are inclined to say, because they had nothing better in mind. But all become functioning economists by becoming part of the conversation of economists.

Introducing the notion of culture

What does it take to be Italian? More than a declaration, or a passport; more than respecting Italian customs and frequenting its squares. You can learn to speak with your hands, be perfectly fluent in Italian, and prefer Italian food over any other, but if you are not Italian, you will be found out. And you will be ever aware of your own foreignness. To be Italian you need to be so Italian that you are not aware of being Italian unless it is pointed out to you. That is culture. I realized what it is to be Dutch only after living amidst Americans. Culture is for humans what water is for fish: we become aware of it only when it does not surround us. Culture sits so comfortably in us that we do not feel it. Likewise, the academic economist needs to grow into and assimilate the academic economist's culture so much so that he or she is unaware of it.

The academically inclined will want to know what I mean by "culture." I must protest a little here: the meanings of "rationality" or "market" are varied and ambiguous, but in the company of economists no one will ask for a definition. To say or write culture without defining it is to have my entire world besieging me for concrete meaning. Economists, especially, are wary, as culture is not part of their conversation (yet). It has no mention in economic handbooks, no entry in the exhaustive *Palgrave Dictionary of Economics*, nor does it appear in the *Handbook of Economic Methodology*. Introducing the notion of culture in the economic conversation is thus a risk.

However risky, I need it. A contested concept such as culture makes the experience of being in the academic economic conversation more clear. Culture is a matter of getting things into the subconscious, of having certain emotions and sentiments arise without having to call upon them. Clifford Geertz, an anthropologist, calls culture "deep play" (Geertz 1973). When Balinese men engage in cockfights – a famous case of his – they play out a distinct variety of customs, values, emotions, stories, and sentiments without necessarily being conscious of them. Onlookers can learn the elements of play, but it is too deep for them to be players without elements of artifice.

I therefore risk proposing a definition: culture denotes beliefs, customs, values, emotions, stories, and sentiments that every member of group (Balinese men,

Italians, academic economists) have in common and, crucially, by which they distinguish themselves as a group. The distinction is a great matter: Italians are quite unlike non-Italians and academic economists are quite unlike sociologists, businesspeople, and non-academic economists. Here, though, the definition has to make sense in usage. What does the introduction of culture do for us in this book?

Conversation, as I am using it, begs for the idea of culture. Besides the casual conversation, the chatting in a café or over dinner, conversation denotes a way of being. To evoke the company an academic economist keeps is to be in that culture, and to be able to perform the deep play of economics without being found out. Being in the economic conversation is like being in a world or, as sociologists like to say, operating in a field. Worlds and fields are fine concepts to make sense of academic economics as a cultural practice, but I prefer conversation because of the linguistic performance that being in a world or field entails. The culture of economics becomes evident in its conversation. An outsider will be lost in its unexpected deep play, and no one prepares anyone for it because no one is much aware of it.

Becoming acquainted with the culture is easy enough. Good teachers of introductory economics do their best to make the subject interesting. They refer to actual economic events and attempt to show how abstract economic concepts apply to the real economy. But infectious exposure to the culture of economics comes with working toward a PhD, when life plans are often rethought and learning the tacit rules of the conversation is a must. Amidst it come the shocks and waves of a new culture.

In the late 1980s, David Colander and I conducted a series of interviews with graduate students. Their frustrations were evident in our conversations. Some acknowledged that they already had given up plans to become policy advisors because that was not the thing to do. Others had given up their reading in other subjects such as psychology, philosophy, and the like because that, too, was not the thing to do. General intellectual curiosity was not appreciated in their new surroundings. To some the experience was downright painful. As one first-year Harvard student so vividly told it:

> It seems to me that the first year is going to shape the rest of our professional career as economists to a great extent. I find it really disturbing. We are being socialized into something, but nobody in the faculty seems to know what that is, except they were socialized themselves five years ago. It's like being brainwashed. You may have heard stories of brainwashing during the Korean War. You are deprived of sleep, you are subjected to extreme stress, bombarded with contradictory convictions – you end up accepting anything. You end up in the middle of the semester completely malleable. You write down whatever you can and try to understand it. If you get your head above water, you survive. But you don't know where you are – all the intellectual landmarks have been leveled.

(Klamer and Colander 1990:94)

Granted, this student was unusually aware of what was going on, and unusually eloquent in expressing it. His fellow students seemed to identify with his observations, though. They laughed in approval at the image of brainwashing.

Although I would not have been able to express my own experience so precisely, I can sympathize with his account. I did not choose economics; it chose me. I did not make the conversation; it made me. And, as there was already so much out there, so very rich and deep in tradition; and because so many people, so many clever, sharp people, had already developed and shaped the conversation by filling countless journals and books with their ideas – wouldn't it be rather arrogant to imagine myself making a difference? As though I had the freedom to choose and make the conversation according to my liking? Like the Harvard student tells it, the conversation overcame and engulfed me. But I grew up and earned my ethos, and introducing a new conversation no longer seems foolish.

The experience of graduate school is not so much about "science as knowledge" as it is about "science as practice."[2] Studying results, findings, and methods consumes the time, but the essence of the experience is reading, listening, talking, writing, socializing, visiting professors, attending seminars, showing off skills and knowledge, demonstrating the proper intentions, and so on. It is the practice of science, not the knowledge of it, that makes economists and reshapes their worldview. They stealthily move into conversation with like-minded people and out of the conversations of so many others, such as sociologists, business economists, psychologists, natural scientists, engineers, historians, and all others they may have once cared about. At a point unknown to themselves, they have adapted and are cloaked in the culture of economics, in its nervous system.

In representing the world we intervene, as the philosopher Ian Hacking argued in one of his books (Hacking 1983). Economic professors intervene by asking for a great deal of study, and they expect, simultaneously, total attention to the acclimatization of their "habitus"[3] and to the shedding of all others'. This is not necessarily wrong – I do the same by wanting others to adjust to the values of "economics is a conversation." But being aware of the intervention is good: it stimulates us to think of science as a practice, and to think of the practice of science as culture.

Academic dogs

To see the academic community of economics as a separate culture it helps to step away from it. Only looking from the outside do we see its strange, different, and unexpected characteristics. We asked "What does it take to become successful as an economist?", offering several options. How graduate students of elite institutions responded is shown in Table 3.1.

The popular press gleefully fell on this outcome and gave it wide notice. How could these budding economists not care about the real world? Were they out of their minds? Journalists saw it as a grand occasion for economics bashing. The implication was obvious: if economics is not about the real world, economists are not of much use.

Table 3.1 Perceptions of success

	Very important	Moderately important	Unimportant	Don't know
Excellence in mathematics	65	32	3	1
Being very knowledgeable about one particular field	57	41	2	0
Being smart in the sense of being good at problem solving	37	42	19	2
Ability to make connections with prominent professors	26	60	16	9
Being interested in, and good at, empirical research	16	50	23	1
Having a broad knowledge of the economic literature	10	41	43	5
Having a thorough knowledge of the economy	3	22	68	7

Insiders, however, read the results quite differently. To them, the students had understood what counts in the conversation and what it takes to sustain that all-important conversation. Practical concerns, such as the latest move of the Federal Reserve or globalization, are distractions for which there is not much time and energy left, at least not in the beginning of a career.

Their grasp of the conversation notwithstanding, the students seemed to be confounded. They came with expectations of becoming policy advisors, social activists, teachers, researchers, or even intellectuals and, in the pursuit, were discouraged. Positive reinforcement led to performance in academic circles, to becoming a Professional Academic. A Professional Academic is strangely unlike others who have undergone tough academic training, such as doctors or lawyers, in that doctors and lawyers are trained to perform for people outside their own spheres. Professional Academics trained to entertain, impress, and intimidate other Professional Academics. Their goals are to teach in the best economics departments, publish in the best journals, and speak at the most important conferences. Extracurricular activities such as the writing of textbooks, consulting, policy advising, and speaking for general audiences jeopardize their academic standing. The focus of the community is inward.

At the time of the survey I had a young, rather ill-behaved, cocker spaniel. I opted for obedience school on his behalf. The experience was analogous to the inward-focused, exclusive academic community. The first surprise was that Fittipaldi had to do undergraduate training (he was put in a class for beginners only; apparently, there existed something like Graduate Obedience.) In these classes, I was struck by the number of exercises that did not serve the simple objectives of the real world – having him heel, come at my command, not bite people.

When I noted the goings-on of the graduate training, it dawned on me that we were being prepared for just that, higher learning, which, in turn, was to prepare us for performances at dog shows. Fittipaldi was being trained to become a Professional Academic Dog, that is, a dog who entertains, impresses, and intimidates owners and dogs of the academic dog world. Having no such ambitions, we abandoned the conversation of dog shows. Fittipaldi, as many will attest to, remained ill-behaved.

About half of graduate students do not quit. They undergo the initiation, master the rhetoric, and go on to be academics, questioning little along the way. As they read academic journals, they observe that the accolades go to theoretical and technical articles. As they note how their professors, often a few years out of graduate school themselves, perform in the classroom, in seminars, and in personal exchanges, they emulate. They listen to the jokes and join in the gossip. And most become Professional Academic Dogs . . . er, Professional Academics.

Academic versus non-academic culture

Part of becoming an academic economist is becoming an academic. Academic economists share a culture that is different from that of economists at banks, government institutions, and think-tanks. The manner of life is different – life at a university is not life at the offices of product-oriented or bureaucratic organizations. It shows in the discomfort that people experience when they move over from one to the other.

Some differences between academic and non-academic economists manifest on the surface. Wandering through a university building (noisy, poster-filled, helter-skelter; and only occasionally does one find faculty members in their cluttered offices) is not like wandering through a bank or government office (quieter, more formal, organized, office-occupied). Academics are looser with their schedules. Faculty members work at home most of the time (or so they say). Many are off at conferences (or so their secretaries think). Vacations are taken informally. In twenty-five years of university teaching, I have not checked with anyone about going on vacation. Could a banker or government employee ever do the same?

Academic freedom has its price. The younger members of faculty may have trouble with the loneliness of their academic existence. It is one reason that some turn back from an academic career, preferring lively teamwork to solitary plodding. An academic is like a self-making entrepreneur. Lunching and talking with colleagues goes on, but the actual work is usually hard to share in process. A colleague is quite advanced in the mathematics of network analysis. No one around understands what he is doing, including me. Now and then he communicates with a couple of like-minded people abroad, but most of the time he works alone.

Underneath the surface are the values, attitudes, and dispositions that constitute the academic life. Habitus is more than mere habit; in Bourdieu's terms, it is more like the interiorization of the exterior. Only when an outsider is in the house do academics, who know how to behave without thinking about it, become aware of the rules. When a mathematical invention in a game-theoretic setting is the issue, someone in the know does not bring up the importance of emotions. No one cites the newspaper, no matter how relevant. The response to habitus violations is usually awkward silence.

Academics do find outsiders out. At a Washington, DC, university, political economists ("policy entrepreneurs," Paul Krugman calls them) came by occasionally to give seminars. Their culture is about political clout, citation in newspapers, and recognition by the general population. The blending of this culture with that of the university seminar room proved to be quite ugly. After a polite presentation come seemingly innocent questions leading to what academics are good at: problematization and scathing and purely recreational criticism. "The statistical methods you used are not quite appropriate." "[An academic economist], probably not known to you, has shown the opposite of what you are arguing here." "Your thesis is blown down by rational expectations." The poor fellow! The argument that worked so well with important politicians evaporates in the presence of obscure academicians. The awkward realization sets in that he does not know the data, has not kept up with the literature, and has no idea what his fellow economists are talking about.

The treatment is reciprocated when academics present their work in a political environment. There no one cares about the technical intricacies of the analysis and everyone demands to know about its practical relevance. "What does this do for us? What bearing does it have on the interest rate, unemployment, justice, global peace?" Honest academics, and those who think of their academic reputation, will refuse to say more. And they will long for the academic community, to whom their performance is entertaining and impressive.

Non-academics do not have a clue as to how the academic community works. "Only a few hours of teaching each week, and you are complaining about being too busy?" Even many academics do not have a clue. A source of confusion is the group whose applause they want to seek and to whom they want to be accountable. Many mistakenly believe that they do the work to impress their local environment: the dean or the colleagues in their department or, if the university is small, the entire faculty. But the opinion of those who are circumstantially nearby does not necessarily have relevance to the caliber of work. Yes, the university pays the salary, and, yes, senior colleagues decide on tenure, and, yes, praise feels warm, but the significant community is often elsewhere. Diana Crane's notion of the "invisible college" is so pertinent because it suggests a world with no walls, scattered as it is over the globe. Collins (1998) more fashionably terms it a "network." Whatever its name, the community that shares a particular area of expertise counts more than the community that shares the immediacies of hallways and cafeterias. The community at large, whose members drift in and out, decides the academic's fate by deciding whether or not to publish work, cite work, and thereby constitute the relevant conversation. Tenure, salary, and what local colleagues think are based, in large part, on how the academic performs in that conversation.

This preoccupation with whom to please makes for risk-balancing behavior. Duties at the home institution are important, but efforts to fulfill them may be at the expense of activities in the academic community. Teaching and serving on university committees may take so much time that there is none left to write papers and be published. On the other hand, time-consuming research may cause the neglect of duties at the university – students complain, colleagues resent bearing the brunt of home duties for those forever away at conferences. In general, it is better to risk the latter. Affronting students and eschewing dutiful behavior is less of a matter to an academic than being overlooked by the academic community.

The academic commons

Being in a community, sharing values and dispositions, implies that the individual academic has a great deal in common with fellow academics. This is particularly manifest with academic economists, who share a distinct conversation. Their oral and written products are a contribution to the common conversation. Academic etiquette requires awarding authorship to contributions by means of citation, but the contribution is a common possession, accessible to anyone. No matter how selfish, narcissistic, and autistic an individual academic can be, it is essential to recognize the communal nature of the discourse in which he or she partakes.

The practice shows in the language. The papers academics write are "contributions" and they are "pleased" to "share" their latest findings with seminar audiences. And, in fact, most are "eager" to share. The commonness of the conversation induces the values of collegiality and reciprocity. I vividly recall my first attempt to get published. The editors requested that I resubmit the paper after having incorporated the comments of referees, and I panicked when they asked for some technical additions I did not know about. I timidly approached Jim Grant, our in-house econometrician. His response was "Sure, no problem!" He sacrificed a solid day to read the paper and an entire afternoon to help make the revisions with me. I knew enough of the academic code to know that the most I could do in return was thank him kindly and acknowledge him in a footnote. Monetary compensation was out of the question. Suggestion of it would have been an insult. Thinking of it would have been a sign of bad faith. His assistance was a gift, not necessarily to me, his colleague, but to the academic conversation. After this, I knew what to do when a colleague asked for my help.

The gift is the means by which individuals support what they have in common with others.[4] Academics give all the time. And they reciprocate. I got plenty of help and have given plenty of help, some of which, I like to think, was significant. I have also worked closely with colleagues who, so I noticed later, unwittingly appropriated some of my ideas as their own. I am sure that a great deal of what I am writing here I owe to them, too, without being aware of it. It is all a contribution to the common good. Ideas are gifts, too.

The giving goes further. I have spent a good deal of time organizing conferences, convening seminars, preparing commentaries, advising PhD candidates, and refereeing papers for journals. Only when reviewing books for publishers do I receive some nominal payment, usually in the form of books. Many colleagues give a great deal more. The community spirit that so many display is remarkable and moving. Editing journals, for example, is hard work and often a thankless job. An endless stream of papers crosses editors' desks. They send them to referees and subsequently have to beg for the comments that never seem to meet deadlines. They deal with the desperation of those facing the "publish or perish" dilemma.

They receive five to ten times more papers than they can publish, and thus are always breaking some poor fellow's heart. Enemies are easily accumulated. Yet it is a gift to the community, with the meager returns of reputation and small change. The same applies to academics serving on boards of associations or, worse, organizers of the major associations' conferences.

Fame and reputation demand a toll and, as a result, gift-giving sometimes has to be deferred. The well-known are inundated with requests to present papers at seminars, give lectures to students, write references for tenure cases, and so on. A stack of papers and letters arrive daily with the kind request for a response. Most of them become quite efficient in responding: "Thanks for your paper. It looks interesting. You seem to have an important point. As soon as I have time, I will give it a serious look." But they can be caught in their routines. A colleague was chatting with a visitor about a paper he had brought to her. The discussion went on for some time and she expressed interest in his ideas. As the visitor was leaving, my colleague was startled when he asked her if she wanted another copy of his paper. With some embarrassment, she realized that while talking she had mindlessly thrown the paper in the waste bin, as was her custom with papers given to her.

Being an academic implies the continuous enriching and sustaining of the community and conversation, the academic commons. Economists who see gift-giving as a market exchange miss the point. The reputation effect is a reward of sorts but is in no way proportionate to the work. The real recompense is the thrill of being part of and contributing to the common accumulation of knowledge. Randall Collins, a sociologist, points to the emotional energy that academics experience from time to time. The excitement comes, Collins suggests, when the academic senses that he or she has hit upon something greater than the individual, something that may significantly contribute to the common conversation. Thus, being part of an academic conversation calls for sacrifices but the return is the emotional energy that gives a sense of meaning and purpose to what academics are doing.

The ambiguity of academic values

The academic habitus implies an academic attitude and the enactment of implicit academic values. Novices interiorize the vaguer rules by practicing. Some values I dare make explicit here: take the relevant literature seriously, be systematic in the analysis, cite generously, do not refer to non-academic literature, adhere to the academic mode of writing, be impersonal, keep the anecdotal to a minimum, be excessive with footnote references, be brief, do not be too inventive (stay within the bounds of the conversation!), defer to the relevant authorities, be a willing referee, be a good colleague, and recognize the circumstances under which certain rules can be broken (as in this book).

Some values are contradictory. Scientists are supposed to be disinterested, objective, and emotionally flat. Yet they have (and rightly so) interest in their own careers and fervently defend their research against criticism. University politics invite emotional argument. Scientific careers require avid self-promotion; each academic needs and wants to be heard. Like everyone else, scientists have passionate political views. How objective can scientists be when their causes inextricably mingle with issues outside the academic community? Emotions are part of eliciting, sharing, and sometimes vehemently arguing about important ideas. Scientists could not do their work without them. Without passion, good science would not come about, as Michael Polanyi (1962 [1958]) more poignantly points out.

Open-mindedness, too, is cherished in the academic disposition. Academics maintain that they are open to criticism and that they eschew the dogmatic. The practice? Criticism is sneered at or ignored. Dogmatism and fortress-holding abound. The dogmatic disposition thwarts creativity, another value preached in academics. Judging how open a scientific conversation is to creativity is a risky matter. A little imagination is all right but leaping too far from acknowledged platforms means leaping right out of the conversation. Creative contributions are cumbersome. To address them is to admit they might be right, to entertain the notion that they have promise. Thus, in the conversation, taking little steps to new ideas is the better approach.

In principle, academic economists are egalitarian and democratic. In reality, academic economists are powermongers. They compete for good positions, funding, spots in journals, and places at conferences. They discriminate in favor of like-minded colleagues and obstruct the entry of dissenters. The suggestion of egalitarianism and democracy is as polite a pretense as the suggestion of objectivity and disinterest. A keen sense of who is worthy lends itself to the quick and relentless judgment of who gets the spotlight. The scientific community is really an aristocracy, ruled by those perceived to be the very best.

Justifying the conversation

When the academic world is besieged from the outside, the academic interest exhibits the most solidarity. All academics stand shoulder to shoulder when politicians or businesspeople question the funding of academia or the importance of what they do. And they are vehement and eloquent about it. Thus, the solidarity of American academic life in the McCarthy period. The vehemence betrays vulnerability: it is hard to defend against accusations that they are interested only in their own petty intellectual pursuits and that what they do contributes little to society at large. How to justify the two-thousandth article on *Macbeth*? Even economists are vulnerable, since little of their work has demonstrable use in politics or business. What is the point?

Like any coherent conversation the economic one requires legitimization and justification toward critics and skeptics. Academic economists need to convince themselves and others from time to time that there is a point to what they are doing, and three topoi lend them a hand. The first is in the realm of the sacred, or transcendental: "We are doing what we do in quest for Truth." Quest for the holy grail? Well, yes, in a way. They may not have the faintest idea what is meant by truth, or may never have achieved the idea. But it gives a religious purpose to their work. While I do not have the audacity to claim I know definite truth (although I claim it in my argument, don't I?), I believe in it. I keep this justification for special occasions, such as when a dissertation student experiences existential doubt about becoming an academic or when I am campaigning for a new academy. Each community needs its religion: the scientific one worships Truth.

Social justification is another topos to use when under question. Academic economists then appeal to something socially relevant, like the task of enlightening young minds, the importance of social policy, the struggle against poverty and inequality (Tinbergen), the impact on financial markets (Black–Scholes) and auction markets (one lone result in game theory). In these cases the economic conversation gains positive and coherent meaning in the social one. Any academic can use the social justification topos. "What is gazing into the universe good for?" a student once challenged her astronomy professor. What does one say to that? Stammer some, and then: "Some of the instruments we have developed turned out to have important applications in health care." True or not, sensible or not, the argument contented everyone. Social justifications are equivalent to the corporate responsibility talk of businesses. We all need arguments to justify our own conversations.

And then there are personal justifications. "I find it interesting." "My parents made me do it." "I have nothing better to do." "It pays the bills." Personal justifications are especially big in the world of the arts. The circle has apparently grown weary of things like "beauty," "political relevance," and "changing the world." A simple "I found this interesting" will do. Economists are usually more cynical by their own model of prudence: "It's a living," or "I've invested in this so I'll keep doing it." I am at a loss when colleagues or graduate students use the topos of income. "You can't be into [academic] economics for the money," I say. I attempt to appeal to the common interest of sustaining the conversation. Personal justification topoi notwithstanding, it has to be about more than making money, or a living. It has to be a way of life.

So what?

This is what: the disagreements, disputes, common history; that is, conversations that distinguish "us" as academic economists – and which are things "they" function without – justify speaking of a "culture." In the elaboration of the phenomenon of culture, I have done more to justify the differentiation of academic from non-academic cultures than to justify a culture of economists per se, exclusive of academics in sociology, anthropology, physics, and the like. That argument comes later, when I address the rhetoric of economists, their unique way of talking. People who talk continuously in terms of rational, self-interested, individual behavior, and imagine the world as one complex mechanical system, will, of course, differ in "deep play" from those preoccupied with social power, human culture, or physical phenomena.

The application of "culture" to academia makes practical sense. It helps to account for differences and to guide the outsider amidst certain curious practices. It makes clearer how much is required to be in the economic conversation and that it involves a change of heart, or even soul. It takes years of training and practice to negotiate the strange contradictions of the academic culture but, once there, one can seriously proclaim objectivity while enthusiastically hustling for status – and not be troubled by the conflict.

Engulfing the gap that separates academic from non-academic culture is no more acutely experienced than by people from the working class. From their own accounts they forever sense a precariousness, rendering their existence as academics awkward and ambivalent. They feel, and are, exceptional in belonging to a world that was so far removed from their childhoods' but they continue to feel like "strangers in paradise."[5] They cannot shed consciousness of the contradictions of academic culture, and often end up disappointed, frustrated, or angry with academic practices. Some confess to an anxiety about being found out, similar to the anxiety of someone who has changed gender. The point: culture is not obtained by desire.

Not convinced that academic culture is different? Read David Lodge's novels. His stories lend the academic experience a genuineness that a scholarly account could never reproduce. *Small World* (not to be read at conference breaks) is the story of Morris Zapp, a well-known English professor (with a remarkable resemblance to the real-life Stanley Fish) who is continually traipsing from one academic conference to another. It is a hilarious account of the absurdities of what goes on at them and may motivate one to reconsider academic ambitions. *Changing Places* is a satirical work on the differences between American and British academic institutions. *Nice Work* juxtaposes an academic with a businessman; only love enables the two characters to overcome cultural prejudices. Whether in realism or parody, the books say, "An academic is different." Having read this chapter, do not respond, "Yes, they have more education."

Further reading

To get an idea of what academic culture is all about, read the novels of David Lodge, in particular *Small World* (Secker and Warburg, 1984), *Changing Places* (Secker and Warburg, 1975), *Nice Work* (Secker and Warburg, 1988), and *Thinks . . .* (Secker and Warburg, 2001).

A good idea is to read (auto)biographies. In the previous chapter I mentioned a few by economists. Particularly interesting is the autobiography of Richard Feynman, *Surely You're Joking, Mr. Feynman: Adventures of a Curious Character* (Norton, 1985). And there a few good biographies of economists, most particularly the three volumes on John Maynard Keynes (Viking, 1983, 1992, 2000) by Robert Skidelsky. I also recommend Bruce Caldwell's *Hayek's Challenge: An Intellectual Biography of F. A. Hayek* (University of Chicago Press, 2004).

Interesting, too, are studies of particular episodes in the development of the sciences, like *The Double Helix: A Personal Account of the Discovery of the Structure of DNA* (Norton, 1969) by J.D. Watson. More data on graduate students and interviews are to be found in *The Making of an Economist* (Westview Press, 1990) by Arjo Klamer and David Colander. If you want to read something by Geertz about culture and deep play, start with *The Interpretation of Cultures: Selected Essays* (Basic Books, 1973). Last, there are quite a few studies on the academic attitude. I mention two: Randall Collins, *The Sociology of Philosophies: A Global Theory of Intellectual Change* (Harvard University Press, 1998) and Frederick Grinnell, *The Scientific Attitude* (Westview Press Collins, 1987).

4   It's the attention, stupid![1]

The name of the game

> Many of you will conjure up reasons why the number of citations should be ignored. There are fads; there are self-citations; there are conspiracies; there are derogatory citations; there are bribes to editors and referees; there are sycophantic students; and there are subjects capable of direct understanding by only a few. But why didn't your paper start fads; why don't you publish more and cite yourself; why did your conspiracies fail; why don't you become an editor; why don't your students care about your welfare; and why don't you insist on writing about obscure issues?
>
> (Leamer 1981)

If the proposals of the preceding chapters – that economics is conversation, academic economists are a distinct culture – have bewildered you, brace yourself for even more confusion. In the conversation of economists, *attention* is what really matters – both getting it and giving it. In a world whose banner is in the largest of letters "truth" and whose primary virtue is in the sternest of directives "disinterest," how far we have strayed. Yet, attention is the name of the game.

What does anyone know when musing, "Ah, the science of economics – I think I will choose that as my lifelong pursuit"? What did I know? Not much. Nothing prepared me for the requirements of getting into the conversation. And surely nothing hinted at the fact that attention was its fuel. Indeed, I was nearly two decades immersed in the conversation before the notion of attention dawned on me. It was because the literature did not mention it, I tell myself, that I was late in the discovery. After all, no book on science, no article on methodology or philosophy of science refers to attention as the pivotal factor to practicing it, at least not to my knowledge. No conversation is about attention, at least not explicitly. Could scientists be ashamed of the fact? Facing up to it must not be easy. But once recognized it is impossible to avoid noting that what scientists do is largely about getting and giving attention.

Being busy and getting lost

When I got into the game I expected professors to be forever locked up in their studies or laboratories, diligently carrying out research in search of truth. They would be disinterested and unassuming in their work. In reality, professors turn out to be quite full of themselves. They like to talk about their work, to suggest you read their work, and, whenever possible, to cite themselves. And professors are quite busy outside the laboratory or study. The well-known professors, especially, are flying around the world all the time, attending conferences, giving lectures, and advising important people. In the meantime they publish one article after the other. All for the sake of the truth, you say? I beg to differ. They're seeking attention. It's as simple as that. They write, lecture, confer, and advise to get attention. Without that effort, they get none. And without attention, they do not exist as scientists. Attention is the lifeline, the proof of existence, the sine qua non of scientists.

Students are more than pleased to get the attention of their supervisor and finish their dissertation with his or her assistance. I was concerned with the attention of no one other than my supervisor, my occasional romantic pursuits notwithstanding. After that accomplishment, my dissertation, came my first publication. I still remember receiving the journal – there they were, my own words, all in print! Available to anyone, everyone! What would people say? Not much, as it turned out. Holding my first book for the first time was even more exciting. In *Conversations with Economists* (1983), all my mental work had become concrete, was ready to be read. Very wrongly, it turns out, I imagined myself having made it into the scientific conversation.

Doing a dissertation is one thing, getting published is another, but getting *noticed* is an entirely different ball game. It had not occurred to me that others in the conversation might ignore the book. But how could this not be? I should have realized this before as a reader. A profusion of bookstore shelves, university library stacks, and catalogues of publishers abound with the work of others seeking attention. How is anyone going to notice a particular book or article when there are so many others?

The story of a fellow graduate student portrays the importance of attention. Ambitious and enthusiastic, he was continually bothering me with his newest ideas, convinced that current economic theories were wrong for one reason or another. He would come up with a grand new scheme; the Nobel Prize was awaiting him. While writing his dissertation he assured me that it would change everything. It would certainly change the profession. Some months later, he dropped by to show me his book contract. His dissertation would be published! He had made it! This was it!

His book did get published. I received a copy and his mother put one on the coffee table (where it most likely remains). The sales amounted to no more than a few hundred (the bulk of it from libraries, probably) and reviews were not forthcoming. I watched his spirits deflate and his work languish. A few years later, he became a lawyer.

I was luckier. *Conversations with Economists* caught the attention of David Warsh of the *Boston Globe*. Leonard Silk of the *New York Times* dedicated two columns to it. *BusinessWeek* listed it in its top ten. *Fortune* magazine gave it two pages of praise. There were reviews. And there was talk. On several occasions I overheard people discussing *Conversations*, even once on a street in New York. "Have you read the *Conversations* book of this fellow Klamer?" people would ask me. But, however great the amount of attention it received, it paled in comparison with conversations surrounding Robert Solow, Amartya Sen, Paul Krugman, Joe Sitglitz, and a few others. I enjoy some name recognition but it means little compared with what their names effect in the conversation. (Outside the conversation is another matter: the better names there are Galbraith, Friedman, and a few others. Thurow was someone, once.) The well-known operate in a constant buzz of attention. My scientific life is quiet in comparison.

What is attention?

"Attention" stems from the Latin *attendere*, which signifies the act of directing one's mind or consciousness to a phenomenon. *Roget's* terms it "mindfulness, alertness, thought"; "concentration of the mental powers on something; heedfulness, regardfulness." Each moment the brain receives a multitude of impulses, as yours and mine are doing right now. Locking the mind on to one of them is the phenomenon of attention. Only a few impulses trigger brain waves in such a way that they leap to notice, or cause thought about a particular impulse. In such a case the mind attends; that is, it pays attention. As one would expect, attention takes various forms and has various levels of intensity. The red dress in today's crowd may scarcely cause a blip; tomorrow, for some reason, it may harness your thoughts.

Psychologists, of course, try to figure out how all this works, why we pay attention to some things and overlook or ignore so many other impulses.[2] They are intrigued by the cognitive problems that humans experience. The concept of attention serves to point to the problematic connection between the stimuli that a human organism receives and its mental state. People receive the same stimuli yet one pays attention while another remains as if nothing happened. Why is that?

Advertisers are among those interested in the answers. How to catch the attention of people for a new product when so many things compete for attention? Marketers know, for example, that it is hard to redirect the attention of people already aroused by some other thing. Those whose home team is in the finals do not see much of the advertisements that interrupt the broadcast; they are too excited to notice or have secondary things to attend to.[3] Advertisers compete for attention by trying to surprise with a joke or an oddity or Britney Spears (a pop star of the day in case you do not know the name). But the too extraordinary does not always work. The attention spectrum stays mostly within the ordinary: what we know and what our brains agree to take notice of. If I started writing in Swahili here, the brain would certainly notice, but it would soon stop paying attention. Swahili is too extraordinary.

Effort is another important condition for attention.[4] We enhance attention when we have made an effort toward it. Effort influences the intensity of attention. Studying a play before going to the theater, learning about its context, reading the reviews, and so on means seeing so much more of it than if seeing it unaware and unprepared. By now I hope you will have struggled enough with "conversation" and "attention" that you notice their ubiquity without having to put your brain to the task. They are familiar to you, and have gotten your attention.

Attention is not the same as information, an association my colleagues sometimes make. It is, rather, the selection of certain data from all the information that comes to us. Information just sits there; it is merely available. If you have no attention for the relationship between the growth of money and inflation, you won't know it, won't recognize it, won't see it – even when reading a newspaper that is full of articles about it. You simply will read over those signs. For me the music that my teenagers know all about is an annoying noise, so preoccupied am I with this book. For them, their books present an annoyingly tedious amount of homework they have a hard time paying attention to when the music is on.

Intense attention is what characterizes the scientific life. The chemist-turned-philosopher Michael Polanyi writes (1962 [1958]: 127):

> Obsession with one's problem is in fact the mainspring of all inventive power, . . . Asked by his pupils in jest what they should do to become "a Pavlov," the master answered in all seriousness: "Get up in the morning with your problem before you. Breakfast with it. Go to the laboratory with it. Eat your lunch with it. Keep it before you after dinner. Go to bed with it in your mind. Dream about it."

He continues:

> It is this unremitting preoccupation with his problem that lends to genius its proverbial capacity for taking infinite pains. And the intensity of our preoccupation with a problem generates also our power for reorganizing our thoughts successfully, both during the hours of search and afterwards, during a period of rest.
>
> (Ibid.)

Come to think of it, I should show this to my wife. Maybe she will understand. And I should have this read by PhD students who think that a scientific life can fit a normal work schedule.

This intense attention that scientific work requires accounts for the autism of so many scientists. They are self-absorbed – and have to be – in order to fix their attention on their problem, to focus on what is really important in their research, thus earning the well-deserved reputation of being absent-minded. They are too preoccupied to pay attention to the other conversations that are going on around them, rendering them bad company in non-academic settings. A scientist deeply and intensely engaged in, say, "evolutionary games" tends to see all the information that presents itself to her in that light. When her partner talks about the troubles that the kids are having at school, she wants to show that they can be explained with evolutionary game theory. Unfortunately, the partner most likely does not see it the same way, and will think that she is full of her own stuff. And she is. It is a matter of different focus, or being in another attention space.

The focusing shows in what I am doing now. I am focused on my computer screen. The table is littered with books, articles, notebooks, and papers. (These words don't tumble out effortlessly, even if they seem to.) I notice Polanyi's book, books by McCloskey, Perelman, Toulmin, Foucault, Habermas, articles by Allan Janik, Bourdieu. I notice little else. And that is the point. I can write only when I block out not just my children (with my apologies!), students, and university business, but also most of whatever else is out there. And what about how much has been written about my subject matter? I should consult it all, but I can't. And won't. Rather, I select a few books, a few articles, and work with those. I choose to be in conversation with a certain few minds, and by doing so exclude all others.

Accordingly, I am seeking and giving attention, as are you. We need attention and cannot live without giving it as well. Ideas exist because people give them their attention, read about them, talk about them, and best of all write about them. When I pay attention to McCloskey's writings on rhetoric, I affirm their existence; when I write about them I do even more by bringing them to the attention of others, given that others pay attention to my writings. The giving and receiving of attention is the mechanism by which the conversation lives and grows.

Attention and the conversation

The conversation is the manifestation of attention. Instead of thinking of attention as something going on in people's heads, as psychologists like us to do, I suggest we think of attention as a characteristic of the conversation. Ideas have attention only if they are in the conversation. Conversations are thus attention spaces. By virtue of the ongoing conversations on game theory, an idea about repeated games has the space to receive attention. Outside such a conversation it would languish. The idea dies out when people stop talking about it. It has left the conversation's attention space.

This is important. Say you have the brilliant idea that returning to the gold standard will resolve all the world's economic problems. You have realized by now that you need to get attention for your idea. It won't do much good to arbitrarily stop people on the street and tell them about your idea. Your chances of getting attention are as good as seeking out a group of men talking in the Italian square. You need a conversation out there somewhere, a conversation you can tap into where your idea makes sense and the people in that conversation are willing to pay attention to it. So you have to get into a conversation, or several conversations, in order to make others part of your idea, and give it a chance to become real. Get economists interested and you have a [fat] chance that the talk spills over into the conversations of policy-makers.

No attention for an idea means that nobody talks or writes about it. Writing an article or spelling out the idea does not mean getting attention. Get the attention of an editor and referees may have to pay attention, but that could be the end. Even if some bother to read the article, they may not cite it. Forms of attention include talk in the scientific community, citations, prizes, labels, new terms. The frequency of the form indicates the intensity of the attention. As I perceive it, attention in science is defined by the intensity with which any product of scientific imagination (an argument, an article, a scientist, a research program, an *oeuvre*, a discipline) is communicated in the scientific community. Attention is in the conversation.

The attention game is a cruel one for most of us. We tell each other that academic life is a matter of "publish or perish." But it is actually a case of "attention or perish." Even if we do publish, the chances are that we will starve for attention anyway. The statistics of academic publishing prove the point.

The harsh facts

One unforgiving reality is the abundance of ideas, articles, books, scientists, research programs, and disciplines seeking attention. The other is the highly skewed distribution of attention. In the attention game the winner takes virtually all.

Each year scientists face about 165,000 serials issued by 80,000 publishers covering 969 subjects ranging from anthropology to zoology.[5] What a nightmarish task for librarians! How can they possibly store all those publications? Of course, not every serial is as important and as scholarly as one would like. Many journals border on scientific journalism: they merely report and popularize ideas (and should not be cited by you if you care about your ethos as a scientist). Of the 165,000 serials, 12,600 journals are registered as refereed journals (refereed means that peers have reviewed and approved the articles). The authoritative Institute for Scientific Information tabulates the citations from the articles of 7,000 journals out of the 12,600 in order to determine the impact of both the journal and the individual article. Thus, these 7,000 journals can be considered the core of the scientific conversation.

These numbers make it impossible for any Renaissance man to fulfill his ambition of keeping up with all disciplines. This abundance forces the selection of a discipline. So, saying you choose to concentrate on economics, the number of journals is trimmed to about 164. But, even then, these journals offer 6,500 articles for the economist's yearly read, an impossible task.

And the abundance is only growing. New journals get added to the pile every year, correlating, I suppose, to the increase in the number of academic economists. Their ranks are swelling with people eager to get a piece of attention, and therefore eager to publish. Their production needs an outlet; more outlets mean more journals. Each new journal, each additional article, each new member of the tribe increases the competition and poses the dilemma of what to pay attention to and what to ignore. As Herbert Simon noted, "a wealth of information, a poverty of attention" (1971: 40).

The distribution of attention is highly skewed. The lion's share of articles suffers a poverty of attention; a precious few fill the attention space. To begin with, 80 percent of all journals have a negligible influence on the conversation. Their articles are rarely cited. The median article gets cited maybe one or two times (self-citations not included). An estimated 40 percent of articles never get cited, rendering them, in effect, non-existent. Only a few articles get a notable number of citations (more than 100 per year). These are the classics, the must-haves, the articles that everyone has to read if they want to stay in the conversation.

The Institute for Scientific Information measures the impact of an article by the number of citations it receives over a period of two years after publication. Using this measure it has determined that the top ten medical journals publish only 28 percent of all medical articles yet occupy 77 percent of the attention space. In economics, the distribution is not so badly skewed; even so, its top ten journals (including the *American Economic Review, Econometrica, Journal of Political Economy, Journal of Economic Literature,* and *The Economic Journal*) publish 16 percent of the articles and take 36 percent of the attention space. With ever more people vying for space, the chance of publishing an article in these prestigious journals – and thus the chance of getting serious attention – has been dropping steadily over the past three decades (Coupé 2000).

If you do get your article published in the top journal, which is the *American Economic Review (AER)*, success is not assured. It has been calculated that only 1.8 percent of the authors publishing in the *AER* can say that their article has become a classic.[6] In the end only 0.1 percent of the hundreds of thousands of articles and books published each year receive a significant amount of attention (Garfield 1990). The majority of research done, published or not, passes unnoticed. I offer hereby the one-in-ten rule: of all articles, books, movies, and songs that are brought out, one in ten will be noticed. Among those, one in ten will receive a great deal of attention. Accordingly, only one out of every one hundred articles hits it big. The rule is by approximation (Garfield thinks it is a mere one in 1,000 articles) but appears to hold up pretty well.

Consequently, the distribution of citations is highly skewed. If we take citations for attention, we might also say that the distribution of attention is highly skewed.[7] In terms of attention the world of science is extraordinarily unjust. The distribution of wealth in the most corrupt country would not be that skewed. In the sciences the winner takes virtually all. For the majority the luck is tough. Even the lucky ones, the successful scientists, have to deal with the attention factor. It is a known fact that successful scientists publish more than others, yet they are known for only a few of their articles. The major body of their work will be overlooked and ignored (Simonton 1984, 1988). Welcome to the harsh reality of the scientific world.

Is science a game of wasteful competition?

When the American magazine *Newsweek* found out that half of science papers are never cited within five years after publication, it decried the waste of research money. It concluded that "nearly half the scientific work in this country is worthless" and went as far as depicting scientists "with their belief in their God-given right to tax dollars" as "welfare queens in white coats" (April, 1991). This reaction is understandable if you approach the game with the expectation that science is about truth and that truth speaks for itself. When you realize that the game is about getting attention, you will be less reproachful. There is similar waste in the worlds of movies, literature, music, and the visual arts. Only a small number of paintings made are bought and only a tiny part of those will get significant attention. Most movies never make it to the local cinema; most books pass unnoticed. The same is true for most commercial products: only a small number of all new products make it to the market shelves and only a tiny portion of those endures.

Asking scientists to limit their production to the winners is like asking soccer players to play only the highlights of their game.[8] The proposal is ludicrous. All the plays are part of the game, including the ineffective ones; the fan understands this and appreciates the battles that are fought on the field, whether they result in a goal or not. The so-called waste is part of the game. And since scientific research, after all, stands to benefit all of humanity, it seems sensible to look at its costs in terms of world income. Let's see. Direct costs, as reflected in serial prices, amount to about $1,000 to $8,000 per article. Imputing $20,000 for the costs of the scientist's time, $8,000 for library costs, and $4,000 for editorial and refereeing costs, the maximum total per article is $40,000. Multiplying that by the 720,382 articles that appear in the 7,000 core journals makes a grand total of $28.8 billion. Total world income was $41,344 billion in 1999. Accordingly, all scientific research does not cost more than 0.0007 percent of world income (see Odlyzko 1997).

Can there be too much waste? Sure. But trimming it is dangerous. It is impossible to predict accurately which play, which book, which product, which article will become immensely important. George Akerlof, for instance, had great trouble getting his "Lemons" article (Akerlof 1970) accepted for publication yet it later became a classic, winning the Nobel Prize. Thus, publication in large numbers, including the questionable ones, counters the unpredictability of success. Publishers take chances in rejecting manuscripts; they may reject another Lemons article. Major motion picture studios do the same, hoping for a "sleeper" (remember the original *Rocky*?). And for them it is a good strategy: one hit makes up for a great number of mediocre movies.

Accounting for the inflation of articles and skewed distribution of attention

Is there a market for attention?

You might say that the skewed distribution of attention is unfair. It is unjust to the hordes of scholars who do their very best and yet do not receive any return for their efforts. If this were to happen in the labor market, we would probably ask the government to interfere by transferring some resources from the rich to the poor. But how could we do that here? You can't walk up to Paul Krugman and ask him to decline invitations or reduce his output just to give others a chance to get a piece of the action.

Franck, a German economist, advances the market metaphor to make sense of the skewed distribution of attention (Franck 1999, 2000). Although I am skeptical of applying prices and products to what scientists do, it goes some distance before it falters. Franck claims that attention is the main input in knowledge production and that attention income is the factor that motivates scientists most.

The analysis is as follows. Attention or recognition must compensate for the pecuniary income forgone (for scientists could make more doing research for commercial companies). Attention does well for their self-esteem and gives them a sense of satisfaction. Accordingly, and here the economic heuristic kicks in, scientists try to maximize the amount of attention they get. That accounts for their frenetic activity in going to conferences, flying around to give lectures, and producing massive numbers of papers. The more famous they are, the more papers they write. (They know what movie producers know: if they want to stay ahead, they have to keep producing in large numbers to counter the unpredictability of attention.) All this activity constitutes the *demand for attention*.

The very same cohort of scientists provides the *supply of attention*. They have incentive to offer attention to articles that will help make their own work better and increase their own chance of getting attention. For example, I do better with this text when I have read the right books and am able to cite the right sources in that you assume I know what I am writing about. Having read the right articles is also important in the socializing with other economists. Scientists earn credit for being able to refer colleagues to relevant papers and show off their knowledge of the literature. They don't want to have to say too often that they do not know the article others are referring to, so they have incentive to supply the attention for what others are doing. Franck imagines that the market for scientific attention operates in an enclosed world, differentiating it from, say, the market for movie attention, where determinations of supply and demand are open to all.

The markets are similarly efficient, according to Franck, when the best articles (movies) win out. Producers may think a movie is great, but the market has the final say: how many people are willing to pay to see this movie above all others seeking their attention? Likewise, a scientist may think his or her paper a revelation but as it competes with numerous other papers its real value is determined by the amount of attention other scientists are willing to pay it. The number of citations it receives approximates its value. The market decides: laissez-faire, laissez-aller.

If we accept this reasoning we accept the skewed distribution of attention as an efficient outcome and are left with the classic Smithian problem: does a "free" market of attention generate optimal outcomes? Franck himself is not sure. He acknowledges that the amount of attention a paper receives is hard to measure. In contrast to a real market, this one has no obvious price. The number of citations is not really a satisfactory measure. Even if a million students have read the paper, citations can be negligible.

I am left with the dissatisfaction that so much economic reasoning can give. An analysis in terms of a market sounds tough and seems to make some sense. But there may be consequences. Suppose university deans take hold of this analysis and decide to reward scientists according to the amount of attention that their work gets? In such a case, the citation game would get nasty. Some will do anything to rig the game to their advantage: "Hey [whoever you are], if you cite me, I'll cite you back." The system wouldn't be made any better. If we all started making each other co-authors, in six months we would all have CVs with 40,000 items!

Moreover, this market account lacks texture. Scientists are into the game for something more than just attention – as so many colleagues have been eager to point out when I presented Franck's argument. There is an intrinsic motivation;[9] there is the passion, the companionship, the being in conversation with like-minded people. All these have their own rewards. The market metaphor engenders cynicism, something too many economists already have too much of. So can we try to make sense of the skewed distribution and the inflation of articles some other way?

Winners take all?

A useful addition may be the theory of superstars. The sciences have their Tom Hankses and Julia Robertses, too. They are the winners who take all, receiving most of the attention and leaving the multitude begging for it. The economist Sherwin Rosen made much of this phenomenon in 1981, claiming that initial endowment differences, however small, tend to be magnified by the market size or the size of the audience for a service or idea. Pavarotti may be only a slightly better tenor than the next guy, yet in the worldwide market he receives an inordinate amount of attention. Just because he is known, every producer wants him on the billboard. Pavarotti draws the crowds that the next best guy will leave at home. The larger the market, the more super the stars. Accordingly, stardom has less to do with talent than with the size of the market. Since the market for attention in economics is expanding, its stars will become ever greater.

This account seems to makes sense. It falls in line with the "Matthew Effect" in science coined by sociologist Robert Merton (1968): Those who have will receive. According to the gospel of Matthew, "For unto everyone that hath shall be given, and he shall have abundance: but from him that hath not shall be taken away even that which he hath." It sounds unjust, yet that is how it works. Conference arrangers know that having a superstar at the proceedings works like a magnet, drawing all the attention. Everyone wants to hear what he or she has to say, pretty much regardless of what is actually said.

Equal distribution of attention would be more just, but it simply doesn't work that way. Our actual attention space is finite and thus we are able to attend to a limited number of articles, scientists, and disciplines. I would like to give more attention to philosophers, psychologists, sociologists, and anthropologists but I have neither the time nor the cognitive capacity to keep up with them all. I need to focus. Furthermore, I have incentive to focus on the same articles and names that my colleagues focus on. When everyone around me is referring to the articles of Bourdieu and Deleuze, I had better read them as well (even though I find their French way of writing annoying). Sharing the attention that is given is more effective. The hourglass (Figure 4.1) illustrates this process. All the scientists grouped on top are in the enormous and ever-busy space of "attention-seek"; those below are in the equally enormous space of "attention-give." The actual attention exchange is limited to the width of the funnel. Those who make it through the funnel are rewarded with exposure to the whole of the attention-give space, a winner-takes-all scenario. The production, the work, the effort, and the energy at the top are never-ending for those who want an opportunity to go through the funnel. A scientist can always do more and work harder. As a consequence, the top of the hourglass gets more crowded with pleas for attention, usually manifested by an increasing number of publications.

Viewed this way the situation looks hopeless. A few take virtually all the attention to be had and the rest cannot do much better than be on the giving side. This account, however, has little to say about how people become superstars and how the rest cope with the skewed distribution. There is more left to say.

Conversations and clustering

What is missing from the previous accounts is the notion of conversation. What we do as scientists is generate something in common, a conversation to which we all contribute and in which we share our research, theories, models, concepts, and stories. Stardom is a threat to the conversation as it undermines the notion of the commons. A winner-take-all system makes others feel left out and underappreciated. After all, the star is a star thanks to all those who contributed to the conversation that made him or her a star. Thus, scientists expect a certain modesty from their famous colleagues. Stardom is better played down on your home turf else you risk being ostracized by fellow faculty members and ridiculed by graduate students. The stars have to prove themselves again each time, putting them on equal footing with the guys just out of graduate school (at least that is the intention). An egalitarian spirit works better to sustain a sense of the commons.

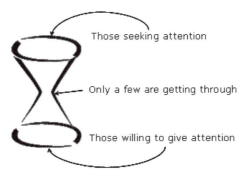

Those seeking attention

Only a few are getting through

Those willing to give attention

Figure 4.1 The attention hourglass

Moreover, the stars badly need the conversation themselves: their existence would have little meaning without it. They need the resources of the conversation and to know what others are doing. They need conference organizers so that they can perform and journal editors so that they can publish. And they need talented researchers who can review their work critically and who are willing to challenge their ideas. They need the companionship of people with whom they can share a conversation in depth, and they need an ever-growing conversation to increase the attention space that they can occupy. Thus, stars usually behave as good citizens. Exceptions exist, but stars who are not willing participants risk a bad reputation. (I'm thinking of a star who cancelled three times on the American Economic Association conference. He may never be invited back.)

Randall Collins points out the importance of clustering in science. When the ability to send printed scientific papers to their audience came about, we might have expected that scientists would no longer have a need to meet. Instead, scientists have always sought each other's company. Collins did an extensive study of the formation of important philosophical schools or networks, such as the neo-Confucians, the German idealists (Kant), and the Vienna Circle. He found that important philosophical schools (i.e., those that survived their times and made it into the textbooks) came about within a restricted time span (thirty years or less) and within a restricted network. Just as we would expect, thinking of the attention space. According to Collins, "[t]he social structure of the intellectual world . . . is an ongoing struggle among chains of persons, charged up with emotional energy and cultural capital, to fill a small number of centers of attention" (Collins 1998: 14). The clustering in personal meetings, professional meetings, university departments, seminars, and lectures helps to focus the attention and develop a common mood, emotion, and intellectual energy. Scientists need each other.

Collins's investigation of "centers of attention" through time adds another interesting insight: important philosophical schools are invariably in competition with other schools, but never with more than two others. This finding Collins calls the "law of small numbers." It appears that three rival schools are all that philosophers can handle. More rival positions would scatter the attention too much and dilute the focus of the conversation to the point of fragmentation and subsequent disintegration. A related consequence is that individuals do not have much of a chance to be in the fray. You generally do better if you are calling for attention as part of a group, that is, if you go under a label, such as new classical economics, evolutionary game theory, or bounded rationality economics. That enables others to place your contribution within their attention space.

The clustering shows in all kinds of ways. It began with the clustering in universities that helped to differentiate academic scholarship from other knowledge activities. Toward the end of the nineteenth century the need was perceived to cordon off economics as a separate discipline with its own departments in the universities. Economists began to form their own associations and to organize their own conferences. As the number of economists increases, we observe a stratification that helps to restrict the attention space. I follow Collins's classification (ibid.: 43):

- scientific stars (small absolute numbers);
- inner core – top producers (1–2 percent of total floating population);
- outer core (20 percent of floating population);
- transients – a few publications or one-shot producers (75–80 percent of floating population);
- audience and would-be recruits (10–100 times the size of floating population).

A criterion for this stratification is the output of the members of the community. The most productive members are at the core. You find large numbers of them in the top departments in economics (Harvard, Massachusetts Institute of Technology, Stanford, Princeton, London School of Economics, maybe). They are in constant communication with each other – by email, by sharing papers, by collaboration, by attending special conferences and seminars. The outer core consists of all the economists who are at second-tier departments, publish regularly, and constitute the audience at special conferences. They may interact with the core but less intensively than those within the core. The transients float in and out. They usually work at second- or third-tier departments, publish now and then (but not in the major journals), and interact only sporadically and superficially with the core. The audience consists of graduate students and all those economists interested in academic work but unable or unwilling to contribute in the form of publications. They make for the large crowds at major conferences. They give the stars and the core the attention they need without asking anything in return.

The clustering goes further. Unless you are a star or a member of the inner core, the stratification is much too expansive to command attention. The outer core copes by specializing and organizing their own attention spaces. They set up subfields, such as feminist economics, urban economics, or cultural economics. They form their own associations, publish special journals, and organize conferences dedicated to their specialty.

I am especially familiar with the example of cultural economics. Even though a few prominent economists in this field, e.g., William Baumol and Mark Blaug, had published in well-known journals, less prominent cultural economists failed to get the attention of core journals. So they formed their own association which issues a newsletter, organizes biannual conferences, publishes the *Journal of Cultural Economics*, and is trying to have its articles included in the Social Sciences Citation Index (SSCI), so that citations to them will be counted. (You now know how critical that is.) The advantage of clustering within the outer core is focusing the attention of a reasonably well-identified group on the subject of their specialty. It also serves as a flag to draw people in from the outside. Researchers and graduate students who develop an interest in the economics of art and culture now have a place to find a conversation and give attention.

Clustering is a condition for making the process of attention-seeking and -getting manageable. As we saw before, stars emerge when there are lots of people who want to pay attention and they in turn inflate that attention by sharing it with others in conversation. Stars, therefore, are phenomena of larges spaces of attention. Small clusters cannot tolerate stars very well, and distribute the attention more equally among the members. The downsizing of clusters, therefore, is an effective response to the skewed distribution of attention.

This clustering also helps to account for the inflation of publications and citations. Each cluster generates its own citations. Those who write in the *Journal of Cultural Economics* cite other articles in the journal (journal self-citations are high). So even if these articles are not cited elsewhere, their citations add to the total (provided the journal is included in the SSCI). As a rule, articles in specialized journals refer to articles in core journals but the latter do not reciprocate. The *Journal of Cultural Economics* and other specialty journals do not have much of a presence in the core. They constitute their own attention space.

How to get attention

The lesson is that, if you do not make it into the core, your best chance is to join one or more specialized clusters, or set up one yourself. Make sure that you walk under one flag or another. Make yourself known as a cultural, Marxist, historical, feminist, or whatever-adjective-you-can-think-of economist. Most economists will decide to drop your work like a hot potato, but that they would have done anyway. This strategy is the best bet to meet other like-minded economists who operate in the same cluster and are more than eager to share their attention with you. So, you give their work attention and they will give your work attention. It makes for a Pareto-improvement.

But once in your cluster don't relax. You will quickly lose attention when you use the wrong names, do not know the right articles, are unscientific in your approach, cannot hold onto your academic job, do not show up at conferences, fail to get your articles published, and so on. You have to know how to stay in the attention space of your cluster.

You may be lucky and come up with a catchy title that everyone keeps referring to. I am hoping that the term "conversation" catches on and that this book is the source to cite. It would not really matter whether people liked it or not. Even if the entire community thinks the conversation metaphor is terrible, people may continue to cite this work whenever they feel like venting their anger. Then again, they may ignore the metaphor altogether. And that's the end of it.

So what?

Do I need to say more? Even if attention is not the sole reward that we scientists are seeking, it sure influences the world in which we are operating. That will not change with the digitization that is under way. With the possibility of making your work available on the Internet, it seems like you can circumvent all the barriers that academics put up to prevent you from participating in their conversation. The promise is that of a more egalitarian world with more equal access. Forget it. Just as after the introduction of printed manuscripts, scientists will find as much reason to cluster in a digitized world as they do now. It is a matter of attention space.

You should rather expect scientists to be more attentive to the need of clustering because of the increasing abundance that digitization entails. There is simply too much on the web. So we will to select even more stringently than we do. The gate-keepers will have to get tougher, the clusters tighter, and the communities closer. Really, attention is the name of the game.

Further reading

This chapter is based on a couple of papers that I wrote with Harry van Dalen: "Attention and the Art of Scientific Publishing" in *Journal of Economic Methodology* 9: 289–315; and "Is There Such a Thing Called Scientific Waste?" *Tinbergen Institute Discussion Paper*: TI 2005-005/1.

In the above papers are further references. Most important among these is Randall Collins, *The Sociology of Philosophies: A Global Theory of Intellectual Change* (Harvard University Press, 1998). The first three chapters are especially relevant.

The classic paper on the economics of stars is Sherwin Rosen's "The Economics of Superstars" in *American Economic Review* 71: 845–58. Also interesting is Robert Frank and P.J. Cook, *The Winner-Take-All Society* (Free Press, 1995).

About citations and related topics there is an extensive literature. See, for example, Arthur M. Diamond's "What is a Citation Worth?" in *Journal of Human Resources* 21: 200–15; and Robert K. Merton's "The Matthew Effect in Science" in *Science* 159: 56–63.

5 A good scientific conversation, or contribution thereto, is truthful and meaningful and serves certain interests

Responding to hard-nosed and lazy-dazy ideas about science

"How about the truth? Isn't that what science is all about? Enough of your talk about conversation, culture, attention . . . it's truth I want to hear about!" The exasperation is audible when these outbursts come. And, invariably and inevitably, they do. When I rummage around, I usually encounter an opinion of science and scientific practice that the preceding three chapters have upset. After all, science has to be something stripped away from conversation to be tougher, more solid, and, indeed, more truthful. A rocket launch to the moon is not a conversation, is it? It must be a product of truthful science.

Exasperation with the metaphor of conversation easily turns into indignation or even condemnation: "We [economists] do science and science can do without all this" and "When are you going to do some serious economics?"[1] Translation: Science is serious and conversation is not. "How about a serious conversation in a scientific setting?" I am tempted to retort. But I fear the cause is lost on these tough-minded economists. "Science is science, and not a conversation." In the philosophical literature, these economists would qualify as "positivists." Lest that term be confused with "optimists," call them "hard-nosed" scientists. For them science is a matter of logic, facts, hypotheses, and empirical tests. Those who do not subscribe to these tenets may simply leave the conversation (read: they do not deserve tenure, will not get published in important journals, and will not be invited to conferences). That is why they deserve the label hard-nosed.

Another type of response to truth comes with sighs and concessions like, "Truth does not exist." "Science is a matter of belief." "It's all subjective." "Truth is just a construction, a fabrication." Students are especially susceptible to this. I suspect they learned in high school that one opinion (i.e., theirs) about a text is as good as any other and therefore one belief is as good as any other. (I contribute to this mindset myself. To convey deep philosophical insight, I taught my children that we do not know anything for certain. They cleverly took advantage: "You don't know vegetables are good for me, so please pass the chips," forcing me to fall back on, "That may be so, but eat your vegetables anyway.") I admit that by stressing the notion of the metaphor I appear to support the mindset that nothing can be known for sure and that all knowledge is subjective. That is not at all that I have in mind, as I hope to demonstrate. But people who do think this way parade in the philosophical literature under the flag of the relativists. (Relative to what is relative.) Call these people the "lazy-dazy" scientists: they take science as it comes.

I am not comfortable with either stance. The hard-nosed may consider how strange the practice of a science like economics looks from their perspective with its disagreements, inconclusive empirical tests, lack of hard facts, and skirting of real laws. Maybe they want to entertain the possibility that science is not as hard-nosed as they make it out to be, that more is at stake than logic and facts. Maybe. But the abandonment of a belief in hard-nosed science based on Truth does not automatically lead to a lazy-dazy position. Even if strictly objective knowledge does not exist, knowledge does not necessarily become subjective. People cannot believe whatever they please. They cannot double prices and expect people to flock to their shops anyway. They can deny the laws of gravity, but they will most certainly tumble when they step off the balcony.

Similarly, in conversation, people cannot get away with saying whatever pops into their heads. If they think they have good reasons to deny the Holocaust, I suggest they be prepared to duck when introducing them in most conversations. When people subject themselves to the conversations of a certain discipline such as economics, they cannot argue that freezing rents will help those looking for cheap rentals, or start talking about reincarnation. If they do, they will surely be out of the conversation and probably shown to the door. As must be clear by now, to share an insight with others you need to be in their conversation. And conversations – scientific conversations especially – constrain what you want to say and how you want to say it. Just as the Italians exclude me in the social conversations of their squares, economists will screen contributions to their scientific conversations and ban all sorts of talk. A practitioner buying in to the idea that all knowledge is subjective will quickly find out that it is, if nothing else, socially subjective. To share subjective knowledge with others, you have to subject yourself to the discipline of the conversation in which you want to be. Life is not as simple or lazy-dazy as some imagine it to be.

How about scientific standards? Go to the practice!

"So, tell us, what makes a conversation scientific?" Hard-nosed scientists are tough and persistent. "How do we determine whether a theory is true or not?" They seem to be asking for some clear-cut, unequivocal standards that distinguish science from non-science, truthful claims from false ones. Oh, that we had such standards! – they would determine whether this book is truer and more scientific than any other you have read! Show the truth and the discussion is closed.

Let's talk about the practice of economics, and the study of economics. Do students ever get a three-by-five card that lists such standards?[2] Of course not. They learn all kinds of procedures, many of which are implicit. They set up models and solve them, do the math, run regressions, do experiments; in short, they learn science by doing it. The initiation is intense and time-consuming; the problems are tough, the mathematics daunting. Students forge ahead, follow the instructions of teachers and later, when reaching for that PhD, they try almost desperately to get the model and econometrics "right" so that the committee will approve. Later yet, in the business of publishing, they will do anything to get the referees to agree. That is the path of getting in the conversation. If asked about the truth, students think, "Honestly, do I have the luxury to care?" The rules and the norms of science? "Sure, those are the ones the referees agree on." Economics is a discipline.

The discipline shows in the continuous and inescapable appraisal. Practitioners continually evaluate models, tests, assumptions, methods, arguments, and even each other. They say things like, "I like that paper very much" or "I do not care much for the work of F____." Appreciation becomes concrete when practitioners bother to talk about a paper, work with it, and assign it to their students. The quality of their attention is what matters. And, as pointed out in the previous chapter, most contributions get no attention at all. Are the decisions of journal editors – who reject the majority of submissions and publish only a handful – based on truth content? Get real, as they say. Selection is part of the game. Bounce around an idea for a model and you will quickly find out whether it finds approval or not. The point: rather than applying standards, practitioners evaluate contributions to their conversation by an assortment of criteria. And usually they cannot tell you what they are.

The hard part of getting into a conversation is knowing how to evaluate contributions, your own as well as those of others. It is similar to grading students' papers – a seasoned professor more or less knows what grade to give; explaining why is the tough part. "The argument does not go very deep," one economist may say to another (or professor may say to student). "What do you mean?" "The model does not do a great deal." "?!" "Read my article and you may see what I mean." The evaluation is diffuse, often inarticulate, and seemingly arbitrary. You learn it by doing it.

Be prepared, though, to legitimize your daily practice. When cornered by a dogged student or challenged by an insistent politician eager to unmask you as a pseudo-scientist, you will have to fall back on the arguments that you have picked up along the way. Then you may want to say that economics comes as close to a physical science as any other, that unrealism of assumptions does not matter as long as theories predict, and that the lack of predictive accuracy is a matter of time. It helps to look a little scientific – distant, haughty, hard-nosed – when saying these things even though this does not do justice to your practice.

Hope and prospects for the science of economics

Give up the metaphors of science such as "mirror and logic" and "body of accumulated knowledge" urged by meta-conversations; stop staring at propositions, statements and sentences as harbingers of truth; stop thinking of the individual as the wherewithal and start thinking conversation, or better, a bunch of conversations. I promise that encouraging vistas will appear on the horizon.

Inspiration may come from philosophers such as Richard Rorty, Aristotle, the

Ludwig Wittgenstein of *Philosophical Investigations* (*Tractatus* had put him in the camp of the Vienna Circle, but *Investigations* proved he had grown with the times), the German hermeneutic philosopher George Gadamer, and American pragmatists Charles Peirce and John Dewey. There are more but we have to start somewhere. They all urge us to look beyond single propositions, to see that there is more in play than logic and facts, and to consider all that scientists argue in the context of conversations, or discursive contexts, as some prefer to say.

The ideas of pragmatist Charles Peirce (1839–1914) were buried during the reign of the Received View but, after the turn to discourse and conversation, they are being unearthed. He draws attention away from the knowing individual toward the community of scholars; truth is what they come to agree upon after arduous research, vigorous argument, and lengthy deliberation. Truth, therefore, is a matter of opinion. Peirce also speaks of beliefs that turn into habits. His pragmatic point is that the truths or beliefs scientists hold must be good for something, must motivate one action or another. In his own words: "[T]he rational purport of a word or expression lies exclusively in its conceivable bearing on the conduct of life" (Peirce 1966 [1878]: 121). Does that make truth relative? That is a matter of perspective. The community of scholars judges each contribution to its conversation. Its members first determine whether the contribution is worthy of their joint attention (and we have discussed how slim those chances are) and then they subject it to their scrutiny, discuss it, and possibly refer to it or apply it in their work.

As Rorty would say, the value of a contribution does not follow from confrontation with the facts of the world out there (as the empiricists would have it) or with logic (as propagated by rationalists), but comes about in social situations. Science, therefore, is not a solipsistic affair in which, one by one, scientists uncover truth, but thoroughly social. As a scientist I am dependent upon the conversation in which I participate. Whether this particular contribution is worth anything is not for me to determine; neither will it be determined by the inevitable few who will kindly tell me it has changed their lives. The conversation in which the book is discussed will be the ultimate judge. The disciplinary character is self-preserving. When a community of scholars gets slack about its selection of contributions, it risks its reputation and may discourage new brains from entering its conversation.

Philosophers will be the first to point out that Peirce is not Dewey and Rorty is more a Deweyan than a Peircean. The pragmatic points stand: truth is established in deliberation within communities of scholars. But it is not only truth that matters in a conversation. More is involved in the assessment of contributions to conversations, and of conversations in their entirety.

Does the philosophizing matter?

Roy Weintraub, my PhD advisor and an economist who switched from general equilibrium theory to history of thought, would insist that the philosophical discussion about truth and all that is of no consequence to what economists do. He

Box 5.1 The history of epistemology in a joke

American intellectuals often use the metaphor of baseball, and the game serves to tell the story of epistemology over time. Understand that, in baseball, the umpire, hovering over the catcher, determines whether the pitches are strikes (coming in over the plate at the right height) or balls (coming in too wide, high, or low).

Three umpires are arguing at a bar over who is the best one. The first, a positivist or traditionalist, says proudly, "I calls 'em as they are." The second, a modernist, says, "I calls 'em as I see 'em." The third, our postmodernist umpire, says, "They ain't nothin' 'til I calls 'em!"

For the traditional umpire there is no cause for doubt. The modernist umpire acknowledges the possibility that he has no direct knowledge of the situation and that his call can be proven wrong. The postmodern umpire is right in that if he does not call anything, the game stops. But this does not mean that he can call whatever he pleases. A few bad calls and he himself is out of the game. Umpires function in the conversation of baseball, and an intense and critical conversation that is. Each call will be judged and discussed by thousands, if not millions, of spectators. Other umpires will be all over the one making the call. Calling pitches may follow a firm standard of truth, but it most assuredly is subject to serious constraints.

got that from Stanley Fish, a literary critic, legal scholar, and rhetorician. McCloskey and I invited Fish to a conference at Wellesley College in 1984 to have him tell us economists about rhetoric and all that. "Forget it," was his message, "keep doing what you're doing and don't be bothered." The methodologists among us may resist the conclusion, but practitioners' lack of interest for what they do suggests that Weintraub and Fish are right. (Then again, what are the consequences of the academic economic conversation on policy and business?) Even so, conversations do influence each other. And reflections on conversations may matter, too.

Truths, meanings, and interests

A contribution to a conversation is like a pebble thrown in a pond. It will cause little waves that expand and fade; one pebble causes bigger ripples than others. Often your pebble will not stir things at all. There are exceptions. Keynes's *The General Theory of Employment, Interest and Money* (1936) caused significant waves. Solow's article on growth caused waves, too, although they took a while to reach shore. The work by George Akerlof on asymmetric information caused waves. None of these contributions appeared to have caused waves merely because they were true. What made the difference in each case?

Box 5.2 A story

If you are pestered by people who want to know what is underneath it all, what the rock bottom is on which the truth rests, or if you pester yourself with the question, here is the story to tell in response. (It originated with William James; I owe it to Deirdre McCloskey who tells it so much better than I can here):

A man came up to the Zen master. He had a question for the master. "So what is it?" "Ah well, here we are, walking on the earth, having firm ground under our feet. What then, holds the earth?" "That's simple, my man, an elephant who carries the earth on his shoulders." The man nodded and walked away. The next morning he came back with another question for the master. "So what is it?" "Ah well, so we are walking on the earth which is held by an elephant on his shoulders. But on what does the elephant stand?" "That is simple, my man," the Zen master responded, "a giant turtle is what the elephant is standing on." The man nodded and walked away to return the next morning. "So what is the turtle standing on? he wanted to know now. "That is simple my man," the master responded patiently, "you are standing on the earth which is held by an elephant who is standing on a giant turtle that is standing on a giant elephant." An hour later the man returned with one more question. "But what then is the elephant standing on?" Now the Zen master showed a slight sign of impatience. And so he responded: "It's elephants all the way down."

It is about meanings, the significant connections that a contribution makes, the values to which it appeals, the associations that it evokes. And it is about interests, the purpose it serves, the action it calls for. Truth is another concern, in some cases more, but usually less, important than the other two. The questions asked, and therefore the questions to ask, are:

- How meaningful, how interesting, is the contribution? And, then,
- What are its interests, or implications for research or policy? And, certainly,
- How true, or plausible, is it (and sometimes, how truthful is the person making the contribution)?

How practical this is. In a seminar conversation, what constitutes a contribution? Say I note that there are thirteen people in the room. Unless someone believes in ghosts, anyone can quickly assess the truth-value of that statement which, unfortunately, is beside the point. The question is rather what I mean to say with this contribution. Do thirteen people ruin the chance that everyone can be heard? Am I disappointed with the low turnout? Do the thirteen make up a significant percentage of a caucus? These questions expose the meaning of the remark because it, too, must have an interest. What do I intend to accomplish with it? Do I want more people to come or am I telling people to think again before coming next time? In those cases, the remark serves the interest of the seminar. Or am I prefacing a philosophical point to serve the interest of furthering philosophical inquiry? A single remark has all kinds of meanings and serves one or perhaps several interests. All this weighs in on the participants to determine whether my remark made a contribution or not. It is not terribly logical; it is, however, quite complex.

In this context, it is useful to know about the speech act theory propagated by the philosopher John L. Austin and further developed by philosophers such as John Searle and Jurgen Habermas. Austin made the point that sentences perform in various ways; they are speech acts. The performance is usually more than referring to some reality out there. When I say, "Get out of here!" I do not make a claim about some truth but intend just what I say: "Get out of here!" He called such a speech act a perlocutionary act. A locutionary speech act involves saying that something is the case, such as "There are thirteen people in this room." If the speech act intends to make some other point (e.g., thirteen is a low turnout), it is called an illocutionary act. A speech act like the remark about the thirteen people is often all three. Although you can talk quite competently without knowing the names of your speech acts, it is important to realize that not all we say has value because of its truth content. There is more.

As soon you realize this, the point is obvious. Claiming the truth about a poem would be presumptuous if not arrogant – as if all other opinions and interpretations are untrue and therefore beside the point. Discussions about relationships are not very different. We associate, muse, argue about what the other really meant. While intimating that it is all about true love, true friendship, we simply are relating to each other. Sure, at times the truth rules, like when you find your partner with your best friend in a compromising position, or when you mistake one artist for another. Even so, any "truth" is subject to interpretation.

Truth is not pivotal in a scientific conversation, either. Truth is not the primary arbiter of debates, nor is it the focal guide in scientific inquiry. In the company of economists, the truth question hardly ever comes up. Rare is the instance when someone will ask, "Is this really true?" Going about claiming the truth is not what you do in a scientific setting. You rather say you have "an interesting result," a "plausible outcome," or a "more fruitful approach." Economists may say that they are right with their theories and others wrong, but woe be to those who dare say their prediction is true. That would be a true faux pas. Virtually all those in the scientific conversation know that the truth is elusive, that new results may prove old results wrong, that theories evolve and change, and that uncertainty is ubiquitous. As philosopher of science Paul Feyerabend noted in *Against Method*, "And as regards the word 'truth,' we can say at this stage that it certainly has people in a tizzy but has not achieved much else" (1975: 230).

So although it is always hard to tell from the outside which contributions will cause waves and which will not, or how high they will be, we can say that effective contributions will perform, as Austin would say, locutionary, illocutionary, and perlocutionary functions, and therefore have to be truthful, meaningful, and of interest. Let me elaborate.

Being truthful

The truth of contribution to a conversation – be it a proposition, a sentence, an entire theory, a gesture, a factual statement, or something else – matters. On certain occasions, it matters more than others. This is the realist point. Truth stands here for truth in the sense of logical consistency, correct calculations, and proper deductions – and in the sense of correspondence with some reality out there. But a truthful statement does not speak for itself and is not persuasive on its own; it needs more.

Being meaningful

A contribution generates meanings all around. This is the hermeneutic point. Meanings are more or less loose connections of a statement, proposition, emotion, concept, text (or whatever) with other statements, propositions, emotions, concepts, texts (or whatever). The truth, or evocation thereof, is only one meaning. Others may prevail. When one economist mentions "Nash equilibrium," other economists may think other things: its logical definition, the vexing issues related to it, or Nash's peculiar life. (He went mad, won the Nobel Prize, and became the subject of an award-winning movie.) Associations constitute meanings. A contribution to a conversation has to be meaningful to be heard and to become part of it. That is why scientists continually interpret, and why it is so important that they find a contribution interesting. They are not just trying to determine the truth value of a contribution but, more importantly, they are trying to interpret what it means in the context of the ongoing conversation, how it stands in relation to other contributions, whether its meanings are more or less in correspondence with prevailing beliefs, and so on.

Being of interest

A contribution has to serve certain interests, or inspire one or more actions. This is the pragmatic point. You might say the contribution has to perform in certain ways. This makes it of interest, rather than interesting. A contribution is of interest when:

- It sustains the conversation by suggesting new research and further argument, offering new heuristics or solving a problem that stood in the way of progress.
- It has consequences for other conversations, such as those related to policy, management, the stock market, journalism, households, unions.

- It contributes to the commons, the values that are shared within and without the academic community (as when an argument supports the value of justice, or Rorty argues for greater solidarity and tolerance). When the implied values of a contribution clash with existing values, the contribution may cause waves because of opposition and resistance. (Gary Becker received a great deal of attention because many took issue with his economistic view of things personal.)
- It serves personal and institutional interests in terms of generating research money, personal satisfaction, and the like.

Little can be known offhand about just what makes a contribution interesting and of interest outside one's own conversation. Where computer scientists find notions such as "inheritance" and "composition" exciting, people on the outside are left to wonder. For insiders, the notions are packed with meanings. They can recount dramas of success and failure, muse about its opportunities, and have a feel for the significance of their discussion on the outside world. How interesting it is, how much it is of interest, and how valuable it is will be beyond outsiders – including those, coming from what they mistakenly see as a loftier perch, who believe that they can step into such a conversation from time to time and judge the essence of it. Likewise, it is almost impossible to gauge from the outside what a new contribution to the literature on cooperative games signifies. The outsider may be dismayed by the wildly unrealistic assumptions in the analysis, but insiders may think it has a profound impact and will therefore be excited when talking about it.

Contributions have to be of interest (Figure 5.1). Recall Peirce (p.69 above): the significance of what we say is the impact on the conduct of life. That is why economic arguments often conclude with policy implications and why research foundations want to know the social relevance of what they fund. Often the claims made are window dressing. Economists claim policy relevance even though they know that the chance that policy-makers will take notice of their argument is negligible. For a long time, methodologists have claimed their discussion would bear directly on the practice of economists. Now we know that that is highly dubious (see Box 5.3). Everyone thinks physics research interests lead to inventing things,

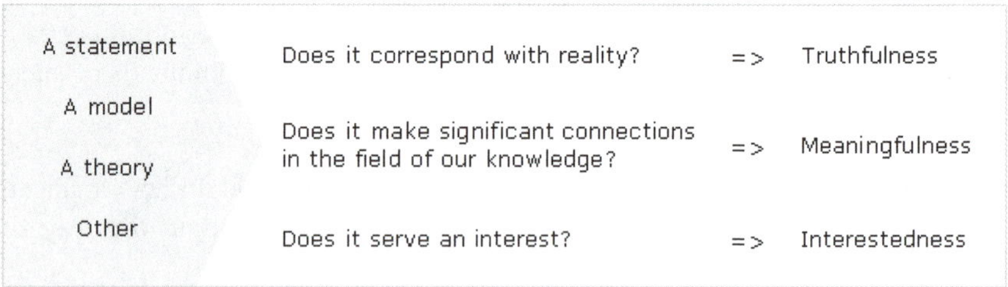

A statement	Does it correspond with reality?	=>	Truthfulness
A model			
A theory	Does it make significant connections in the field of our knowledge?	=>	Meaningfulness
Other	Does it serve an interest?	=>	Interestedness

Figure 5.1   A contribution to a conversation has to be truthful and meaningful, and serve an interest

Box 5.3 Science as a pick-up game

The pick-up game of basketball is common practice in the US. Having gathered at a court, teams are formed by having two people alternately pick the players. Another method is for everyone to shoot a foul shot: the first five to make their shots form team one; the second five become team two. The people left over form a third team, which plays against the winner of the first game. (The rule is somewhat strange in that the better players tend to end up on one team and may continue winning till the bitter end.) Before the start of the game, the players agree on some basic rules such as "loser takes out" (the team that got scored against gets the ball). Most rules, however, are tacit. For example, when someone fouls you, you are supposed to make the call yourself. There is no referee. Usually the calls are honored, but when someone appears to abuse the rule, people will make comments, argue, get mad, or even get into a fight.

Think of economists playing a pick-up game. People like the methodologists are watching the game. And here is the difference. Some of the methodologists yell at the players, telling them how to play the game. They, after all, know the rules because they are philosophers and can tell a good move from a bad one. They at times give the impression of wanting to jump and participate as referees. The players, however, do not pay any attention. They continue to violate and vitiate all kinds of rules and do not seem to be bothered. Only when one of them stops and makes suggestions about one rule or another do they pay attention, like when Milton Friedman tells them that accurate predictions, not realistic assumptions, are key. Then the other players get into the discussion and an argument ensues. Subsequently, the play changes somewhat. Players will invoke the argument when disputes occur. ("Hey, listen, the realism of assumptions doesn't matter, don't you know? Let's go!" "Wait a minute, Samuelson pointed out that it does matter. So let's see whether what we are doing here is right." "C'mon man, let's just play.")

In the meantime, methodologists are busy critiquing what the players said, and yell again that they are mistaken, that Friedman did not mean it that way, that what he says does not make sense anyway, that the rules really are different. But the players do not hear and do not care.

I wonder what this says about the games of economists and methodologists. Apparently, the latter are involved in a game that has little to do with the game economists are playing. That does not mean that it is irrelevant. The endless talk about and around a game like basketball may have no influence on how the game is played, but it sure is important. The game would mean little without all that talk. Methodological talk may not be as important for the game of science, but science is inconceivable without it.

With the discursive turn, students of economics have become more modest and extensively study the games economists are playing while withholding judgment. They can only hope that the players will learn from such studies, are inspired by them, or may realize when they are repeating the discussions and even the mistakes of previous players.

Consider the philosopher your therapist. Rorty does not know how to do economics, nor do any of the others cited above. (They are all standing on the sidelines of the game, if present at all.) Then again, you do not expect your therapist to live your life for you. If you realized the mess they probably are making of their own lives, you would not want them to. Even so, they may give you insights into your own life, hand you some concepts, and make you face up to your problems, confusions, and doubts. (Dr Phil: "We all have our doubts. But we want to go with life, don't we?") Philosophy of science is a source for economists who want to understand what they are doing, what this science is all about. It helps the hard-nosed scientists to tone down somewhat. (Dr Phil: "You're a little arrogant, aren't you? And you don't want to be that, do you? So for goodness' sake, change your tune.") And the lazy-dazy people will be encouraged to get more serious about the social character of a conversation.

and medical research interests promote health. The influence takes years to be effectuated and, even then, often occurs indirectly and haphazardly.

One consequence: how to be critical

Since a contribution has to be not only truthful but also interesting and of interest, criticisms can be directed at all three dimensions. When you want to be critical of a particular conversation, say Marxist or neoclassical, you could try to argue that its claims are false. Capitalism works and the rate of profit is not falling, you could posit to discredit Marxist economics. Or you could point at crises in capitalist systems to undermine neoclassical economics. Don't expect your opponents to surrender. However truthful your claims are, truth is not all that matters.

Instead of exposing the untruth of a conversation or a contribution thereto, you could question its meaningfulness. The contribution may fail to make relevant connections, may conflict with important values, or may simply fail to interest

Box 5.4 Statements are always positive and normative

Every student of economics is exposed to the distinction between positive and normative statements. Positive statements supposedly state things as they are; normative statements state things as they ought to be. Scientists "should" stick to positive statements – at least that is what students are taught. The previous discussion shows that this is impossible. Even a most empirical, and therefore positive, statement about the number of the people in the room implies an "ought" (there ought to be more/fewer people), which is the interest or purpose that the statement serves, the action it calls for.

A mathematical equation appears decidedly scientific and objective (positive it need not be as it may not be an empirical statement) but, for a first-year student with a blind spot for formulas, notice its normative implication ("If you cannot learn the mathematics, you do not belong here"). The writing in mathematics evokes the scientific values of rigorous, abstract, and usually reductionist reasoning. It is not free of values.

Thus, the positive–normative distinction cannot be interpreted to imply that scientific practice should be without values. Every practice, every utterance, evokes or communicates one value or another, like a scientific value. The distinction tells us something different. What we want to convey with the positive–normative distinction is the importance of sticking to the economic conversation as much as possible. The distinction, therefore, is normative! We are telling our students and each other:

> Do not let the concerns of other conversations interfere in your economics. Do not bring in the values you negotiate with in your political, artistic, religious, or personal practices; keep out religious, political, and personal meanings and interests as much as possible. And when someone suggests that the theory under discussion is discredited because the party, big business or trade union won't like it, beware. The positive–normative distinction will readily appear just to discipline such an interference.

Keep the economic conversation pure! There is much to say for that. I tell my students as much, especially those who arrive with strong beliefs about a free (unjust, cruel, perfect, whatever) world. But I would like to say the same to those who come in with a firm belief that mathematical modeling is the only sure path to the truth. "Don't be so normative," I'd like to say. "Don't think that we necessarily have to bring in the values, methods, and ideas of the discipline of mathematics. Be open-minded and see what else the economic conversation has to offer." In the end, we all have to be normative; we all have to assume a standpoint, whether it is for the scientific conversation, the free market, the rationality assumption, or something else entirely.

you. When I asked Sir John Hicks how he responds to the notion of "conflict," he reacted with irritation and mumbled that he had nothing to do with that (Klamer 1989). In this way, he made clear that a Marxist discourse would not interest him, regardless of its truth-value. Likewise, some people may be uninterested in speaking about humans as if they were computers or about economies as if they were game-theoretic. In the former case, the would-be participant has little interest in the abstract discourse of neural systems; in the latter case, he or she will most likely not find any neoclassical conversation compelling.

Another way of being critical of a conversation or a contribution thereto is to direct your arrows at the interests it serves. Critical friends such as Jack Amariglio will point out that I am too nice in this book. Why not speak of powerful and overpowering interests? Why not recognize that some conversations, like the current neoclassical one, overpower, crowd out, and silence other conversations? They want me to hammer home the point that conversations are exclusive in some way or another. To which I say "yes" and "yes" and "but." From the point of view of heterodox economists like institutionalists, Marxists, post-Keynesians, feminist economists, and cultural economists like me, the neoclassical conversation is dominant to the point of overpowering. Its protagonists make sure that their interests are served. In 2003, one of the rare bastions of heterodox economics, the University of Notre Dame, isolated itself to make space for a more conventional economics department. But, while all this is going on, the point is that not merely that the truth is at stake; neoclassical economists communicate distinct meanings and do well serving their own interests. I do not want to come on so heavily. Neoclassical economists should also be able to be comfortable reading this. That is my interest.

So what?

To appreciate a conversation like that of academic economists, it helps to look beyond logic and fact. Neither the hard-nosed scientist nor the lazy-dazy scientist is right. I suggest that both consider the metaphor of the conversation. It will mellow the hard-nosed scientist somewhat (at least so I presume) and get the lazy-dazy scientist to pay attention. The metaphor of the conversation compels us to realize that contributions have to be not only truthful but also meaningful and of interest. When you recognize that the meanings of what you say are important, you will understand why you have to submerge yourself in a conversation, for only then will you be able to appreciate the nuances and the refined meanings that are being shared in that conversation. You also will understand why scientists want to claim more for their contributions than a sober observation will establish. Scientists, too, want to believe that their work is good for something beyond the conversation in which they are participating. Some may stress the value of science; others will talk about values such as justice, freedom, emancipation. Rorty speaks of the edifying and therapeutic values of participating in a scientific conversation. I would be more than content if such were the values that a discourse like this realized.

Appendix

Those unfamiliar with the philosophical and methodological discussions about knowledge, truth, and the standards of science may find this appendix helpful.

Eavesdropping on the conversation of philosophers and methodologists

Economists learn to present their discipline in a scientific light. Never mind what it is they really do. Introductory chapters of economic textbooks are scattered with terms like "induction," "deduction," "falsification," and "positive versus normative statements." Regarding the positive–normative distinction, economists want to say that science is about positive statements, i.e., statements about the world as it is. Normative statements – those about the world as it should be – are to be avoided and expunged. Science, after all, has to be value-free (scientists assigning a value to their contributions to conversation notwithstanding). This aversion to normative statements does not prevent the hard-nosed from evoking scientific terms when their image needs legitimizing.

The hard-nosed did not invent their image of science. With their tough pronouncements on science, these practical men, who believe themselves to be quite exempt from any intellectual influence, are actually the slaves of some defunct philosopher.[3] What does or does not constitute science – induction, deduction, empiricism, and so on – is in the conversations of philosophers. Library shelves are filled with books on the subject. The *Journal of Economic Methodology*, among others, is dedicated to it. Numerous well-known economists have contributed to these meta-discussions ("meta" is Greek for "after," as in metaphysics). John Neville Keynes, for example, introduced the distinction between positive and normative statements; Milton Friedman has argued that the realism of assumptions does not matter (to which Paul Samuelson responded that operationalization of theoretical terms is the key); Deirdre McCloskey has called attention to the rhetoric of the discipline; Mark Blaug has admonished economists to be more serious about subjecting their theories to empirical tests.

Eavesdropping on the conversation of philosophers of science and (economic) methodologists

How did the idea of science and scientific knowledge come about? The idea of "science" is not all that old, less than three centuries. The idea that the economy can be the subject of scientific inquiry is even more recent, going back two centuries or so to Adam Smith's 1776 publication, *The Wealth of Nations*. The notion of scientific inquiry was, at the time, a direct challenge to the authority of the church. With God as the supreme and all-knowing Being, humans had no need to find out for themselves. All they had to do was open their minds, ignore preconceived notions, and see what God had in store for the world. For people with a religious belief, truth is a *veritas divina* – truth is divine. Such truth manifests itself. Knowledge comes about by studying the sacred books such the Bible, the Talmud, the Koran, or the Veda, and by praying or meditating. The enlightened see clearly, like the Buddha (who did not have an image of God as in the Judeo-Christian and Moslem traditions). With the conception of science, our ancestors left divine inspiration for what it was and went out to find out for themselves. Some were burned at the stake for such sacrilege, or excommunicated.

The first inklings of modern-day scientific awareness came in the sixteenth century. Philosophers routinely call upon the spirits of Francis Bacon and René Descartes to tell the story. Bacon (1561–1626) admonished his contemporaries to look beyond the sacred books and read the "Book of Nature." In saying that we might just as well open our eyes and look around us to find out what is there to be known, Bacon laid the foundation for the empirical and experimental approach of science.

René Descartes is the other inevitable character in the narrative, and justifiably so. His *Discourse on Method and the Meditations* (1968 [1621]) is still a good read. He tells about his Jesuit education, the readings of Aristotle and other ancient philosophers (noting that "to *converse* with those of other centuries is the same as to travel"),[4] his love of mathematics, and proceeds to his experience one day in Germany, "whither the war." He was in the army at the time. Stuck in a room "heated by an enclosed stove . . . where I had the complete leisure to meditate on my own thoughts," he tried to determine what – of all the knowledge he had acquired during his studies – he knew for certain, and discovered that he could discard all but one truth: *cogito, ergo sum*.

"I think therefore I am" is arguably the most famous sentence of all philosophy. The method Descartes subsequently envisioned, and to some extent implemented, was the deduction of other statements from what he knew for certain. The method is that of mathematics: begin from axioms – statements that are evidently true – and then derive other statements that, by virtue of the rules of logic, have to be true as well. Knowledge is something of the mind, Descartes concluded, and the mind is the thing out there, distinct from the body. Thus the mind–body problem came into the world. Since there is a gap between us (thinking) and the world out there, how can we be sure that what we think represents the world as it really is (Figure 5.2)? According to Descartes, reason is the key.

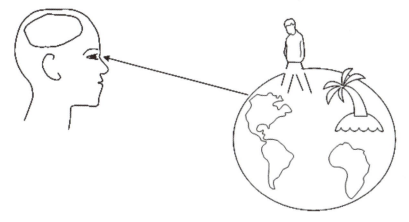

Figure 5.2 The gap between the mind that wants to know and the world to be known

Because Descartes stressed the role of reason, philosophers call him a rationalist. Bacon is an empiricist because he stressed observation as the source of our knowledge. Both gave impetus to epistemology, the branch of philosophy dedicated to questions about knowledge such as "How do we know?" and "How do we know we know?" Ancient philosophers had already paved the way. Socrates, in the texts of Plato, had pointed to the problem of knowledge with the story of the cave: we humans are like prisoners in a cave who are doomed to observe the world out there in the form of shadows projected by a fire on the wall we face – we cannot know any better. Aristotle was the precursor of Bacon, as he pointed frequently to reality as he saw it. But it took centuries before Bacon and Descartes would alert us to the responsibility we have for knowledge. Bacon told us to use our senses and Descartes told us to use our brains.

We recognize their rationalist and empiricist threads in current practice. Think, for example, of economists who like to work with data and propagate measurement without theory. They could be called empiricists in the tradition of Bacon. The theorists – those economists who hope to come to know the world by means of elaborate mathematical models with axioms, lemmas, etc. – operate in the spirit of Descartes. Notice that the narrative is working its way toward a vision on science that suits the hard-nosed economist. See in this Rorty's metaphor of knowledge in Chapter 2 as "mirror and logic". Bacon was for the mirror and Descartes for the logic. Getting them into one system of thought was now required: enter Immanuel Kant.

Kant is the philosopher of philosophers; he is a tough read. Key is his famous maxim: "Perceptions without conceptions are empty; conceptions without perceptions are blind." In other words, scientists need the empiricism of Bacon as well as the rationalism of Descartes. Some statements are true by virtue of their logic – these he called analytic statements; the truth of what he called synthetic statements is contingent, dependent on what the facts tell. Scientists make use of both.

It gets tougher when he probes the truth of synthetic and analytic statements and comes up with the notion of synthetic statements that are a priori true. He suggests that the human mind is equipped with some categories for time and space that are true even though they are not true logically. Economists would later use the argument to suit their needs, in particular by arguing that certain of their assumptions, like the one of self-interested agents, are a priori true. Most important for the narrative is that science requires both logical or mathematical derivation and confrontation with the facts. We see here the image of science that the hard-nosed propagate.

The confident picture of science and what it generates in terms of certain knowledge culminated in the views of a group of philosophers in the 1920s. As they gathered in Vienna, they go by the name of the Vienna Circle. Logical positivists is another name for them, as they are relentless in their insistence that science restrict itself to entities that can be observed and follow the rules of logic. Science is to be grounded in logic and facts, as it were. Here we discern the solid foundations the hard-nosed economists have in mind for their discipline.

The philosophizing that went on in the Vienna Circle was intense, complex, and involving. You have to get into that conversation to appreciate a book like *Tractatus* by Ludwig Wittgenstein, not an immediate member of the circle but a brilliant Austrian philosopher who had a great impact on their conversations. Much of the discussion in *Tractatus* focuses on the role of language. Earlier philosophers had pointed to the gap between the mind and the world out there, wondering how humans think to bridge it. The logical positivists pointed out that language is that bridge; everything we think to know we express in sentences, statements, or propositions. We now say that their input marks the linguistic turn in epistemology (Figure 5.3). The analytic approach to philosophy that ensued calls attention to the intricacies of language, to the issues of representation, meaning, and so on. What does "yellow" mean? How does it come to mean just that, the color yellow? The analysis can become extremely complicated. The issues were intricate, as when they tried to figure out how we can observe the unobservable. Physicists have their forces, relativity, and strands; economists have their preferences, demand and supply forces, elasticity, and so much more that we cannot observe directly. Have you seen a demand force? Elasticity? The logical positivists dealt with these issues, among others. In another venture, Russell and Whitehead tried to show that mathematics is all logic, that proof is important if logic is the foundation of all deductive reasoning (they failed). I could go on. The point is that these people were serious about getting to the foundations of knowledge.

The hard-nosed scientists must like the idea of foundations and the privileging of science. For that is what logical positivists became known for. Any statement, proposition or sentence that cannot be verified by facts, so they urged, is either analytical (i.e., logical) or meaningless. It is fine to argue, "I love you," "God exists," "The cat is on the mat," or "When price goes up, quantity demanded goes down"; the question is whether there are facts to support it. Only positive and logical statements count.

The influence of these philosophers was profound, so much so that their way

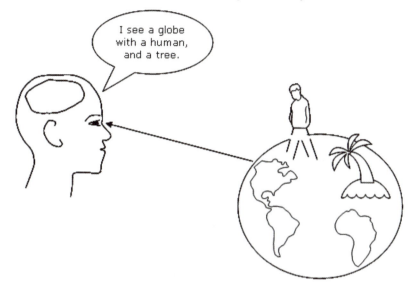

Figure 5.3 The linguistic turn highlighted the role of language in the process of knowledge

of thinking became the Received View for the next half-century or so. There were some amendments. The intervention of Karl Popper, another Austrian who ended up in London, was important. In 1934, he wrote his *magnum opus, Logik der Forschung* (translated in 1959 as *The Logic of Scientific Discovery*), but it took a while before it caught on. I learned about it through my teacher, the methodologist Joop Klant, and the writings of Terence Hutchison, another economic methodologist. They were the Popperians among economic methodologists, and that is what most economists would become, whether they knew it or not.

Popper inserted a little bit of modesty in the Received View. He evoked the "Problem of Induction," which David Hume (a contemporary and friend of Adam Smith) had pointed out, and that implied that we could never prove a general statement by means of observations. With the statement, "All swans are white," you can go on observing swans till you are quite fed up with traveling to lakes but you can never be sure that you would not see the black swan. Popper proposed, therefore, to replace the criterion of verifiability with that of falsifiability: A statement qualifies as scientific when it can be falsified, or proven wrong, by the facts. Economists have taken this criterion to heart. After running a regression they will never, ever write, "The test has proven [verified] the theory" but are content with the more modest, "The test has failed to disprove the theory." A modicum of modesty cannot hurt the hard-nosed scientist.

Popper is about more than the criterion of falsification. He also articulated the hypothetic–deductive method, which now comes almost instinctively to the economic scientist. You do not go about collecting data to do research but you try to formulate a model about some phenomenon, say the importance of a political union for a monetary union. You deduce from your model a hypothesis, e.g., a monetary union cannot succeed without a political union. And then you subject your model to the most rigorous tests possible to see whether the hypothesis can be falsified. If it cannot, you have made a contribution to economics. Whether it actually works this way is another matter. In reality you may begin with a hypothesis, develop a model to fit it, and maybe do some empirical tests to see how the model holds up. Popper was adamant about his procedure. He maintained that science progresses only by a process of conjectures and refutations. The principle makes excellent advice to students who face writing a thesis or term paper: be bold; make a conjecture with which people can disagree or that is surprising in some way, and then do whatever you can in terms of tests to refute or disprove the claim. When you fail to refute your conjecture, it really means an advance in our knowledge.

Notice how the normative sneaks into the story? The philosophers of the Received View had distinct ideas on what constitutes science and what does not. Science was mirror and logic. Popper wanted to see more conjecture and more integrity by expecting scientists to do everything they could to refute their conjectures – no easy confirmations but really tough tests. He wanted a science that stands strong against dogmatic, totalitarian, and quasi-scientific thinking such as in Marxism and Freudian psychology.

Economic methodologists took this stance to their conversations about economics. When I tried to enter their conversations in the mid-1970s, the quest was for the rules that would make economics a science. Methodologists such as Joop Klant and Mark Blaug (and, somewhat later, Daniel Hausman and Alexander Rosenberg) wanted to provide economists with clear standards for differentiating economic science from economic non-science and for choosing among competing theories. The idea was that science is a rational enterprise and disagreements find resolution by the application of some objective standard. The hard-nosed scientists must have felt reassured at this stage of the meta-conversation.

When I got around to doing my dissertation in the late 1970s, the hype was Lakatos and his notion of a research program. You might consider Lakatos Popper with historical perspective. The notion of a research program suggested that the relevant objects of study are not the single propositions or theories but a constellation of propositions and theories. Lakatos called such a constellation a research program. Falsification of a single proposition does not mean that an entire research program has to be abandoned. Rather, researchers will find ways to amend the theory so they can hold onto the basic assumptions that they are accustomed to and which form the hard core of the program. The hard core of neoclassical economics would contain assumptions like constrained maximization as the explanation of behavior. Nothing will convince the researchers in that program to give up the hard core, no matter what evidence comes in. A research program will be sustainable as long as its theoretical content shows progress and empirical work continues to add confirmations without too many falsifications. All that seemed eminently reasonable, and a few of my fellow students set out to show that Lakatos's research program accurately describes what happens in economics. At first I had the same idea (with new classical economics as the case), but I gave it up when it hit me that the conversation of philosophers had been changing, that the Received View had been unraveling, and that the discussion had moved beyond Popper and Lakatos, making a discursive turn. The attention had shifted away from the logic of scientific argument to scientific discourse, that is, everything that scientists do to communicate their findings, concepts, and ideas.

Hard-nosed science loses its footings

In the meta-field at large, doubts about the logical and factual foundations of science had begun to gnaw much earlier, when Einstein came up with his relativity theory. With this reorientation of the notions of time and space, it dawned on philosophers and scientists alike that much of what was held to be true was only true by approximation. It took a while before these doubts were able to break into the Received View. Thomas Kuhn drove the point home in 1962 with *The Structure of Scientific Revolutions*. He introduced the notion of paradigm to indicate that scientists work in a framework of assumptions, exemplars, methods, and beliefs, and that a framework may be upset and rendered obsolete when a new paradigm comes about. According to Kuhn, scientific knowledge progresses via a series of small revolutions punctured by a major revolution from time to time. His examples were drawn from physics.

Not surprisingly, Kuhn's account caused a stir. If revolutions occur in physics, they must occur in a less sure-footed science like economics. Revolutions are no fun, at least to those who are revolved in the process. The very possibility of their occurrence makes any normal scientist shiver. Just imagine – you have studied equilibrium theory cum constrained maximization and dedicated your entire professional life to developing that paradigm. Then something happens, new ideas come about and take over, constrained maximization suddenly proves to be a sterile and inadequate representation of economic behavior, and all your students jump on the new bandwagon. In one stroke, all the literature you know, all results, all methods, all class notes, all lectures have become obsolete. And you have become obsolete as a scientist. Apart from retraining, your best alternative is to retire and wonder what your economics was good for. How appalling an experience! Yet it happens. It happened when Keynesian economics became the dominant paradigm in the 1950s and when game theory took over in the 1980s; it happened to Eastern European economists when the fall of the Wall marked the end of the Marxist economics they had been teaching and developing. In each revolution, economists had to discard an entire literature and learn a new one just to stay in the conversation.

In the meantime, the Received View took one internal blow after another. Its carefully constructed framework unraveled and its optimism about establishing firm foundations for scientific knowledge faded. Gödel's theorem, with its argument that no complete proof is possible within a logical system, unsettled beliefs in a complete logical system. Disturbing to the empirical sciences, including economics, was the Duhem–Quine thesis, which stated that falsification of a theory is impossible: because every empirical test requires various auxiliary hypotheses, in the end you do not know whether any of the latter are responsible for a falsification. The econometrics used could be wrong; the specification of the model could be mistaken. So much is involved in the testing that all kinds of factors can be wrong. Consequently, falsification no longer sufficed as a criterion for choosing among competing theories. The backbone of hard-nosed science was gone.

Related is the problem of what is called the theory-ladenness of the facts. When economists speak of "wages" and "prices," they refer not to the facts seen by anyone but to facts that have been constructed with the aid of the index methodology. The index methodology is tricky and depends on various assumptions. How grounded, then, are the facts? And how reliable are the tests based on these constructed facts? You suspect some circularity: scientists use theories to determine facts and then turn around to use those facts to test the theories.

Language, the intermediary between the mind and reality out there, proved to be problematic as well. Fixing the meanings of words is difficult, if not impossible.

Box 5.5 As a matter of fact

Virtually all facts that economists rely on are constructed through surveys, guesses (e.g., "How many hours did you work last week?"), and calculations. Economists toss out numbers on economic growth as if they were facts, but they depend on numerous decisions and difficult procedures that took decades to construct and continue to be subject to debate and change. Only recently did economists come to acknowledge that the procedure for determining the consumer price index was off; as a consequence, inflation had to be significantly adjusted. Even some "fact" like the price of sugar is dubious. For what sugar, in which store, in what area is that price fact? How to adjust for differences in quality? Does price include brown sugar, granulated sugar, sugar lumps, packets of sugar? What is the price that the researcher should use? There are procedures for a researcher to find statistics on the price of sugar over time. These statistics, however, do not report direct observations alone; they reflect intellectual efforts (i.e., judgments) as well.

Well known is the problem with measurement of the rate of return on capital. Economists can determine that rate only if they have a measurement of the capital stock, and that measurement requires knowledge of the rate of return (considering the value of capital to be equal to the total of future earnings discounted over time). The same problem occurs with all aggregated figures used in economics. Aggregation procedures are suspect, yet most practitioners prefer to overlook the problems as they otherwise would get stuck. Yes, you can be too honest a scientist.

French philosophers such as Jacques Derrida made a career out of pointing out the complexities in our texts. Meanings change. Terms such as "the market" can mean all kinds of things. Some people will think of demand and supply, whereas others will think of a Walrasian equilibrium mechanism; most non-economists will make associations with business, commercial life, privatization, competition, money and profit, and consumer orientation. That is why some philosophers call upon the method of hermeneutics, which urges the student of economics to interpret the meanings that words and texts generate.

Related to hermeneutics is the rhetorical approach. When Deirdre McCloskey wrote of economics as rhetoric in 1983, she (although at that time she was still Donald) shocked her colleagues. The very idea that they, scientists, were in the business of persuasion and used a variety of rhetorical devices – including non-scientific ones such as metaphors and narratives – as means clashed with the image of cool, detached, and rigorous. Even so, McCloskey's arguments showed clearly how rhetorical devices are ubiquitous in the scientific writings of economics. In a way, Milton Friedman had argued something similar when he purported that economists reason "as if the realism of assumptions does not matter." "As if" is the figure of the metaphor: reasoning about one phenomenon in terms of another.

The rhetorical approach calls attention to another gap. Whereas Plato and many after him pointed to the gap between our minds and reality out there, the use of rhetoric points to the gap that exists between you and me. I may be convinced that economists engage in conversation and may present powerful arguments in support of that; you may still misunderstand me, make associations I wish you would not make, or see the consequences more clearly than I do. There are all kinds of reasons for such a gap to exist. You and I come to the exchange with different experiences, different knowledge. I cannot make you think exactly as I do, or stop you from thinking the wrong associations (rhetoric makes you think "demagoguery" or "mere style"). The rhetorical approach calls attention to the fact that I use an excess of devices in an attempt to make you see the science of economics my way. Even so, my meanings will be distorted in the process. Just carry out the post-lecture experiment: ask audience members to tell what they learned. You will be astonished to find how many got the main message wrong, how they stress different points, remember anecdotes best and sometimes, seemingly, have attended entirely different lectures. The stabilization of meanings is tough to achieve in face of yawning gaps between different minds (Figure 5.4).

Hard-nosed economists elect for mathematical formulations as a way of dealing with the unstable and varied meanings of words. But even the language of mathematics is not a firewall; that much the philosophical and rhetorical investigations have pointed out. Mathematics is more than logic. Its proofs are rhetorical and subject to interpretation as well.[5] There are good proofs and bad proofs, and mathematicians can disagree on which proof is which. Another problem with the language of mathematics is that it restrains us in what we can express. When the mathematical formulation of a phenomenon is prohibitively complicated, this does not mean that the phenomenon is irrelevant. I would not disregard the feelings I have for my wife if they could not be articulated mathematically. When passions

Figure 5.4 A gap exists between the brain and reality as well as among brains

are believed to drive the stock market, it is really too bad if the mathematical model cannot account for them. These limitations of the language of mathematics have not held mainstream economists back. The stress on formal reasoning, on tightly articulated models, on lemmas and proofs is stronger than ever. If this practice depends on a hard-nosed image of science, it has lost its backing in the meta-conversation.

That backing is worn thinner when eavesdropping on the meta-conversation of economic methodologists. Mark Blaug continues to rail against excessive formalism and too little empiricism in economics as he, like Popper, wants to keep the barbarians from the gate. He does not, however, appear to be maintaining his original agenda of handing economists a few standards on a platter. He, too, has had to acknowledge that it was far too ambitious. Klant foresaw this denouement in his 1979 *Rules of the Game* (translated from Dutch in 1985). No economic methodologist still claims to know the foundations on which hard-nosed economic science can rest. Uskali Maki carries on with his campaign for clarity of language, well-defined terms, consistency in argument, and conviction that we are all scientific realists after all. Even if we have to give up hope for firm foundations, we do not have to resort to a form of instrumentalism, that is, the conviction that theories are merely instruments to control and manage processes in physical and social life, and that their truth value does not matter. After extensive debates I have come to the recognition that he is right: I too refer to some truth out there – as I will stress below – but we both agree that this does not mean that science is firmly grounded and that scientists follow clear rules. Wade Hands entitles an extensive survey of the literature of the meta-conversations *Reflection without Rules* (2001) to underscore the point. There simply is no three-by-five that lists the rules by which economic scientists can distinguish true theories from false ones. "Pluralism rules" is the conclusion of Bruce Caldwell and Sheila Dow, among others. The hard-nosed scientists are left on their own.

Richard Rorty, a soft-spoken American philosopher, added insult to injury in his book *Philosophy and the Mirror of Nature* (1979). He debunks and subsequently tramples the metaphor of knowledge as mirror of nature. There is no basis for the belief that the world out there is reflected in our minds and is captured in the language we use to express what we think we know. With that there is no basis to believe in foundations and hence to privilege scientific representations of reality over others. There is no philosophical reason to believe that knowledge provided by science is more truthful than what we come to know by reading poetry or novels. Therefore, there is no reason for scientists to go to philosophers for definite answers to their questions about science and knowledge. If they want to know how to do better in their science, they should study the practice of successful sciences and scientists.

Many students of economics as a science have done just that. Rather than holding on to the philosopher's armchair and pronouncing judgment on the practice of economics, scholars such as E. Roy Weintraub, Phil Mirowski, Esther Mirjam Sent, Sheila Dow, Robert Leonard, Dave Colander, and myself (if you'll allow) have turned to studies of what is going on in the field of economics. We go into archives to find out who said what to whom and when. We try to figure out why disagreements persist, why Cambridge UK lost the battle on the so-called capital controversy to Cambridge US (even though it had superior arguments), how war agencies appear to have influenced the course that economic theorizing took in the fifties, and what is happening in graduate school.[6] These studies may be very instructive in scientific practices in economics but they do not provide the foundations that hard-nosed scientists need to hold onto their claim of having privileged knowledge and following privileged procedures.

Nowadays the field of meta-science is wide open. The study of social settings in which science comes about is popular. Latour and Woolgar, for instance, work like anthropologists observing what goes on in laboratories. In the previous chapter, I referred to the impressive work of Randall Collins, who has sorted out the networks in which major contributions to the conversations of philosophers came about. Feminists have shown the gender bias in science and have advocated a feminist standpoint for science. Followers of Derrida, Deleuze, Foucault, and other difficult French scholars continue to take apart and turn upside down whatever claims, concepts, and models science generates. Others are looking at cognitive science and artificial intelligence to learn about mental processes by which we come to think we know. One group is even trying out the merits of an economic perspective on the work of scientists.[7] After all, money plays a role, and economists have incentives too. For anyone interested in joining those conversations, a lot of work remains to be done. Don't expect any definite answers, though, on what makes economics work as a science.

With the hard-nosed scientists hanging in the ropes, you would expect the lazy-dazy scientists to manifest themselves. And they do. Not that you see economists parading with Feyerabend, who became known for his campaign "against method" and for "anything goes." Economists as a group remain tough-minded and insist on some approach – preferably a mathematical one – but you can spot the cynicism that has crept into the profession. When asked what the point of their research is, too many economists are saying things like "It's fun"; "It keeps me off the street"; "They pay me for doing this"; "Who cares?" They do not say, "to know how to improve the world," "to provide a rationale for economic policy," or even "to make sense of the world." Don't expect the confessions when the discipline is called into question, when an alternative approach to economics challenges, or when research funds have to be secured; in face of those quandaries, economists, even the lazy-dazy, toughen up. Then they are adamant that what they do is scientific and everything else is not. Internally, however, doubts about the scientific mission prevail. They add to the strangeness of the discipline.

Further reading

I started my inquiry with Klant, *The Rules of the Game: The Logical Structure of Economic Theories* (Cambridge University Press, 1985). Klant pointed me to the early work of Terence Hutchison, *The Significance and Basic Postulates of Economic Theory* (Kelley, 1965 [1938]), a book that is still of interest. Blaug's *The Methodology of Economics* (Cambridge University Press, 1992) is a good and mundane introduction to the field of economic methodology. If you are not afraid of delving deeper and becoming aware of the limitations of the field, read Wade Hands's *Reflection without Rules: Economic Methodology and Contemporary Science Theory* (Cambridge University Press, 2001). (Note the title and realize how far we have come since Klant wrote his book in 1979.) A good collection of papers in the field can be found in Bruce Caldwell's *Appraisal and Criticism in Economics: A Book of Readings* (Unwin Hyman, 1984), including classics such as Friedman's "Methodology of Positive Economics" and McCloskey's 1983 article on rhetoric. For recent work, consult the *Journal of Economic Methodology*, or *The Handbook of Economic Methodology* edited by John B. Davids, D. Wade Hands, and Uskali Maki (Edward Elgar, 1998).

The philosophical literature on the subject fills entire bookcases. I still find Popper useful to read. His classic is *The Logic of Scientific Discovery* (Hutchinson, 1959); his *Conjectures and Refutations: The Growth of Scientific Knowledge* (Basic Books, 1962) is more interesting. Richard Rorty's *Philosophy and the Mirror of Nature* (Princeton University Press, 1979) is the classic for a critical perspective.

A classic, too, is Thomas S. Kuhn's *The Structure of Scientific Revolutions* (University of Chicago Press, 1970 [1962]). Here you find the introduction of the notion of "paradigm." Also interesting is Kuhn's *The Essential Tension* (University of Chicago Press, 1977).

For the notion of research program, read Imre Lakatos in *The Methodology of Scientific Research Programmes Philosophical Papers* (Vol. I), edited by J. Worrall and G. Curie (Cambridge University Press, 1978).

For a serious challenge of your conventional notions of science, read Paul Feyerabend's *Against Method* (NLB, 1978).

6   The art of economic persuasion*

About rhetoric and all that

Truth and persuasion

The truth is: we study economics to find out what other economists have to offer in the bunch of conversations that are about truth. Graduate school sucks students, willy-nilly, into the conversation of economists. They want to know the truth and find themselves writing term papers, a thesis, and then more papers, and then research proposals. Instead of asking questions like, "Is this really true?" they find themselves asking, "Will my writing interest them?" – "them" being teachers and, later, colleagues, referees, editors, other researchers, economists at large, and, who knows, those guys in Sweden. Instead of looking for the thrill of knowing it all, students (and economists) are looking for good grades, refereed publications, tenure, grants, conference invitations, citations, fame and, why not, the Nobel Prize. In the process they find out how tough it is, how seldom papers get accepted and cited, how reluctantly "they" embrace your ideas. So they keep on talking, writing, talking again, writing more. When will it ever stop? When will they know the truth?

The metaphor of the conversation intimated it all along: getting into a conversation, assimilating its culture, knowing how to get attention, and being attentive to the truthfulness, meaningfulness, and character of your contributions – the topics that it has stimulated thus far – implies communication. Scientists settle into an endless process of communication with other scientists. That is how it is. That is how it has to be.

And where there is communication, there is miscommunication. Everyone knows that. We experience its consequences every day. We go along, constantly trying to get what is in our own heads implanted into the heads of others. We want to convey what we feel, we want others to see things our way, or understand what others want us to do. So often we fail. "My mother doesn't understand me." "You're not listening!" "How can these students not get it? I couldn't be any f***ing clearer!" But then, don't we also have difficulties understanding what is in the mind of someone or something addressing us? I can be dense too, closed off

---

*Reader's note: This chapter appears to be longer than the others. If you pass over the boxes it is not. Then again, I added the boxes for good reasons. You judge for yourself.

from an eminently clear message – my students or, better, my wife, will attest to that. But it is not for lack of trying. If only humans could understand each other.

Science was supposed to solve the problem. By using logic and fact we would be able to share identical scientific knowledge. Communication problems would cease, at least as far as science was concerned. Agreement would be a matter of being rational and adhering to the principles of logic. Descartes (1596–1650) and, especially, Spinoza (1632–77) saw in the method of geometry the means to generate expressions that would be universally true, that is, true for everyone at any historical, geographical, or cultural coordinate. Leibniz (1646–1716) preferred mathematics as a way to make or be sure, as a way to express universal knowledge. Mathematics has since been the favorite language for scientists.

And just as surely as we got a lot of science from it, we got lots of talk and interaction that surpasses the realm of logic and fact. Science stands for all sorts of activities, institutions, people, and conversations. Its practice tells you that there is simply too much variation, too many impermanences in meaning and too great a divergence in interests for logic to be its only guide to truth. There is an entire conversation going on or, better, a bunch of conversations.

And what do we do when we are writing and talking with fellow economists? We're applying research methods, constructing arguments, searching for interesting concepts, citing the right sources, justifying the methodology – all in the hope of . . . what? Persuading the audience and bridging the gap between human minds. In short, we are practicing rhetoric – as I am at this moment – whether we like to admit it or not.

Rhetoric introduced

In common parlance, "rhetoric" has negative connotations. When a politician's speech is judged "mere rhetoric," we are made to believe that it is "style" without "substance." Rhetoric is used to stand for "trickery" and "demagoguery." When you apply rhetoric you supposedly apply tricks to manipulate and fool your audience. This is rhetoric in its negative sense. With the rhetorical figure of exaggeration, you can vilify, denounce, and ridicule anything. Surely, democracy stands for endless talk, anarchy for bomb throwers, capitalism for greed, and religion for war. Add a series of powerful anecdotes and the audience is ready to believe the (mis)characterization. People can be convinced with half-truths (democracy indeed stands for endless talk, but also for more than that), or even lies. But will the arguments stand up to scrutiny? The president of a large country may be able to fool people with ill-founded arguments to push through a major reform of welfare or justify a war, but risks losing the next election when found out. It may be possible to fool people once but, when the conversation continues, he or she cannot continue fooling them. I'd almost say, "The truth wins out." I should say, "In the end, good rhetoric wins out."

Rhetoric refers to the craft of working with words or any other means of communication. Gestures and facial expressions have rhetorical functions, too. "Rhetoric may be defined," said Aristotle in his treatise with the same title, "as the faculty of observing in any given case the available means of persuasion." So rhetoric is a faculty, an ability that each of us masters, more or less. Being a faculty, it is something we work on. And it is directed at persuasion; it is about finding the means to convey something to another, to get an idea, theory, or insight across, to get another to do or believe something.

If we think about it we realize that we need the faculty of rhetoric all the time, whether to convince friends to go to a movie, to convey love (may a poem do the trick? or a mere look?), to persuade the officer to scrap that speeding ticket, or to get elected to some office. Persuasion is what markets are about, as evidenced in the chattering, shouting, negotiating, and cajoling that accompany market activities. Persuasion defines the proceedings in court. Persuasion is what science is about. Having an idea is one thing, having others pay attention to it is quite another. The scientist, accordingly, learns to master the faculty of rhetoric.

Box 6.1 Placing rhetoric

After I had almost completed a dissertation on the argumentation in new classical economics (monetarism cum rational expectations), my advisor, Roy Weintraub, showed me a research paper by the famous economic historian Deirdre McCloskey entitled "The Rhetoric of Economics." "This shows what you are trying to do," he added. I had never paid any attention to rhetoric, did not really know what it was, and probably used the term in the negative way that so many others do. Then a new world opened up. I suddenly discerned all the rhetorical moves that participants made in the debate about the neutrality of money and the ineffectiveness of government interventions. (I also wanted to toss the dissertation because McCloskey was saying it so much better and was so rhetorically superior. Weintraub convinced me to hang on; after all, I had a case worked out and that was good enough for a dissertation.) McCloskey and I subsequently organized a conference (culminating in *The Consequences of Economic Rhetoric* in 1988) and, a little later, a conference in Iowa City brought Clifford Geertz, Richard Rorty, Thomas Kuhn, and many others to the table, with *The Rhetoric of the Human Sciences* in 1987 as its visible result. Journals were started. People in all conceivable disciplines were doing rhetoric. After being subdued for centuries, the conversation on rhetoric had resumed.

The going has not been easy. The talk about rhetoric met a great deal of resistance in and outside economic circles. Analytical philosophers considered it trivial. Although sympathetic, Uskali Maki subjected McCloskey's argument to a series of analytical tests and found it wanting. Interestingly enough, his criticism was published in the prestigious *Journal of Economic Literature* in 1995. (Did the editors intend to marginalize the idea?) Most economists simply did not appear to be interested, and when confronted with the rhetoric in their discipline did not appear to get it. "We practice science," the hard-nosed insisted, "not rhetoric." But McCloskey, I, and others who had joined the cause stood firm. "You use metaphors. You use rhetorical figures to make your point."

The idea that rhetoric is about mere style proved pernicious. The source of this misconception is to be found far back, some 2,400 centuries ago. Find a copy of the collected *Dialogues of Plato* and look for the one called *Gorgias*.[1]

What you find is a conversation – it even has the form of one – between Socrates and Gorgias, a famous rhetorician at the time. First Socrates let Gorgias recognize that the truth is what we are after, and that the truth of a subject is particular to that subject. Gorgias insists that rhetoric is a craft in and of itself, independent of any subject. In section 457 he says,

> The rhetorician is competent to speak against anybody on any subject, and to prove himself more convincing before a crowd on practically every topic he wishes, but he should not any the more rob the doctors – or any other craftsmen either – of their reputation, merely because he has his power.

Here Gorgias suggests that the rhetorician is like the modern debater who is skilled in arguing and debating any proposition. For or against the death penalty, utility maximization or not, he will passionately take a stand. It is understandable that Socrates takes issue with this. I would, too.

Socrates proceeds to show in subsequent conversations (with others joining in) that what matters is to be truthful. In the end, it was Gorgias who did not do justice to the discipline of rhetoric. He made it seem that the rhetorician is a specialist who can be hired to make a case on any subject and be persuasive without any deep knowledge of the subject. Gorgias, as Plato portrayed him, gave rhetoricians and sophists (groups to which Gorgias belonged) a bad name. Rhetoric came to mean demagoguery and sophistry, something akin to senseless and even deceitful talk.

Get into the contemporary conversation about rhetoric and you will notice that Plato and Socrates are made out to be the villains – perhaps unjustly, as the reading of the *Gorgias* suggests – and Aristotle the hero. Aristotle dedicated an entire treatise to the subject. Even so, Aristotle shares in the responsibility for the marginalization of rhetoric. The very first sentence put us on the wrong track. "Rhetoric is the counterpart of dialectic." Dialectic in his usage is the art of reasoning well, and is distinct from analytics, the discipline of reasoning logically and completely. Dialectic we can discern in the practice of economics, but rhetoric . . .? Aristotle did not see rhetoric as an element of everything we humans do; he delegated it to special occasions. He distinguished between deliberative (as in political speeches), forensic (as in the court of law), and epideictic (as in laudations at funerals and wedding) oratory. Science was not to be the realm of rhetoric. It took us twenty-three centuries to get over this false start.

Even so, *Rhetoric* remains the book of choice to launch its exploration. It has a great deal to say about a great variety of rhetorical figures, invention, and composition. And it is the first treatise on psychology. For, as Aristotle points out, to bridge the gap so one can persuade another of an insight, we had better know something about psychology, particularly emotions. That remains an important point to keep in mind – we run into a wide range of emotions in the company of economists.

Throughout the next twenty centuries, rhetoric remained the mainstay of classical education. Along with logic and grammar, it constitutes the classical trivium. The dismissal by Socrates and Plato has not been lethal – yet. For many centuries to follow, students would learn about arrangement, invention, style, delivery, and memory. They would study the works of Cicero, the famous Roman orator, and Quintilian.

It was Cicero who warned against the separation of rhetoric from a discipline such as philosophy. He attacked Socrates as the source of this misconception. "What would have become of Socrates if Plato had not used his rhetorical skills to compose the dialogues?" he asks rhetorically. Rhetoric is a part of anything we do. Cicero spoke of "the undoubtedly absurd and unprofitable and reprehensible severance between tongue and the brain, leading to our having one set of professors to teach us to think and another to teach us to speak." The point is to combine the thinking and the speaking, as the sophists had argued and as Socrates had demonstrated so well.

The classical tradition held firm until the eighteenth century. Adam Smith still wrote about and taught the subject. But the emergence of the scientific spirit with its aspiration for universal and definite truths brought about the demise of this rich tradition. The faculty of rhetoric was considered subordinate to those in pursuit of the truth. Truth, in and of itself, is eloquent – that was the belief, and has been the belief, until recently. In the meantime we know better.

The last century saw a revival of the conversation on rhetoric. Get into that conversation and you encounter the names of Chaim Perelman, Wayne Booth, Stephen Toulmin, Kenneth Burke, Stanley Fish, and others. In collaboration with Olbrechts-Tyteca, the Belgian philosopher Perelman wrote a tome entitled *The New Rhetoric: A Treatise on Argumentation* (1969). He began wondering how we reason about values, and reached the insight that all reasoning is rhetorical, including scientific reasoning. Logic and facts will never be sufficient to breach the divide between separate human brains. For a communication to be effective, or persuasive, it will require the application of a variety of rhetorical figures. And that is where we stand. The idea of a scientific discourse that relies entirely on the use of logic and the reference to facts has ceased to make sense. We know better, we know much more. We know, for example, how daunting the task of persuasion is, how rare persuasive contributions are.

Accordingly, rhetoric is not just a faculty of being crafty with words. Being conscious of the rhetorical dimension of what scientists like economists do is to be conscious of the complexity of communicating ideas. It makes us think of conversations, of the culture of conversations, of the importance of getting and giving attention.

What can rhetoric mean for us?

Suppose we suspend, for the moment, all disbelief and doubt toward rhetoric and go along, just for now, with the idea that scientific practice is thoroughly rhetorical. What would that mean?

Any scientific practice is rhetorical to its core

It should be clear by now: science is not simply scripting a model, performing the empirical work, writing up the results and sending the paper off to a journal. It is about joining a conversation and knowing how to contribute to it, knowing how to draw attention to it. "Science is an instance of writing with intent, the intent to persuade other scientists, such as economic scientists" (McCloskey 1998 [1985]: 4). Having a good idea is great, but the skill is giving the idea such a form that it will be noticed. Even the best-known economists will find that the attention given to the bulk of what they have written is little to none. That is not to discourage, but to persuade how rhetorical the task is.

Argumentation drives the scientific conversation

Students usually have to learn this point the hard way. They like definition discussions ("Let me first define what a museum is"), indulge in surveys, or wallow in historical descriptions and then look puzzled when asked, "What for? What is the argument?" "No, you see, this is just a historical description." "All right, but why do I need to read it? What claim does it support?" I often refer to Popper's *Conjectures and Refutations* as a motif for scientific practice. Dare to advance a bold hypothesis, argue it, and see whether it can withstand the most serious challenges, both theoretically and philosophically. Arguing is an art in and of itself.

Practicing science is performing science, and the performance is, in large part, rhetorical

Figuring out the model, compiling the data, running regressions, or doing whatever statistical operation is called for – all that is part of the daily scientific practice. But there is so much more. As practicing economists, we find ourselves in streams of discussions with fellow economists over lunch, in the office, near the coffee machine, at seminars, during conferences, through email, and via the phone. In each, we have to perform in some way or another. We will need to find the words to get the point across, and we need to be able to hear what others are trying to tell us, including the innuendos and hidden messages. Even unexpressive people will find themselves constantly asking, "What would other economists think of what I am writing?" Whoever it is, whatever the type of person, he or she will have to know how to perform in a seminar, as both speaker and participant.

Writing and speaking scientifically calls for the rhetorical skills of arrangement, invention, and style

How to begin a paper, where to place the lemmas, how to cover a weakness, which literature to cite, and where and how to conclude the paper – all are matters of composition and invention. Some are more skilled than others. The title is a matter of invention. A seemingly silly-sounding title like "The Lemons" may become a classic.[2] The skill of style shows in the presentation. Here, too, some excel whereas others disappoint. Economists expect economists to present spontaneously; philosophers are expected to read their presentation literally. The rhetorical skills of an economist, therefore, differ from those of a philosopher. Maybe because I grew up an economist, I prefer to speak with, at most, a few notes in front of me. A recitation easily becomes mechanical, making it easy for both audience and speaker to let their thoughts wander. But, in unscripted presentations, the sentences tend to be less well crafted, speakers more easily indulge in distracting asides, and how to conclude is sometimes elusive.

"But what does all this have to do with the truth?" you might say. "It's all about style and performance!" I agree. But what if you deliver your "truth" in such a way that no one pays attention? What if you present your "truth" mathematically when your audience doesn't know mathematics or, worse, hates it? What if you start to mumble, get lost in your presentation, or simply don't know what the appropriate arguments are? Do you think your "truth" will still bear out, just like that?

Effective rhetoric requires knowing the audience

This is a key insight of the rhetorical perspective. Scientists seem to write for eternity, meaning, for a universal audience. After all, shouldn't knowledge be

---

Box 6.2 How to order a presentation

(This is something I learned from rhetoric and teach my students.)

Exordium: When starting, grab your audience by the collar; make them want to pay attention. Do not start with, say, "This essay is about . . .," whereupon they will immediately want to tune out. Tell them what your point is or intrigue them with a problem, an anomaly, or a puzzle.

Narratio: Briefly write about the context of your argument to motivate its relevance; cite some data in support of it; discuss what others have said and written about the issue; appeal to some authority.

Probatio: Make your case; present your arguments. This part may include theoretical, historical, and empirical arguments (see also Box 6.3). The inclination of many students is to cover what everyone else has said and, toward the end, when the reader is exhausted, stake their claim. Turn the order around; start with your own arguments. The presentation is more effective and the audience is ever more captive.

Refutatio: Deal with possible objections; use the occasion to amplify and strengthen your argument. In scientific arguments, however, you need to acknowledge the limitations and caveats of your argument. A scientific audience tends to be convinced if you offer your awareness of the discussion's problems and limitations.

Peroratio: A good ending can save a dull argument. You can do better than, "So that's it, folks." A joke is nice (and works in the *exordium* as well); demonstrating how much your audience learned is advantageous; revealing the powerful implications of your argument leaves them pondering your work. Know how to end. I sometimes forget this and have to end abruptly, leaving everyone, including myself, unsatisfied.

universal? Perhaps, but the reality is that academic economists write for other academic economists, game theorists write for each other, and each group asks for a specific rhetoric. If an academic economist writes for politicians or the newspaper, he or she had better omit the equations, solution concepts, elasticities, and all the other things that go down so smoothly with colleagues. Doing so may win the attention of the non-academics but risks losing the academic audience. The rule of adjusting the rhetoric to the audience is one of the more important lessons that Gorgias, Aristotle, and the other great rhetoricians had for us. And it is, of course, implied in the metaphor of the conversation.

Establishing and respecting ethos matters

The authority of the speaker matters: "ethos" is its rhetorical term. Getting a PhD is a necessary start in seeking ethos in the academic conversation. Working on reputation matters, although being knowledgeable on a particular topic does not guarantee stealing attention from a more famous – but less knowledgeable – colleague. The latter's ethos makes the difference, not necessarily the superiority of argumentation. Academics know how to assess credentials such as where PhDs came from and where they subsequently teach. Being an editor of a good journal may make a difference; having won a Nobel Prize makes all the difference. Some gain ethos by appearing to be nice and social, others do better by seeming tough-minded. Just as establishing ethos requires work, recognizing ethos requires involvement in the conversation. Being able to appreciate the obscure mumbling of the intellectual giant is the reward.

The style of reasoning implies a rhetorical choice

Recording an idea as a mathematical model has rhetorical consequences by more or less defining the audience. Mathematics tells people who do not get it to study more of it, and might narrow the range of topics for discussion and analysis. Mathematical modeling tends to generate interest in the modeling and its properties per se, such that the conversation may easily veer into solution concepts and existence theorems or new mathematical methods. The choice is rhetorical because it serves the interest of a particular conversation and therefore excludes others. Austrian economists, for example, will ignore such a mathematical argumentation on the grounds that it is irrelevant to understanding markets and entrepreneurship. Old-institutionalists, a number of feminists, and quite a few Marxists will maintain that an analysis of economic processes calls for more qualitative arguments. When one economist insists on full mathematical articulation of the model and another does not care, the communication derails. The parties find themselves in different conversations.

Box 6.3 Culture matters

The differences in styles across cultures are intriguing. They are evidenced particularly in oral presentations: American scholars trying to be lively and argumentative, Italian scholars showing off their verbiage, French scholars trying to be fundamental and usually obscure, Dutch scholars trying to be slightly boring to seem serious, Japanese scholars showing off the latest trends in a seemingly rambling fashion, and Finnish scholars trying to be long-winded and excruciatingly boring. (My prejudice calls for exceptions such as Finnish friend and colleague Uskali Maki.) These differences are not merely stylistic, but suggest different conversations. Apparently, it takes more than learning a language to be in conversation with Finns, Italians, or the Japanese.

I have learned to speak American English, the lingua franca for scientists, and to write in the Anglo-Saxon tradition. Thus, this account is biased. Even so, the tradition dominates the world of the sciences today.

Rhetoric includes knowing the topoi

Participation in a conversation requires knowledge of the commonplaces, or topoi. When economists' assumptions are challenged for being unrealistic, they simply return Friedman's well-known phrase that the "realism of assumptions does not matter." They may not know what it means or what its philosophical implications are; they say it for the approval of their audience. (When further challenged about the statement, they shrug their shoulders and go on with their exposition.) For example, when people complain about pollution, an economist might say something like "pollution needs to be priced" for that is the topos that makes him or her an economist. Good teachers have a good collection of topoi to streamline their presentations and handle questions. They determine the quality – and winner – of a debate.

Economics, like any other science, is literary

This is the major point that Deirdre McCloskey (1983, 1990) tried to make when she called attention to the rhetoric of economics. She showed that economists employ metaphors just like poets do, and tell stories just like novelists do. Not every economist was ready to hear this, since it seemed to undermine the scientific status of economics. The response has some merit. Economics is, after all, quite unlike poetry because the conversation of economists is quite unlike the conversation of poets. Even so, McCloskey rightly points out the ubiquity of metaphors in economics and the importance of narrative.

Participation calls for persuasive and interpretive skills

Economists must know how to read a text critically and decipher its message. A rhetorical reading is difficult and time-consuming. Its rewards are great. Such a reading does not aim at a summary of the main argument but focuses on the construction and composition of the text to determine what messages it contains. Why did the author do what he or she did? What does the text reveal? Or conceal? The craft of interpretation also goes under the name of hermeneutics. Authors of scientific articles benefit from doing the hermeneutics. They know how other authors construct their texts and that style, choice of rhetorical figures, voice, and composition reveal a great deal. They become more watchful of their own writing.

Argumentation drives the scientific conversation

One important consequence of perceiving the rhetoric in the conversation is discovering how argumentative economists are. And naturally so: persuasion requires argumentation. A group of young socialists, upon hearing that markets are efficient allocators, and certainly more efficient allocators than governments, want to hear the reasons for such an outlandish proposition. Academic economists told that the market system is responsible for conflicts the world over as well as massive poverty want reasons. They will differ, depending on the audience and the case you want to make. A mere assertion will be ignored; the arguments make the difference.

Argumentation is not specific to scientific discourse. Whether I want more money or want someone to remain my lover, I will need to argue. The question is which arguments are persuasive. A gun at someone's head may work in some situations, but usually falls short as an argument; tears can be an effective argument in the personal sphere but they emphatically do not work in the seminar room. In science, special argumentation is called for. If I want to be good at it, if I want my ideas to be heard, I must argue scientifically and argue well. Box 6.4 provides the components of a scientific argument; the examples are particular to the conversation of economists.

Box 6.4 The structure of argumentation

*The **claim** is the point of the argument,* what the argument is about. The scientific claim is the conjecture, the hypothesis, or the prediction. Examples:

- Budgetary policies have no effects on real economic variables such as unemployment and economic growth.
- Privatization of public utilities will reduce energy prices.

- The giving of Christmas gifts causes a welfare loss equal to one-third of the welfare loss due to income taxes.
- The metaphor of the "conversation" is superior to other current metaphors.

*The **grounds** provide a first justification of the claim*. These can take various forms: pointing out an anomaly (a conflict between existing theory and certain data), evoking historical trends in support of the claim, producing data, appealing to common sense, citing an authority, referring to other research. For instance:

- Milton Friedman cast doubts on the effectiveness of budgetary policies in the long run, but his argument still relied on adaptive expectations; with rational expectations the results may be even more damaging to Keynesian policies.
- Privatization of other companies brought about lower prices for consumers, too.
- Does anyone ever get what they really wanted? The waste of all those silly and useless gifts must add up to a welfare loss.
- Economics is an inexplicable discipline when viewed by means of the standard metaphors.

*The **warrant** makes the (theoretical) case for the claim*. It shows how the claim follows from regularity, a law-like statement, a model, a full-blown theory, or a principle that has general validity. The warrant usually has the form of an "if . . . then . . ." statement, where the "if" spells out the general principle, model, or theory as well as the conditions under which each is applicable. Warrants too can take all kinds of forms:

- a Lucas-type model with rational expectations, an endogenous money supply and future generations;
- an econometric model specifying privatized and public companies as well as their consumer prices;
- a model that stipulates the utility functions of recipients of gifts and makes assumptions as to the ability of donors to assess those utility functions (with grandparents being quite bad at it);
- how this book develops a full-blown conceptual framework with "conversation as the key metaphor" and additional notions such as "culture," "attention," and "rhetoric."

*The **backing** is supposed to render the warrant trustworthy, plausible, evident, or empirically grounded.* Usually it takes the form of an empirical test, empirical findings, cases, historical research, or observations of some kind. Thus:

- After having estimated the parameters of the model and run some simulations, we have confirmed the hypothesis that . . .
- Regression analysis of the equations shows that privatization has a significant effect on consumer prices.
- Look at what economists do, consider your own experiences and see how well the reality of doing economics corresponds with the conceptual framework presented in this book.

*The **modals** articulate restrictions and caveats of the argument.* Since the warrant includes simplifying assumptions and depends on specific conditions that are not generally valid, and the backing relies on dubious data that allow for a margin of error, the argumentation is less than logically compelling. Thus, a scientific argumentation usually includes modals, such as:

- The empirical test has failed to reject our initial claim (i.e., we have not proven the claim beyond any reasonable doubt).
- Further research has to bear out whether the results will hold under general conditions and less restrictive assumptions.
- "Evidently . . ."; "Very possibly . . ."; "At the very least . . ."; "On the face of things . . ."
- Admittedly, the argumentation has to be developed further and empirical work is in order, but it appears that the metaphor of conversation works pretty gosh-darned well.

*The **rebuttals** deal with possible objections, alternative claims, and counterfactuals.* Often a scientific argument is directed at alternative claims and arguments. The rebuttal addresses the strongest alternatives and shows why the argument presented is superior. For example:

- Keynesian arguments insisting on sticky prices and long-term contracts fail to make sense if we assume rationality on the part of agents.
- Furthermore, models with sticky prices do worse in simulations than models with flexible prices.

- When a realist insists that the truth claims are decisive in scientific discourse anyway, I will insist that we cannot account in that case for the peculiarities that registered in Chapter 1.

The **consequences** *point at the relevance of the argument beyond the claim advanced.* Economic arguments will often require spelling out policy implications, but it is also possible to point at possibilities for further research or the implications of this argument for a research agenda. For example:

- Given these results, the government does better to stick to budgetary rules rather than attempt to influence the economy by means of discretionary policies.
- When the econometric methods used here are applied in other research, the results may change.
- This analysis shows that the standard economic argument is flawed and needs to be discarded.
- Stop thinking about economics as you were used to, and see how therapeutic and edifying the notion of the conversation can be. You too may change your economic metaphors.

You need a claim. You want to be able to say what your paper is about. Your fellow economists (or students) will want to know. "What's your point?" they'll say. Students tend to have a hard time with this crucial part of their argument. After all, what authority do they have to make an economic claim; what do they know? Their doubts are justified. Getting to your claim takes usually time and requires extensive reading, research, and talking with fellow economists. PhD students often begin with a subject because it seems interesting to them. "I'd like to see whether I can apply game theory in the case of privatization." Only later, sometimes at the very end, do they realize what their claim or the point of their thesis is – something like "the institutional context is critical for the outcome of privatization." The point: without a claim, you do not have an argument.

But a claim does not materialize from the air; it has to be placed in the ongoing conversation. As I say to my PhD students, "Motivate your argument; persuade me, the reader, that the argument is of interest. Tell me about the problem you are addressing or the anomaly you are distinguishing. Make your claim plausible in one way or another." Motivation is a big part of the persuasion. I tried to do this in the first chapter by calling attention to the peculiarities of economics if approached with the common assumptions and metaphors. This is the grounding of the claim.

The truly scientific work is the development of the warrants. The warrant is the result of theoretical work. In standard economic conversations, the convention is to formulate the theory in terms of models, be it a general equilibrium model or a game-theoretic model, or whatever model best fits your idea. Economists like to see a model as the argument, and preferably one that meets economic criteria.

The quality of the warrant tends to be a decisive factor. In a seminar, the attention will focus on that. Are the assumptions plausible? Are the methods correct? Does it take into account pertinent discussions? Is the argument consistent, relevant, and interesting? Being inside the conversation is the only way to know what is expected from a warrant; even then, some grand masters have been mistaken and have had their papers rejected by referees. That is why it is important to test the inventions with fellow economists, present the warrants in seminars, and submit ideas to journals.

In these endless trials and errors, the importance of the rhetoric of science is revealed. The audience and its readily assembled walls of miscomprehension are inescapable. For it matters whether or not the means of the argument is a game-theoretic model; it matters how mathematically advanced the argument is, what concepts it employs, and which assumptions it needs to work. A plausible assumption in one conversation may be laughable in another. The mathematics that was impressive in one seminar can be objectionable in the next.

The art of persuasion is in knowing what warrant is called for. Certain claims call for a taxonomy or characterization. "Kids are like durable goods and therefore can be viewed as commodities" requires a warrant that first shows that kids have the characteristics of durable goods, after which the demand for and supply of kids can be identified.

Beware the gaps

All this can be taken in one's stride if we cling to the hard-nosed version of science: argumentation is a matter of logic. And, if so, the warrants are consistent and the evidence is conclusive. But the argument of the previous chapter has alerted us to the hazards of that thinking. Gaps abound. There are logical gaps in the logic of the argumentation and there are gaps between people, like you and me. That's why economists

– just like lawyers – use a wide variety of arguments and rhetorical devices, some of which are not logically consistent or even coherent.

It helps to imagine yourself standing in the court of reason, somewhat like a lawyer standing in the court of law. You're arguing a case before a jury of your peers. Imagine who your opponent is, that is, the position that you want to reject, if not demolish. The only clear element about it is that there is no decisive evidence. You cannot win by sheer logic. You need to make the case. What are your warrants? What are your backings? How will you get the jury on your side?

Most likely, you will operate in different domains of argumentation. Initially, you will argue your assumptions and the set-up of your model in the theoretical domain. You may then move into a more technical domain, developing lemmas, sorting out solution procedures, and the like. This must sway the technically minded on the jury. When pressed for empirical backing, you will have to enter the domain of econometrics and statistics – an entirely separate argumentation with its own issues, assumptions, techniques, and literature. In the case of a hostile jury, you have to reach into the domain of methodology. There you find the arguments to justify a mathematical approach, an unusual assumption, an empirical argument. (Is it okay that you used a survey? Does the Monte Carlo method make sense?) For the laypeople in the jury or students, you will bring in everyday arguments, appeal to common sense. You will need to invent some policy implications if you want to be persuasive in the political or bureaucratic realm.

The important point is that these domains are disconnected. Gaps between the theoretical and empirical arguments have not been bridged, policy implications do not necessarily follow and methodological arguments are, for the most part, seriously flawed.

Accordingly, strictly logical criteria do not suffice for the jury. They have to weigh and judge the entire constellation of arguments to determine who is right. The judgments need to cover the various gaps in the argumentation for which there are no hard and fast rules. Unanimity will be rare. Some will like the argumentation; others will be less charmed. The art of economic persuasion is no effortless matter.

Box 6.5 Know your metaphors

Yes, metaphors. Frankly, I did not quite know what metaphors were until I read McCloskey's article "The Rhetoric of Economics" in 1983.

I never had a reason to think of such a rhetorical figure. Now I realize that I use metaphors all the time. This book, one might readily say, is all about changing the metaphor of economics from that of a body of accumulated knowledge to that of a conversation. Saying that economics is a conversation does not imply that economists are literally having a conversation, although they might be. The metaphor gets us to think about certain things that we otherwise would not be thinking of, such as rhetoric, metaphor, attention, and the like.

The two distinct domains my metaphor connects are economics and conversations. The difference gets us thinking, which makes metaphors indispensable for thought processes. We use them all the time, in work and in everyday life. Lakoff and Johnson's *Metaphors We Live By* (1980) captures the essence. "GNP is up," the newspaper tells us. "Things are looking up," a friend says. How so, "up"? Should we look to the sky for GNP and things? How is it that Alaskan liquid assets are not always frozen? In attempting to retrieve our deepest thoughts, should we buy a shovel? And when prices in the area are inflated, do we see buoyant tags on our goods?

Children often do not get the metaphors. "We're going to visit someone above New York," I told my then six-year old son when we were living in Washington, DC. "Are we going to take a helicopter?" he asked. Getting the metaphors takes some education. Let's consider the most famous economic metaphor of all (Figure 6.1). It tells the audience to think of a market in its terms. It does not intend to say that a market is literally a diagram. The point is that it triggers us to think of all kinds of processes. It serves as a heuristic and is therefore a heuristic metaphor (see Box 6.6).

Figure 6.1 A market

To say education – or marriage or crime or religion – is a market offers the market as a metaphor. It instructs people to think in terms of a product, the demand for the product, the supply of the product, and the price of the product. If marriage is a market, the price of attractive partners and the willingness of candidates to pay for them frame the thinking of it. Economists are most creative in working the metaphor of the market.

They also like to upset the uninitiated by saying such things as "individuals are rational calculators" or "children are durable goods." People are of course emotional, and we prefer to think of our children in more loving terms. But if the metaphors work in the economic conversation, we have no reason not to use them.

Even to speak of "the economy" or "economics" is speaking metaphorically. Each concept stands for a complex of phenomena varying from people shopping to presidents launching war. The notion of the economy and economics is recent. (My children are still baffled, making it difficult to explain what Dad is doing. "Computer," in my five-year-old's vocabulary and syntax, translates to "Da is computering!") "Economics" was an invention. Alfred Marshall (1842–1924) coined the word when the term "political economy" was current. He thus suggested that "economics" is a discipline on its own, not necessarily geared toward policy, or political in kind. The result was that separate economics departments sprang up, and that economists became a distinct group of scientists. The invention of a new word to match a class of phenomena is called catachresis (see Glossary, p.122).

Some metaphors are more important than others. Economists like the island metaphor to, say, prompt thinking about information problems, or, as I have noted, have Robinson Crusoe do his economics. Thinking of an elastic cord when pondering the responsiveness of demand to a change in price may help with the metaphor of elasticity, but it is not crucial. An economist speaking of the price mechanism or transmission mechanism triggers the calculation of price and interest rate changes. Thinking about oligopolistic competition auctions and how wars occur is now in terms of "games," another productive metaphor. Ignoring those metaphors implies being locked out of the standard conversation of economists (but not necessarily heterodox economic conversations).

Knowing all this is useful. Surely, generations of economists have done well without the notion of the metaphor (but, then, businesspeople do well without knowing about elasticities, price mechanisms, and games). But they would have done better realizing the metaphors by which they think. Why?

Metaphors are fun to know about. Isn't it interesting to realize how many daily expressions are metaphors? "Things are looking up." "He seems down." "How depressed I feel." "Love is a journey." "Metaphors simply go on and on."

Correct interpretation of metaphors – knowing what "game" implies, and what it does not, for example – is requisite to being in the economic conversation. Attach the wrong meanings to a metaphor or interpret one literally and you may as well bellow, "I'm an outsider!"

Knowing the right metaphors matters too. However strong their beliefs that we are moral beings, economists know that the metaphor does not belong in the standard economic conversation.

Metaphors are indispensable as instruments to begin thinking about something as complex as the economy. A good metaphor sets forth possibilities – something the metaphor of conversation proves in this book. Inserting the metaphor of the market in a health care discussion (or art or the environment) introduces new ways of thinking about it.

Metaphors also help bridge the numerous logical gaps on the way to conclusion. Indeed, thinking strictly deductively or inductively is impossible; most thinking occurs by means of metaphors, that is, abductively (see Box 6.5).

All major breakthroughs in economic thought have been the result of a new metaphor. Think of Quesnay's circular flow (inspired by what he found out as a medical doctor), Smith's idea of value as embodied labor, Marshall's supply and demand diagram, Hicks's IS/LM diagram, Muth's rational expectations, von Neumann's game, Becker's time as an economic good, and Simon's metaphor of cognitive agents.

Friedrich Nietzsche famously said:

> What then is truth? A movable host of metaphors, metonymies, and anthropomorphisms: in short, a sum of human relations that have been poetically and rhetorically intensified, transferred, and embellished, which, after long usage, seem to people to be fixed, canonical, and binding. Truths are illusions we have forgotten are illusions; they are metaphors that have become worn out and have been drained of sensuous force, coins which have lost their embossing and are now considered as metal and no longer coins . . . The drive toward the formation of metaphors is the fundamental human drive, which one cannot for a single instant dispense with in thought, for one would thereby dispense with man himself.
>
> (Nietzsche 1999: 84–9)

Box 6.6 A brief guide to begin thinking in and about metaphors

Aristotle defined metaphor as follows: "Metaphor consists in giving the thing a name that belongs to something else; the transference being either from genus to species, or from species to genus, or from species to species, or on grounds of analogy" (*Poetics* 1457b). A shorter definition that I found in more recent literature is "the expression of a term of one domain in terms of another domain."

For example, "time" is a term to be associated with the domain of phenomena such as history, clocks, past, and future. "Money" is a term to be associated with an entirely different domain of phenomena like currency, coins, banks, finance, income, and wealth. "Time is money" is a metaphor; we are made to think of time in terms of the money domain.

The question that has preoccupied philosophers and literary scholars is what a metaphor does. Surely, time is *not* money and John is clearly *not* a dog. The statements are literally false. Here the hard-nosed scientist pounces: "Metaphors are untrue? Then out they go. Science is about truth!"

Hard-nosed philosophers have suggested that metaphors can be made in normal statements by translating them. "Time is money" is, say, "Time imposes an opportunity cost." The latter statement is straightforward and can be true or false.

But a literal translation does not do justice to the metaphor. Metaphors do more. They transfer and create meanings. Etymologically, metaphor means "to transfer" or "to carry over." Poets know this all too well:

> He was my North, my South, my East and West,
> My working week and my Sunday rest,
> My noon, my midnight, my talk, my song;
> I thought that love would last forever: I was wrong.[3]

Here a poet evokes meanings, images, and associations that a straight sentence would never trigger. Extensive research in cognitive science, semantics, and epistemology notwithstanding, we do not know how this really works. Our brains appear to work in a less logical fashion than the hard-nosed may want to presume. They jump around, make surprising connections, and associate. Metaphors stimulate that process. As I. A. Richards and Max Black, two stalwarts in the philosophy of metaphors, point out, metaphors make us think by their very nature, for they compel us to connect disparate domains.

Consider the "time is money" metaphor. Black names "time" the principal subject, and "money" the subsidiary subject of the metaphor (Figure 6.2). According to Richards and Black the metaphor engenders an interaction between the meanings associated with the domain of time with those for the domain of money. The interaction is the point, for the metaphor stimulates the thinking about time in terms of money as well as money in terms of time. The metaphor may call attention to, say, the time dimension of the money business. The impact is cognitive. Seeing time as money affects our notion of time and our notion of money.

The working of the metaphor shows the logical gaps in our thinking processes. By handling metaphors, we handle the gaps. In case of the "time is money" metaphor, both terms have many associations and attributes as their domain (Figure 6.3).

So what are the relevant attributes and associated concepts that are evoked by the metaphor? The metaphor itself does not say. Metaphor does not command; it suggests. "Time is money" could imply that "a clock has a price" or that "a calendar is like green paper" but, of course, it intends neither of these interpretations. We settle for the improbable connection of "the passing of time" with "opportunity costs." Who would think of that? Yet that is how it works. When a confused someone rings me to launch into a long criticism of this book, I will mumble something about "time is money." They get the message: my opportunity costs of the conversation are, apparently, too high to listen.

But it can be different. Picture a Buddhist monk sitting at the bank of a river watching the water flow by. You are trying to tell him what you just learned about metaphors, when he notes, quietly and serenely as only old wise people can, that "time is money" adding, "I have lots of time, so I must be a rich man." The monk changes the meaning of the metaphor by stressing another association with money, that is, the

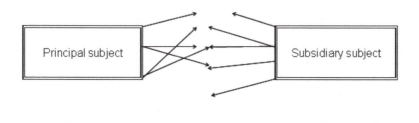

Figure 6.2 The structure of a metaphor. A metaphor consists of giving the principal subject a name that belongs to the subsidiary subject

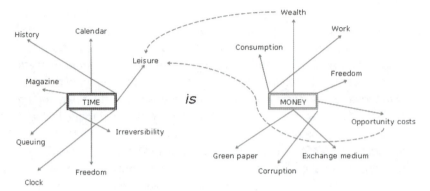

Figure 6.3 So what's an economic metaphor? The principal and subsidiary subjects in the metaphor <time is money> have many relevant attributes and associated concepts. The metaphor suggests one connection but leaves open the possibility for other connections

one of wealth. You get the point: instead of feeling like hurrying up, the Buddhist reading invites you to relax and take all the time to enjoy it as richness.

Their creative potential renders metaphors unstable. Their meaning depends on the context in which they are used. That should make scientists nervous. And that is why so many railed against metaphors in their language. Yet, we now realize it is impossible to think without metaphors, especially in a science like economics. As McCloskey showed, economic discourse consists of metaphors up and down, deep down especially. Note the metaphor.

Most particularly, models are metaphors or, better, expanded metaphors. No economist thinks that markets are literally a system of equations, but many find it helpful to think "as if" they are. Aristotle suggested speaking in this case of analogy as the emphasis is not on the mapping of attributes from one domain to another but on relations.

A model is an analogy is an expanded metaphor

An analogy is an expanded metaphor in which relations pertaining to one domain are mapped onto relations of another domain. William Jevons, the economist, recognized this: "analogy denotes not a resemblance between things, but between the relations of things" (Jevons 1958 [1874]: 627). To say "the atom is a solar system" is to speak metaphorically. When a teacher develops this classic metaphor by drawing the solar system on the blackboard, complete with the sun and elliptically orbiting planets, he or she proposes an analogy that captures and makes explicit some, though not all, of the "associated commonplaces" suggested by the metaphor. Not all of these correspondences will be appropriate. Gravity does not bind electrons to the atom's nucleus, as it does planets to the sun, nor is the atom's nucleus hot with thermonuclear fusion. Likewise, the solar system's moons and asteroids have no obvious counterpart within the atom. On the other hand, less than perfect congruity can also prove to be a virtue, providing insight that a literal rendering cannot achieve. Electrons don't spin on their axes like a planet does, but conceiving of them in this way provides the best current explanation of an electron's angular momentum and its magnetic field. Economic models work like that. Whatever the case, they are metaphorical to start with.

Analogy is an expanded metaphor; more precisely, analogy is a sustained and systematically elaborated metaphor. An economic model is an analogy.

Types of metaphor

There are all kinds of ways to distinguish metaphors. Dead metaphors are, for example, metaphors that people no longer recognize as such. (Economists are particularly good at suffocating metaphors, literal-minded as many of them are.) When I confine myself to metaphors as they operate in a scientific conversation like economics, I prefer to distinguish them according to their functions. That appears most helpful. There are three, at least in my list:

- *Pedagogical metaphors* serve to enlighten and clarify an exposition and can be omitted without affecting the argumentation as such. Good teachers have many. To get the idea of a stable equilibrium they draw a picture of a bowl in which a rolling ball inevitably comes to a rest on the bottom. I like the bathtub as a metaphor for an accounting system to illustrate how flows out (money down the drain) and flows in (but watch the faucet) relate to the level in the bathtub (the balance of stocks). Students are often invited to think of cobwebs, saddles, and sliced watermelons. They are taught to think like economists by means of metaphors. When the hard-nosed insist that we can do without these, they are right. Metaphors are not essential. They are flourishes – but they are important flourishes in the process of persuading the non-initiated. I doubt that even a hard-nosed economist can do without them. The following two, however, are essential. Scientific thinking is inconceivable without them.

- *Heuristic metaphors* catalyze our thinking, stimulating researchers to approach a phenomenon in a novel way. (A "heuristic" is a guide for thinking.) Benjamin Franklin coined the metaphor "time is money" to admonish young Americans to use their time efficiently; Gary Becker used it as a guide to explore the economics of time in his classic article, "The Allocation of Time" (1965). The metaphor apparently connected with his conceptualization of economic behavior. When Alfred Marshall drew the demand and supply diagram, he intended to reconcile a supply-based theory of value and a demand-based theory of value. It proved to be a powerful heuristic (in the sense of a guide for thinking) that helps economists and their students thinking through events such as a change in a price or the imposition of a sales tax. Currently, the metaphor of a game drives a great deal of economic thinking. Human capital proved to be another powerful heuristic metaphor, followed by social, cultural, emotional, and a string of other capitals. Generally, in the context of contemporary economics, a metaphor becomes heuristic when it stimulates the construction of an analogical system. Heuristic metaphors remain heuristic as long as their users see them as such, as instruments to jump-start an analysis. "Hmm, what do we make of this . . . Well, let's think of it in terms of a market . . . Or shall we think of it as a game?"

- *Constitutive metaphors* underlie all thinking to such an extent that thinking without them is inconceivable. They are those essential conceptual schemes through which we interpret a world that is either unknowable (the strong position, per Nietzsche) or at least unknown. To say anything about the world we must characterize it. But because we cannot literally know the nature of the natural and social worlds, we resort to the figurative. The metaphors that constitute our thinking lie so deep that we are usually unaware of them. Only in confrontation with others who think in different (constitutive) metaphors might we become aware of them. Sir John Hicks (1904–89) did not care for the notion of "conflict" and preferred to think in terms of stocks and flows. Accounting was his constitutive metaphor.

Economists tend to see the world in terms of rational individuals seeking maximum gain and looking for moments of exchange. The combination of those two figures – maximizing individuals in moments of exchange – suggests the constitutive metaphor of standard economics. (It is in the end almost impossible to say what the constitutive metaphor is exactly.) Again Marxists see the world differently, more in terms of classes, power, and struggles. Psychologists will not see much if confronted with either constitutive metaphor. They rather think of emotional processes, family constellations, and the like.

Constitutive metaphors usually inform heuristic metaphors and determine which of those look promising or not. "Time is money" proved to be a powerful heuristic metaphor in standard economics because it connects well with its constitutive metaphor. "People are emotional beings" will fare less well. However convinced psychologists are of the role of emotions in human action, having been taught to think in terms of maximizing individuals in moments of exchange renders it nearly impossible to think fruitfully with emotions in the analysis. Therefore, apart from the usual exceptions, few appear in economic journals.

Differences in constitutive metaphors account for major disagreements within and without economics. Staying in conversation with someone who thinks by a different constitutive metaphor is nearly impossible, and assuredly frustrating.

Getting the stories right

Finally, the rhetorical perspective alerts us to the importance of narrative in a persuasive account. The narrative, the story, plays a critical role, albeit often suppressed or hidden. Deirdre McCloskey, a poet at heart, was thrilled when the rhetorical perspective helped her to see that metaphors pervade the talk and work of economists. As she had less affinity with stories (novels were not quite her, and especially his, cup of tea), it took her longer to see the narrative in what economists do. Yet five years after her *Rhetoric of Economics* (1998 [1985]), she squared with the narrative dimension of economics in *If You're so Smart: The Narrative of Economic Expertise* (1990).

A good anecdote, that is, a quick story, in a speech usually keeps us awake. A worthy story draws us in, allows us to identify with the action, and gets us connected with the presentation. A story gets us motivated to follow suit. That's why scientists (or mathematicians for that matter) want to get the story in a seminar before the actual exposition of the paper. "So what's your story?" is a standard and most legitimate opening question. It compels the presenter to tell the theme of the paper, its setting, the main characters, the event triggering the action, what happens next, and the denouement. "Well, I start from a basic new classical set-up, presume a technological shock, apply a new algorithm, and find out that discrete changes in government spending have a lasting effect on real output." "Interesting. Can you show the argumentation?" Sometimes it's sufficient to tell the plot: "It's about the mess we get into when we allow for some interaction in a non-cooperative game."

Most economists' stories nowadays are of this genre: mechanical, abstract, devoid of fascinating characters, and plot-uninspiring. ("After all this work, policy implications remain uncertain." "The effects of a free trade zone are small.") Sometimes they incite action, such as lowering taxes, eliminating tariffs or changing institutions. In stories based on game-theoretic set-ups, there's a temptation to give an if-only-people-were-a-little-more-trustful sigh. The featured character is Max U, as McCloskey called it ("it" because Max U has no gender, no feelings, no social background, no friends, no colleagues, no morals, and no history). Max U stands for a mechanical maximizing character equipped with unidentified preferences and subject to some constraints. Max U can be anything – a consumer, a worker, a manager, a firm, a politician. The only thing "it" is not is an economist (at least not yet). Max U is good for a technical story and liking it allows excitement in the world of contemporary standard economics.

Looking more closely, economists come up with broader stories that betray their positioning toward life in general and the economy in particular. Milton Friedman tells about a world in which government is the bad guy, the antagonist who spoils everything, the market the good guy. It is a romantic story in the sense that the little people, you and I, will triumph if only the government will stay out. It warns us against overzealous bureaucrats and politicians. When the government dominates the narrative, the plot takes a bad turn. A free market stands for a wonderful world. Indeed, it is a story about freedom and unfettered individualism.

The Austrian story is similar but their characters are more human. Entrepreneurs have success against all odds; individuals act in uncertainty and prevail anyway. The story hypes the belief in individual creativity and imagination, and supplements suspicion of bureaucratic systems. (Ayn Rand's *Atlas Shrugged* or *The Fountainhead* gives the story.) McCloskey has recently changed her story to a more Austrian version by stressing the virtues of her characters, the bourgeois virtues in particular.

Robert Solow, Robert Samuelson, Joseph Stiglitz, and other Keynesian-minded economists have quite a different narrative. In their account the government is dressed in white; she comes to the rescue where the market fails. The agents of the market appear more erratic than in the story of freedom. Many live with the threat of being squished by the forces of the market. The story tells about injustices, instabilities, and imperfections. This, too, is a romantic story (or at least it was in its early version), for here the government comes (supported by the narrator, the Keynesian economist) to set things right, to correct imperfections and injustices, to stabilize and thus to make the world better. In recent decades, the story has looked less persuasive. The narrators have a less triumphant tone and, even while continuing to stress her chaste role, the white dress of the government has become a bit smudged. The story is not yet a tragedy – hope glimmers here and there – but it intimates that economists have little to contribute. No wonder the Friedman story does better in economic circles.

Tragedy thrives in the company of radical economists and their gloomy world of doom. Dark forces are ever gathering to throw the system into crisis. Big business is the enemy and government too is suspect because of its alliance with big business, a theme shared with Milton Friedman. Workers are the good guys but the enemy is always trampling on them. The workers constantly have to watch out. With its elements of power, struggle, drama, and tragedy, the story wins the economic Booker Prize. The good guys are set up to lose and, OK, maybe they win out after the revolution, but who still believes in that? Businesspeople tend to like the story, if they don't know it's about radical or Marxist economics. They take to themes of power and conflict, which are all but absent in the other stories.

In contrast the economists' technical stories are remarkably bland and devoid of drama. They are ironic in the sense that they suggest a great deal by setting up a significant problem and then concluding that it doesn't matter all that much. As Jean Paul Sartre said, "In irony a man annihilates what he posits within one and the same act; he leads us to believe in order not to be believed; he affirms to deny and denies to affirm." The technical story is impressive, promising something substantive, something scientific, only to end up as another result-meager exercise that begs for more research, more chatter. Rather too loudly it says, "I want to get published."

Much storytelling in economics is self-referencing. Papers are written to identify with other economists. "We have a problem," they say, "because we cannot account for some phenomenon." Economists are, therefore, the main character. *They* have a problem – not policy-makers, investors, workers, or common folk. Their stories may also place themselves vis-à-vis the rest of the world. Keynesians like to portray themselves as in the know, characters who can tell governments what to do. Chicago economists, on the other hand, loathe that story. "We do not have that knowledge," they maintain, "and therefore cannot presume to know better." McCloskey speaks of the Tinbergen vice, referring to the noble Dutchman who saw economic science as a means to rationalize economic policy. Keynesian economists are selling snake oil, she argues. Chicago economists prefer a story in which academic economists dwell in the ivory tower, without desire to intervene, to ponder the miracles of the market and the rationality of agents. "Laissez-faire" is their motto.

Let me summarize a few of the reasons we need to know about stories:

- It is fun to know about the stories that economists tell and be alert to the differences among them.
- Knowing the story helps to understand what an argument is about.
- Being able to tell the differences between stories helps to sort out the reasons for disagreements, conflicts, and tensions among economists. For example, many disagreements are due to differences in stories not about the economy but about economists.

- You need to be able to tell your story when presenting your paper. Be prepared. And be forewarned. There are good stories and bad stories and how yours comes out may depend on your audience.
- Realize the power of the anecdote. This is especially important in your presentation, and it decidedly bolsters the informal conversation of hallways, cafeterias, and conference check-ins.
- Master your stories, work on them – it is the narrative in your work that will have the most emotional appeal. A gripping one will be especially important when wanting to spur economists, politicians, or students into action. Stories, more than metaphors or whatever arguments, have the power to convey a sense of power; if told well, they have emotional force.
- People probably cannot think without stories or outside stories. You and I – we need a good story to feel alive. Economists are no different.

So what?

"No one said it would be easy" is a song by Sheryl Crow that sings through my head. No, life ain't easy – conversing economically isn't either. Those of you planning to get into the conversation must recoil somewhat from reading about all the rhetoric to be mastered. Then again, remember how impossible it is to get into the conversations on the Italian square if you're not a native Italian. Getting recognized as an economist is a good deal easier than that. A funny English accent will not hold economists back as long as they master the various arguments, know their metaphors, and are able to tell the right story – and have the proper passions. But, then again, that is another story.

> Eloquence without knowledge is hollow and empty; but knowledge without eloquence is mute and powerless, incapable of effect in men's lives.
>
> (Vico)

Box 6.7 What and how about stories? A brief guide to thinking in and
about stories

"Once upon a time . . ." Upon hearing that, the reflex is to lean back and listen. The promise of a story makes us surrender. We grew up with stories. Fairy tales and bedtime stories filled our world. "The mean stepmother had Snow White eat the poisonous apple. She fell into a deep sleep. And guess what? The handsome prince appeared. He woke her up with a kiss and they lived happily ever after." We needed the stories as children (mine were more about seafarers or cowboys and Indians) and we still seek them as adults. People go to theaters, rent movies, and read detective novels to get their dose of stories. Journalists get stories and we pick up the newspaper or turn on the TV to get it from them. We tell each other about what happened. Stories and anecdotes, their shorter version, fill our lives. Animals do not tell stories. How could they? Storytelling is a human activity. As MacIntyre put it, "Man in his actions and practices, as well as in his fictions, is essentially a story telling animal" (MacIntyre 1981: 201). *Homo fabulans* joins *Homo economicus*.

The exception is science. Or so we are led to believe. Surely, stories are fantasies and do not belong in the sphere of science. Science is about truth. And truth comes by means of hypothesis and empirics, and not in stories. In science, logic and fact are decisive. If scientists tell a story, such as the one about Robinson Crusoe, it is only for the sake of illustration and embellishment. That is the story for science. And, yes, it *is* a story about scientists not telling a story. In an amplified way this is how it may go:

> "Listen, when the scientists turn to their work, they forget about their personal values, they forget that they like poetry and love a good novel, and they apply scientific methods in their quest for the truth."

> "Really? Are they really trying to get the truth? And do they find it?"

The literature about narrative and story – their structure, their constructions, their constituting elements, their meanings, their role in political and business processes – is immense. An entire intellectual life could be dedicated to the narrative. I scouted that literature but will not pretend to be an expert (even as I buy into the narrative of scholarship that says that making assertions without knowing the literature puts you in a bad spot).

Story is the colloquial variant of a narrative. The latter is more structured, and sounds and looks like an ordered and self-conscious account of what has happened. Stories – while they may come in fragments, be incoherent, and even lack a plot – do pull certain events together, signal roles and characters to people, and are about a change of some kind, an event. (I often speak of story when I mean narrative.) Some things to look for:

- *Stories have a beginning, a middle, and an end.* "Once upon a time . . ." is the formula that announces the beginning of a fairy tale. A detective may begin with a murder and a life story usually begins with a birth. Then something needs to happen. A person intervenes, someone dies, war breaks out, or the central bank announces a cut in the interest rate. The event actuates a change, usually an action of some sort. And then the story moves to its conclusion, for it has to end somewhere. For the fairy tale the standard formula is "and they lived happily ever after." In an economic argumentation the story may end with QED (*quod erat demonstrandum*).
- *Stories are always constructions.* This characteristic may be obvious but let me state it anyway. The world does not present itself in stories; we humans construct the stories ourselves and impose them on the world. The storyteller decides where to begin, what action to focus on, and where to end, and by means of such decisions constructs and composes the story. All these decisions are interventions.
- *Stories, at the least, approach a plot.* Stories are more than chronicles; they are interpretations, or at least impose them. Chronicles are listings of events, usually diachronically, that is, over the course of time. Although the choice of events to be listed is a sort of ordering, stories do more with the events by suggesting some kind of coherence. This refers to the plot, which is difficult to define but generally indicates the structure and character of the story. In a romantic plot the hero wins against all kinds of odds; in a tragic plot the hero succumbs or perishes in the end. A story with an ironic plot undoes what it promises to do. Economists are particularly good at these.
- *Stories come to life with characters.* The protagonists of the story are its heroes; they are usually the good guys. The antagonists are their opponents and, therefore, usually the bad guys. Myths portray archetypal characters, such as the Hero (Heracles), the Tragic Hero (Oedipus), the Wanderer, the Victim, the Sorcerer, and so on. When people, such as economists, tell stories about themselves, note how they cast themselves (and the others). Are they Heroes or Victims? Sorcerers or Wanderers? Everyday stories have everyday characters, like Entrepreneur, Manager, Scientist, Therapist, Housewife, Worker, and so on. Such characters tend to be stereotyped and have assigned roles.

The Entrepreneur, for example, can be cast as Hero (as in an Austrian story) or Villain (as in a radical story).

- *Stories may have themes*. The themes tell what the story is about. The theme of a detective novel is murder and solution. The theme of an economic story can be the *practice* of science, technical prowess and astuteness, governmental inadequacy, the wonders of globalization, or whatever.
- *Stories motivate more than any other rhetorical figure*. The Jewish rabbi likes to instruct by means of story. Fairy tales tell about life, and about the good and the bad in life. Tragic stories deter, romantic stories inspire. "Stories impart meaning, which is to say worth," as McCloskey (1990: 27) put it. Economists tell stories to propel governments to action, or deter them from it. There is nothing better than a good story if you want something done or undone.

We tell stories for all kinds of reasons. I distinguish three functions that are analogous to those for metaphors:

- *Pedagogical stories* help to clarify a theoretical argument. We tell our students about Robinson Crusoe to motivate our treatise of rational choice and the production possibility curve. It is a good story that happens to have little in common with the actual one told by Daniel Defoe (which is about a guy in search of his father and God). A good teacher has an arsenal of such stories to enliven his class. Each of them can be omitted without effect on substance.
- *Heuristic stories* serve to guide the thinking, or the analysis. Lucas began telling about people living on island to get us thinking about information problems. Townsend and others told a similar story when they tried to account for the use of cash. Economists tell the heuristic story when they try to summarize their paper. "So, this is basically about . . ." and there comes the story.
- *Constitutive stories* underlie all thinking. These stories are rarely told explicitly. You need to extract them from what people say. They are the stories with which you and I make sense of our lives and our world. For Chicago economists it is a story about free individuals making the best of their lives in markets with the dark forces of the government ever threatening them. There is perhaps a deeper story there. A psychoanalyst surmises a

story about a son trying to rid himself of the authority of the father, seeing the market as the mother figure that meets all his desires. (I owe this account to Susan Feiner, a radical economist.) In radical accounts a story about struggle, power, and injustice emerges – it is a more dramatic story that incites some kind of action, even revolution.

Glossary of selected terms

Allegory   A long or extended metaphor, in which the principal side of the original metaphor has been lopped off or "forgotten." Examples are the fables of La Fontaine, Orwell's *Animal Farm*, and the island story (Crusoe) that is common in new classical accounts. The expansion comes in the form of a narrative, and is not systematic. Allegory belongs more to poetry just as analogy belongs more to science.

Analogy   A sustained and systematically elaborated metaphor, in which one system of relationships is joined to another. As Jevons argues in *The Principles of Science*, "analogy denotes not a resemblance between things, but between the relations of things" (Jevons 1958 [1874]: 627). Whereas allegories continually remind us of their metaphorical beginnings (and thus prevent a literal reading), analogies are usually less gracious to their original metaphor, which is easily forgotten. The atom–solar system analogy is one of the more famous. In economics the analogy usually comes in the form of a model.

Catachresis   The metaphorical use of existing language to fill a gap in the vocabulary. Referring to the support of a table as a "leg," or to the base of a mountain as a "foot," was, at one time, a catachrestic act. John Muth found the need for catachresis when he conceived of expectations that are consistent with the outcome of his model. There was no name for such a phenomenon so he coined the term "rational expectations." (The expression is also metaphorical because expectations, which usually are thought to be emotional, are given an attribute that appears to belong to another set of phenomena.) Catachresis occurs all the time in economics – think of the multiplier, human capital, cooperative games, calibrating – and, because the name is usually borrowed from an unrelated domain, a metaphor is at work as well.

Constitutive metaphor   A metaphor that frames the thinking about its principal subject to such an extent that the principal subject cannot be considered without it. More broadly, it is the conceptual scheme we use in characterizing a world that is unknowable or unknown. (Note that constitutive metaphors will typically generate or inspire the heuristic metaphors.)

Enthymeme   An incomplete syllogism.

Ethos   The character of a person, usually a speaker. The ethos of the speaker influences the nature of the message. Ethos is an important rhetorical device, though not a trope per se. Students of economics quickly learn to establish the ethos appropriate to a professional economist, meaning writing in an impersonal voice, deploying scientific language wherever possible and appealing to the appropriate authorities. The latter are economists with an acceptable ethos (not John Kenneth Galbraith, therefore, but serious economists such as Robert Lucas).

Heuristic metaphor   A metaphor that works by motivating inquiry into the principal subject by juxtaposing attributes or relationships of the subsidiary subject. In economics the heuristic metaphor will usually be developed and elaborated into an analogy or model, as with the "human capital" or "work is a market" metaphor. Because heuristic metaphors are not literally true, reasoning as if they were implies that economic models are fictions.

Hyperbole   A figure that relies on calculated exaggeration. Aristotle probably considers it a type of metaphor (species to genus) in citing "Truly ten thousand good deeds has Ulysses wrought" (*Poetics* 1457b), where "ten thousand" represents "many."

Irony   Words that say one thing and mean precisely the opposite, or an unusual incongruity between actual and expected outcomes.

Metaphor   The expression of a term of one domain in terms of another domain. In the metaphor "time is money," "time" and "money" are terms of different domains, yet the latter is used to say something about the former. Etymologically, metaphor means "to carry over," a language process whereby attributes of one object (subsidiary subject) are transferred to another (principal subject). In Richards's and Black's accounts, the two subjects then interact to create new meaning. This figurative meaning has cognitive import because it cannot be achieved by some literal equivalent. Metaphor is the most fertile and powerful of all figurative forms because, in Max Black's terms, the "associated commonplaces" are potentially unlimited when two previously unrelated domains are joined.

Metonymy   A figure in which the name of an attribute or adjunct is substituted for that of the thing meant. "Buckingham Palace denied the allegations" is an example, or "This department needs some new blood." "Labor supply adjusts to a change in expected real wages" is metonymous, if individuals – not the concept of an aggregate schedule of hours worked at a given wage – adjust. When a student says, "I read Barro last weekend," he or she is referring metonymously to an article. Consider "The market sailed into uncharted territory today." The whole expression is metaphorical, given the juxtaposition of sailing and a capital market. "Market" is a synecdoche for a price index of selected stocks (say, the Dow Jones Industrial Average), and "uncharted territory" is metonymous for unattained index levels.

Model   An explicitly, and in economics often formally, articulated analogy. A model is typically characterized by "as if" reasoning.

Pedagogical metaphor   A metaphor typically employed to clarify a difficult, though otherwise understood, exposition, relying on the transparency of resemblances or correspondences between its principal and subsidiary subjects. An example is the "circular flow diagram" of macroeconomics, or the expression "time is money." A pedagogical metaphor, once interpreted, has served its function; it does not lend itself to systematic elaboration as heuristic metaphors do.

Poetic metaphor   Deliberate alteration of language to evolve new meaning and achieve emotion in art (T. S. Eliot). Poetic metaphors are not designed for subsequent analogical elaboration and typically exploit the instability of the meaningful connections between its principal and subsidiary subjects.

Pragmatics   The study of the use of language (words, concepts, metaphors).

Rhetoric   The art of "discovering all means of persuasion in any given case" (Aristotle). In the modern definition rhetoric is viewed as pertaining to all modes of discourse, including scientific. Rhetorical devices include logical operations, metaphors, ethos, and narrative.

Simile   A metaphor that is trivially true when a metaphorical relationship is made explicit by "like" or "as." Examples are "time is like money" and "think of a child as a durable good." The addition of "like" weakens the metaphor. By the explicit comparison in "time is like money," the speaker evokes similarities and simultaneously warns for dissimilarities – as if to suggest that one should not take the comparison too far. Similes are always trivially true because some likeness or similarity can be found between any two subjects. Metaphors may convey a metaphorical truth, but they are almost never literally true.

Syllogism   A logical argument of the form "if . . ., then . . ." with all the if necessary statements specified.

Synecdoche (Greek for "taking together")   A figure that occurs when we substitute a part for the whole (see Aristotle's "genus" and "species") or vice versa. "All hands on deck" is an example. "Technical change" in the production function is a synecdoche in the sense that it stands for all the influences that are unaccounted for by the stated factors of production. Synecdoche is probably best considered as a class of metonymous speech.

Further reading

A good place to start is *The Rhetoric of Rhetoric: The Quest for Effective Communication* by Wayne Booth (Blackwell Publishing, 2004) and McCloskey's *Rhetoric of Economics* (University of Wisconsin Press, 1983, 1998 [1985]). For more general reading, see *Rhetoric of the Human Sciences* edited by John S. Nelson, Allan Megill, and Donald McCloskey (University of Wisconsin Press, 1987), which I briefly refer to in the text. It includes an interesting paper on the rhetoric of mathematics – for anyone who wants to believe that at least math is beyond rhetoric – and my article on the metaphor of the rational individual in neoclassical economics. *Passion and Craft: Economists at Work* edited by Michael Szenberg (University of Michigan Press, 1999) contains interesting accounts of economists at work. To further explore argumentation and rhetoric, entire libraries are at your disposal. Look at *The New Rhetoric: A Treatise on Argumentation* (University of Notre Dame Press, 1969) by Perelman and Olbrechts-Tyteca, or Perelman's shorter book, *The Realm of Rhetoric* (University of Notre Dame Press, 1982).

The classification of an argument I derived from Toulmin's *Uses of Argument* (Cambridge University Press, 1958). More accessible is the textbook he wrote with Alan Janik and Richard Rieke, *An Introduction to Reasoning* (Macmillan, 1979).

To learn more about metaphors you will first have to face a daunting mountain of reading. In collaboration with Tim Leonard, I tried to master the field in an article called "So What's an Economic Metaphor?" in *Natural Images of Economic Thought* edited by P. Mirowski (Cambridge University Press, 1994). See also D. A. Schön's "Generative Metaphor: A Perspective on Problemsetting in Social Policy" in *Metaphor and Thought* edited by A. Ortony (Cambridge University Press, 1979); M. B. Hesse's *Revolution and Reconstruction in the Philosophy of Science* (Indiana University Press, 1980); M. Black's *Models and Metaphors* (Cornell University Press, 1962); and *Metaphors We Live By* (University of Chicago Press, 1980) by Lakoff and Johnson.

The issue on the gaps between different domains of argumentation was pivotal in my dissertation. An abbreviated (but sufficient to the point) version appeared in *History of Political Economy*, "Levels of Discourse in New Classical Economics" (Duke University Press, Summer 1984: 263–90).

In *Keynes, Knowledge and Uncertainty* (Edward Elgar, 1995: 318–33), I do a critical reading of the Samuelson article titled "The Conception of Modernism in Economics: Samuelson versus Keynes." Also study McCloskey's rhetorical readings of economic texts in her *Rhetoric of Economics* (University of Wisconsin Press, 1998 [1983]).

The suggestion that a discursive practice revolves around, or is framed by, constitutive elements is not novel. In 1962 and 1970, Thomas Kuhn implied as much with his notion of the "disciplinary matrix," as did Imre Lakatos in 1970 with the notion that a "hard core" of unquestioned assumptions constitute a research program. Yet neither Kuhn's nor Lakatos's conceptual framework explicitly captures the metaphorical character of discourse framing, that is, the viewing of the principal domain in terms of another domain. More promising in this respect are Michel Foucault's *The Order of Things: An Archaeology of the Human Sciences* (Vintage, 1970) and *The Archaeology of Knowledge* (Pantheon, 1972), and Stephen Pepper's *World Hypotheses* (University of California Press, 1942). Foucault and Pepper both make serious attempts to elucidate the metaphors that frame discursive practices.

The source for abduction is Peirce's "How to Make Our Ideas Clear" in *Charles S. Peirce, Selected Writings* (Doubleday, 1966 [1878]).

Susan Feiner offers the best accounts you can find when you step away from the discipline, look for the margins, and eavesdrop on feminist and radical circles. Here you find the interesting readings of standard economics. The agents themselves usually do not quite know what it is that they are doing. One recommendation is *Out of the Margins: Feminist Perspectives on Economics* (Routledge, 1995), edited by Susan Feiner, Notburga Ott, and Zafiris Tzannatos.

7 Why disagreements among economists persist, why economists need to brace themselves for differences within their simultaneous conversations and their conversations over time, and why they may benefit from knowing about classicism, modernism, and postmodernism

Why indeed?

Two academic economists meet on the plane headed for the mammoth annual meeting of the American Economics Association. The usual chitchat ensues. "So where do you teach?" "At [prestigious American east-coast university]." "How is it over there?" "Pretty good. There are a couple of people I can talk to." "You're lucky. I don't have that," the other responds, seizing the occasion to launch into an exposé of his research. Something about a game-theoretic set-up. His fellow economist listens politely, nods a few times, but says little in response. This, clearly, is not a guy he can talk to. As the conversation languishes, they are drawn back into their reading.

How remarkable that is. Amidst all the economists at this meeting – all of whom are interested in things economic, all of whom are in the conversation – there are but a handful any one of them can talk to. The difficulty of finding good sparring partners was a harsh reality in my budding life among economists. I expected intense interactions, heated exchanges, interest-sparking spectrums of communication. How little of that was realized. Now and then, I meet a fellow economist I can have a real conversation with. (To see who they are, read the acknowledgments.) I am tempted to declare economists autistic, impossible as it is to get a real conversation going with most of them. But that's frustration talking. There are good reasons, I now know, for the stand-offs.

One is personal difference. Some people are too pushy (casual, overbearing, withdrawn) for my taste. Differences in passions and emotions stand in the way. Differences in social background can stand in the way, too. I am most comfortable talking with people who share an intellectual middle-class background and who are intellectually open-minded. I also like getting personal but that, in the academic setting, seems taboo. (Again, check the acknowledgments for the few welcome exceptions.) I was naive enough, early on, to think that personal differences would fade away in the face of reason and logic. They do not. Economists are humans, after all.

Another reason has to do with the character of the conversation. The economic conversation comprises diverse specialties, topics, themes, and research methods. It is therefore unreasonable to expect one economist to engage in a number of them, or a random selection of economists to engage in one in particular. The economics of crime (social security, real estate, high finance) is fascinating to those who are into such topics, but since I am not I quickly tune out of their conversations. Similarly, not all fellow economists are enthusiastic when I bring up the economics of the arts, or the conversation of economists.

The most serious reason for persistent disagreements and communication problems among economists is that economists are in a bunch of conversations and talking across them is problematic if not impossible. The conversations between, say, feminist economists and hard-core neoclassicists are simply too different to expect interaction. They generate miscomprehension, irritation, and sometimes anger. (Attempts to converse will mostly go unnoticed – ignoring a challenge is still the most effective rhetorical strategy.) One advantage of knowing about the rhetoric of economic conversations is being able to anticipate and recognize differences. The obstacles are rhetorical; at least, that is how they become noticeable.

This chapter consists of two parts. The first focuses on differences between conversations that go on simultaneously. Knowing about them is practical, at least if you are interested in the conversations of economists. The second and less practical part is about differences that occur over time. It may help if you are interested in the history of economic conversations. It will also help if you live a long life, for it will show how to anticipate the (perhaps dramatically) changing conversation. Both apply the lessons on rhetoric of the previous chapter in interpreting economic conversations. Hint: think metaphor and narrative!

PART 1. A BUNCH OF CONVERSATIONS IS GOING ON AND SWITCHING FROM ONE TO ANOTHER IS NOT AS EASY AS IT SEEMS

When I tried to sort out the pernicious disagreements between new classical and new Keynesian economists, I conducted a series of conversations with the protagonists (Klamer 1983). The personal differences were revealing. The vivacious Robert Solow (with a taste for the quick quip), the serious Robert Lucas (never less than self-composed), the chatty Franco Modigliani (not shy of self-promotion), and the unassuming James Tobin (wanting an interview at least as long as Lucas's) quickly taught me how trenchant the rhetorical differences were. After hearing Solow's remark, comparing Lucas to a lunatic who wanted to get

him involved "in a technical discussion of cavalry tactics at the battle of Auster-
litz" (Klamer 1983: 146), what, I thought, would Lucas say the next time he faced
Solow? The academic world frowns upon smacking opponents, but smacking, in
this case, might have been warranted. Lucas has probably said nothing about it,
restraining himself to a few polite remarks. (Years later, when I interviewed Chicago students, they told me how offensive Solow's remark was but that it had not
prevented them from taking his work seriously.) Solow's joke went straight to the
jugular. He knows as well as anyone that Lucas is not a lunatic, but it was *as if* he
were. Lucas's way of talking is so different from Solow's that Solow loses himself
when engaging in it and perhaps becomes mad himself.

Let this sink in for a moment. Here are two highly intelligent, well-trained,
professional academic economists who are unable to talk to each other in a meaningful way. Obviously, logical differences don't stand in their way. The difference
must go deeper.

Rhetorical obstacles

Think rhetoric and you are considering rhetorical differences. Recall the lessons
of the preceding chapter, and you surmise different *constitutive* metaphors and
constitutive stories at work. As discussed, constitutive metaphors and stories define a conversation. Once inside a conversation we cannot think without them.
And we can be inside the conversation only if we understand how to work the
constitutive metaphors and stories. That's what graduate school instills: how to
think the constitutive metaphor and enact the constitutive story without being
aware of it. It's like riding a bicycle; people do it without thinking how they do it.
We may be so steeped in our own conversations that we cannot imagine that others think and talk differently, that there are other serious conversations out there.
Yet there are.

The rhetorical gap appears when we try to engage people who are wont to
think another constitutive metaphor and enact another constitutive story. They
are as unlikely to get what we are saying as we will be to hear them. Confusion
ensues. The rule is that people in the dominant conversation cannot be bothered
by the differences and the confusions: they simply ignore the alternatives. People
in the alternative conversations, on the other hand, tend to be obsessed with the
way their conversation is different from the dominant one. The result is minimal
engagement across conversations. The rhetorical obstacles are simply too great.

Consider the rhetorical divide that separates the new classical conversation
of Lucas from the new Keynesian conversation of Solow. Lucas appears to think
in terms of a deep structure that underlies the complexity of economic phenomena. He is interested in finding out the parameters that mark that deep, invariant
structure. The notion that agents maximize objective functions under all kinds of
constraints is part of that deep structure. Accordingly, he is thinking *as if* that deep
structure underlies economic processes and *as if* people are fully rational agents.
The "as if's" indicate the constitutive metaphor that inform his and other new
classical economists' thinking.

Lucas's constitutive metaphor is accompanied by a constitutive story that motivates and legitimates such thinking. In wanting to explore the deep structure of reality, he casts himself in the role of the serious scientist who is not to be distracted by practical concerns or politicians. It is a story about the search for the Holy Grail against all kinds of odds. It is a story that Lucas tells with conviction. "We do not get distracted by what people in Washington want from us," he tells new graduate students at Chicago, "we are serious about economics here." The implication is that other economists, like Robert Solow, are not serious.

Solow's new Keynesian approach tells a story in which economics serves the goal of human betterment, and economists feature as policy advisors. In that story going back and forth between Washington and academic institutions is a positive sign. It is good when economists advise governments what to do. That's the point of all the work. Because he seeks to get a grip on real-world phenomena, Solow is less strongly committed to the constitutive metaphors of new classical economics. He is more pragmatic and, to get relevant outcomes, he allows for the use of realistic assumptions that do not resonate well with Lucas's hard-core neoclassical thinking. In Solow's conversation, an argument that points out market imperfections and calls for government action makes sense. Lucas wants to know what in the deep structure might account for phenomena that seem like market imperfections, and expects that a fully rational explanation leaves no room for effective governmental intervention. Not surprisingly, Solow's new Keynesian conversation speaks more to those who like to see in economic analysis a tool for economic policy.

The difference appears to be a matter of style, the style of Lucas being more formal, more mathematical, than that of Solow. But don't be fooled by this: the form of argument betrays a vision of what science is supposed to do. By being formal, Lucas makes a methodological argument about what constitutes good science. By caring more about realistic features of the model, Solow takes issue with Lucas's argument. For Solow the servitude of economic analysis toward policymakers is critical; for Lucas it is not.

If we drift over to the conversation of Austrian economists, we find even more serious rhetorical walls. Although Austrian economists share with Lucas a constitutive story in which economists are foremost intellectuals seeking the truth regardless of what politicians call for, their constitutive metaphor is quite different. Rather, they picture people as individuals seeking the best for themselves in a world of uncertainty. That is why they like to think of entrepreneurs – people who are enterprising, inventive, and creative. Entrepreneurs are their heroes. Lucas and Solow do not know any heroes in the economy; they know only anonymous economic agents. Austrian economists are inspired by an organic vision of the world; their constitutive metaphor is cast in anthropomorphic terms and makes us think of people who are equipped with emotions, subject to uncertainties, and knowledgeable only in a limited sense. In contrast, the constitutive metaphors of Lucas and Solow come in the form of systems of equations and conjure up images of machines, of humans as calculating robots and a mathematical system. In that respect, they both buy into the neoclassical view of the world. The Austrians do not.

In yet another (entirely) different conversation, feminist economists make gender a critical feature of their constitutive metaphor and project themselves as advocates of a worldview in which gender figures prominently. While feminists may get some sympathy in the conversation of Solow – for the argument that women are systematically underpaid, for example, or that women play a critical role in the development of Third World countries – their conversation will run into a stonewall of miscomprehension with economists who are into the new classical conversation. Gender does not fit in the machine-like world of neoclassical economists.

A visit to the shelves stacked with economic journals alerts you to the many different conversations that are going on. Where the journals *Rethinking Marxism* and *Radical Political Economy* feature concepts like class, power and conflict, the *American Economic Review* and other hard-core new classical journals give them nary a mention. There are journals for neo-institutional economics, experimental economics, behavioral economics, econometrics, social economics, evolutionary economics, and so forth and so on. Economists are truly in a bunch of different conversations.

Switching conversations may require a conversion

Most students get into a conversation without being aware of the consequences. They do not choose consciously or merely follow their professors. Some students fret about where to go, though. I had once extensive conversations with a very bright student who could easily do the math required of hard-core neoclassical economists but was attracted to the political economy as practiced by Michael Piore and Samuel Bowles (both radical economists, more or less). He wanted to know more about the cultural economics that I was doing. He wrote a paper on some labor issue using notions of class and conflict. But a lack of confidence and worries about getting into a good graduate school altered his course. When I saw him a few years later, he confessed that he had given up on what he truly wanted to do and had gotten himself to write an econometric thesis. It was something he was good at. He was apologetic about it, as if he had sold out. He ended up with a good job, but each time we meet he makes me feel as if I am his conscience. He is in a conversation but not wholeheartedly so.

More than once have I found myself in a confessional with fellow economists. They talk about feeling lost, doubtful that what they are doing amounts to anything. This is a period that sensible human beings experience from time to time – I have them about every other week. But sometimes the agonizing is more serious: they have grown disenchanted with the academic world, or with economics. Or they realize that their research does not allow them to ask the questions that interest them. In that case, they appear to be in the wrong conversation. I broach the possibility carefully for, if they face up to it, they are in for a difficult period. They will not switch conversations easily. And if they quit academia, then what? If they like being scientists, can that change? When neoclassical economists want to join the conversation of feminist economists, they have to wean themselves from a host of deep-seated patterns related to the constitutive metaphors and stories of that conversation, and assimilate the ways of talking and thinking that character-ize the feminist conversation. *That is hard work.* Deirdre McCloskey's *Crossing* (2000) evidences just how hard it is. Her story is not only about changing gender but also about changing her conversation to a more open-minded one, one that is more about value, virtue, and even love. Leonard Rapping – at the frontier of research in new classical economics, a recipient of major grants, firmly positioned at a prestigious university, widely appreciated, and clearly part of the inner core of the research community right alongside Bob Lucas – had the war in Vietnam begin to weigh in on him. He had questions about its legitimacy and realized that his way of thinking – his constitutive metaphors and stories – did not help him gain an understanding of what was going on. He made up his mind and quit what he was doing. This is how he told what happened then:

> It was an awful experience. Very difficult. I had never experienced depression before. I did then. It took me many years to recoup from that. For about six years I just read; I didn't write anything. It was a dark and painful period. It was hard. I was afraid. Everything I had learned seemed inadequate, given the war. I concluded that I was inadequately educated and that I had to search further for the truth. I searched to the left and read and thought about that point of view. But I would never again embrace an extreme ideology. To understand the experience you could think of a football player who suddenly decides that football is not his cup of teas and tries another game. The adjust-ment was tremendous. For a long time I was without any defenses. I was intellectually exposed. I disassociated myself from a whole set of friendships developed over a 20-year period. Everytime I made a move I was accused of inconsistency or disloyalty. I was frozen out of the "money river." I felt like a pariah.
>
> (Klamer 1983: 227)

Rapping experienced what it is to give up a conversation. He could not throw himself into another and kept on wandering till he died. A gripping story, isn't it? Imagine how all those economists in the former Soviet Union must have felt when they were forced to give up their Marxist conversation to become neoclassical economists after the communist regime fell. Everything they had learned lost its meaning and interest. They could throw away entire libraries and had to return to class to learn an entirely new economic language and new research methods. Most of them gave up. You do not think in different constitutive metaphors and enact a different constitutive story just like that. For most of us, one conversation is all we can muster in a lifetime.

That the message comes through: differences do matter

It is the drum of difference that I am beating in this chapter. Be aware of the different conversations that are going on: that is the message. People may take issue with the characterization that I am giving of the various conversations; they may point out that the constitutive metaphors are quite different from what I am stating here. That's okay with me. Constitutive metaphors are never made explicit. You cannot ask people what constitutive metaphor constitutes their thinking: they will not know. But ask them what notions such as "rationality," "power," "culture," "emotion," and "conflict" mean to them and you quickly find out where they are. I asked John Hicks, shortly before he died, about the notion of conflict (Klamer 1989). No, he could not do anything with it. He was seemed irritated that I had even asked him. I had expected that, for why would he, one of the founders of modern neoclassical economics, have any affinity with the Marxist way of thinking? But I was surprised to find out that the notion of rationality did not do much for him either. It affirmed my suspicion that he was more akin to the Austrians than to neoclassicists such as Paul Samuelson. When I pushed him, he revealed that he preferred to think like an accountant, think in terms of balance sheets, stocks, and flows. For him accounting shaped his constitutive metaphor (for this see also Klamer and McCloskey 1992). The reason he felt misunderstood by Paul Samuelson was now clear: he worked with a different constitutive metaphor. This goes to show that seeking out the contrast with other conversations helps uncover what constitutes a conversation. There you find the differences that make conversations incommensurate.

I am beating the drum ceaselessly because the message of difference is not coming through. At least, so it seems. Many economists will maintain that there is only one serious scientific conversation out there, really, and that is the hard-core neoclassical conversation with its penchant for tough mathematics and econometrics. A case in point is *A Guide for the Young Economist: Writing and Speaking Effectively about Economics* (Thomson 2001). When I saw the title I was afraid for a moment that I need not write this book, that the message was all there. But it turns out to be a guide on how to write down the mathematics and how to present a mathematical model in a seminar. It has admonitions like "Write so That You Will Not Have to Be Read," "Show Clearly Where Each Proof Ends," "Use Pictures," "Watch your Superscripts and Subscripts," and "Choose Mnemonic Abbreviations for Assumptions and Properties." Nowhere does it point out to the Young Economist that there are other conversations out there, other roads toward the economic truth. The Young Economist is made to believe that there is only one serious scientific conversation and that is the highly abstract, mathematical conversation learned at graduate school.

When the AEA began publishing the *Journal of Economic Perspectives* in 1987, it looked as if the profession was about to open up to alternative perspectives. Since then, the neoclassical hard core appears to be hardening and tolerance for other perspectives decreasing. Economists who are into other conversations go under the banner of heterodox economists to stress the dominance of the orthodoxy. They are driven to the margins of the profession, if they were not already there. The University of Notre Dame housed a strong contingent of these heterodox economists, but the administration decided in 2002 to sideline the group and hire orthodox economists to make orthodoxy the core of its graduate program. Something similar is happening at the Riverside branch of the University of California. Heterodox economists have a difficult time getting positions at mediocre universities and can forget about a position at a top university. Clearly, one conversation appears to be overpowering others. But I say "appears" as everything is relative.

PART 2. CONVERSATIONS CHANGE OVER TIME – WHO SAYS THE CURRENT ONE WILL LAST FOREVER?

Even if one conversation is overpowering the others and appears untouchable, those outside it rest assured (and those inside it be aware): conversations never last. Conversations change over time, ultimately unraveling to make way for another conversation. Some historical experiments make the point.

First go (once again) to the library stacks. Choose a long-standing journal, such as the *Economic Journal*, or the *American Economic Review*, and pick volumes at five-year intervals. The conversation changes in front of your eyes. Articles from the late nineteenth century– when journals got started – are wordy and long-winded. They contain few statistics and very little mathematical notation. Articles of the first few decades of the twentieth century contain page after page of statistics. Economists are into numbers, and collect all kinds of statistics. The 1920s and 1930s spawn a great number of articles on accounting issues. Then comes a new genre, standing out because its articles are short and contain extensive mathematical equations. In the 1980s and 1990s, this genre begins to dominate. Statistical tables become rare. In the 1990s, an increasing proportion of articles contain econometric tests of some sort.

Join me now in the second experiment. This time, collect books by Adam Smith, Milton Friedman, and Robert Lucas. All of them extol the miracles of free market and the importance of free choice and bemoan the disasters that government interventions bring, so these economists, you often hear, have the same point of view – Adam Smith is just a Milton Friedman with a wig on, and Lucas is the modern version of Friedman. Now leaf through their books. What do you see? First of all, Smith's *Wealth of Nations* (1776) is voluminous. Apparently this guy needed lots of pages to get his laissez-faire message across. And they are all filled with – words. You will look in vain for equations and only if you look carefully will you find some statistics. Scan it and you will see how Smith argues by way of anecdotes, a concept here and there, and not all too extensive an analysis. No models here. Now look at Friedman's *Monetary History* (1963). This is voluminous as well, but that is because of its numerous statistics. Friedman worked with numbers, lots of them. Then pick up Lucas's *Models of Business Cycles* (1987). It is relatively slim. And there you have it, one model after another, all neatly formulated in mathematical terms. These guys may have similar ideas but they are in different conversations.

And the conversations are what count, at least if you are living the life among the econ. Friedman was a towering figure in his days at Chicago, but the kind of conversation that he liked and pushed is now known as the "Old Chicago" economics, for it was drowned out by the conversation of New Chicago economists: Robert Lucas and his cohort. Friedman left for Stanford University. He is still revered in the corridors of the economics department at Chicago, but his way of doing economics is out. All he railed against – Walrasian general equilibrium economics instead of Marshallian partial equilibrium economics, heavy-handed theorizing, and modeling geared to expose deep structures rather than pragmatic modeling intended to make a point in the course of an argument – prevailed in the end. And what about Adam Smith? Imagine him waking up today as a Rip van Winkle. He would not have a clue as to what is going on. The mathematics would be gibberish and he probably would turn into a historian or stick with the moral philosophy that he was interested in to begin with. As these experiments demonstrate, the conversation has changed dramatically.

We could leave it at that. We could conclude with the hard-nosed economist that the New Chicago economics, the game theory, the behavioral stuff, and all the heavy-handed mathematics and econometrics are simply the culmination of a long process. This is as good as it gets, and it will only get better. Knowledge accumulates; science advances. (Remember this metaphor from Chapter 2?) But what about the other conversations that are going on simultaneously? Are they necessarily inferior, false, meaningless, or misguided? How do we know for sure? We learned that no decisive empirical tests, no data conclusively prove that one theory is superior to another. Someone like Milton Friedman will have doubts about the formalist turn that the conversation has taken, as will many others. Are these critics mistaken? Are they scientific retrogrades hanging onto old times? Or is something else going on?

I maintain that something else is going on, that the metaphor of the conversation intimates a different perspective on these changes over time. More particularly, I want to suggest that the changes occur because they are meaningful in view of what is going on in society at large. Economic conversations do not change in isolation!

Look beyond economics and see the parallels

To argue the point, we have to cross disciplinary boundaries, and compare and contrast what is going on in other disciplines, or conversations. As I like to think about and look at or listen to art, I cross over to that conversation. I could just as well have chosen another scientific discipline such as physics or mathematics, or taken you to the world of design (e.g., of cars). But the arts will do nicely.

Consider Figure 7.1. The left picture is obvious for it represents the market. The right picture is a painting by Piet Mondrian, a famous Dutch artist whose work is found in all the best modern art museums. Mondrian painted this in 1931. The

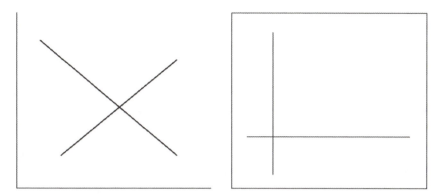

Figure 7.1 What do these pictures have in common?

demand and supply diagram first appeared in 1890 in Alfred Marshall's *Principles of Economics* – in a footnote. I imagine that Marshall was being a little coy, representing something as complex as a market with four lines. That is why he put it in a footnote. The little diagram was more like a pedagogical ploy to illustrate his reconciliation of two accounts of exchange value, that is, the hedonistic account (based on the notion of marginal utility) and the one that focuses on the costs of production. At the time, such a highly abstract representation must have looked weird. How could it do justice to everything that is going on in a market?

It took decades before the diagram became common fare in the teaching of economics, thanks to Paul Samuelson, who made it a central feature in his first economics textbook in 1947. Now economic students take the representation for granted. They get the abstract metaphor and are used to thinking in terms of (serious) movements along and shifts of the curves. Who bothers to remember that it's unrealistic?

Put the same students in front of Mondrian's painting and you get comments like: "What's so special about it?" "My little sister did better in pre-school." "This has *meaning*?" "Isn't it [yawn] time for lunch?" Yet Mondrian made a move similar to Marshall's. He, too, sought to represent a complex reality in the most abstract manner. And, like Samuelson, Mondrian wanted to get rid of all clutter, all references to things realistic – such as the human figure. With a minimum of forms, colors, and straight (vertical and horizontal) lines, he sought to represent the deep structure of reality, which to him was spiritual. The developments in physics inspired him, as they did Samuelson. For physicists had shown the light, representing the deepest structure of physical substances and processes in highly abstract mathematical formulas. They conveyed the message that, if we really want to understand what is going on, we should not describe things in everyday terms but take recourse in scientific jargon and use the abstract language of mathematics. Not just artists got the message; scientists in all disciplines did. Economists were among them.

The economic writing in terms of diagrams and equations, therefore, did not come about in isolation. Economists such as Samuelson and Debreu, and Arrow, who propagated an axiomatic approach to economics, were not alone in their exploration of reality by way of abstract representations. Their rhetoric resonated against what was going on in other fields, in physics, mathematics, and also the arts. I do not want to suggest that Mondrian caused Samuelson, Arrow, and Debreu to seek abstract forms. They may not even have known about Mondrian's work. It is rather that the quest for deep structures under the surface of things and the penchant for the abstract were in the air. Had they presented their mathematical and axiomatic models a decade earlier they probably would have been ignored by economists, because at that time statistical and historical work appealed to the imagination and abstract theorizing would have looked absurd. It did not when the time was ripe, when scientists in other disciplines were making similar moves and when art turned abstract. Remember, it is not the truth of an argument that renders it persuasive, but the meanings it evokes and the kind of conversation it engenders. In the late 1930s an abstract representation had become meaningful. It resonated with the Zeitgeist. And it furthered the conversation among economists.

All kinds of isms characterize historical phases in economic conversations

I am saying nothing original here (does anyone ever?). Many scholars have observed and argued something like it. The label that gets attached to this movement toward the abstract is that of *modernism*. The term is generally used to characterize the intellectual imagination that came to dominate the twentieth century – in the Western world, that is. The general understanding is that leading figures in the arts and sciences took issue with *classicism* as it prevailed in the nineteenth century and radicalized ideas that had begun to percolate in the Enlightenment of the seventeenth and eighteenth centuries. Many believe that, in the meantime, modernism made way for something else, *late modernism* or perhaps *postmodernism*. And classical elements are making a reappearance. The scenery is, as a result, somewhat chaotic and fragmented.

Before the narration of the advent of modernism in economics and its displacement by a form of late modernism at first and possibly postmodernist elements, I share a warning that I owe to my friend Jack Amariglio, a postmodernist at heart and a Marxist to boot (see, for example, Ruccio and Amariglio 2003). Jack warns against totalizing stories that tell us how classicism was overtaken by modernism and how modernism was overtaken by postmodernism. The problem with such accounts is that they ignore the modernist and postmodernist elements that can be discerned in designated classical periods and how classical and modernist elements continue to operate in the postmodern period. He suggests we speak of postmodernist moments and of classical and modernist moments to acknowledge that different imaginations can operate simultaneously and that any of these moments can be discerned at any time. I suggest we heed that warning. After all, it goes along with the earlier argument that different conversations operate simultaneously. Thus no totalizing story. *Panta rhei.*

Box 7.1 A primer

- *Classicism* appears in the form of classical art, classical music, classical architecture, and classical economics. It represents the search for absolutes: absolute truth, absolute beauty, absolute right. It includes respect for authority and tradition.
- *Enlightenment* was the intellectual project of the sixteenth and seventeenth centuries, originating mainly in France and Scotland. Its purpose was to elevate reason as human's best resource. It marked the beginning of the demystification and rationalization of modern life.
- *Modernity* represents the age of innovation, technological advancement, scientific progress, mechanization, and industrialization, beginning somewhere in the eighteenth century.
- *Modernism* is the dominant form of scientific and artistic expression in the twentieth century. Its characteristics are preoccupation with the problem of representation, a predisposition toward abstract and formal representation of the invariant, belief in true representation and one scientific method (positive science), a meta-narrative of progress, liberation and emancipation, humanistic values (see also Box 7.2).
- *Late modernity* (or late capitalism) is an economy revolving around information and knowledge, mass commodification, and globalization.
- *Late* (or high) *modernism* is a radicalization of modernist thinking, such as the predisposition toward minimalist and abstract representations, yet without the meta-narrative of progress and emancipation.
- *Postmodernity* represents the end of ideologies, a word centered around creativity, innovation, communication, the Internet, multicultural societies, a borderless world, the generic city, global markets.
- *Postmodernism* is modernism without its meta-narrative, modernism and late modernism without their rigor and abstraction. Its key words are pluralism, fragmentation, deconstruction, pastiche, collage, simulation, and simulacra.
- *Neo-traditionalism* (or neoclassicism or neo-Aristotelianism) is the reappearance of classical moments such as interest in and respect for traditions, but now with the recognition of their

continuous changes. It is a historical perspective, a reevaluation of values and virtues, a revival of the notion of the economy as being moral and cultural, a focus on what constitutes the good life and good society therein.

The advent of modernism

For classicism – the antidote to modernism – we think of classical economics, Michelangelo's *David*, the Parthenon or, for that matter, any building with pillars, domes, and imposing entrances. Classical economics was about value: what determines the value of things? The physiocrats saw God, or nature, as the creator of value; humans transformed the given value of something like leather into a useful thing like a shoe. Classical thinking is concerned with right and wrong, with the essence of something like the economy, with tradition, and therefore with values. A classic building like the Parthenon honors principles of symmetry and stands there for eternity; classical music spells out harmony and shows closure. Classical thinkers and artists invest a faith in something permanent and in the absolute, as in absolutely good and absolutely beautiful.

Throughout the history of humanity, philosophers and artists have taken issue with classicism. Montaigne's sixteenth-century French thinking called into question the certainties of classicism and challenged reigning traditions. Martin Luther did something similar when, according to legend, he took on the traditional bulwark of the Catholic Church by hammering his "Ninety-Five Theses" on the door of the chapel in Wittenberg. Most significant, however, was the move of French philosopher Descartes, made at the beginning of the seventeenth century. His *cogito ergo sum* (Chapter 5) sparked the Age of Reason that ensued. "I think therefore I am" upstaged God and the sacred text as the source of knowledge. Humans had to think for themselves. Socrates had suggested something similar two thousand years earlier, but the idea settled with Descartes. The Enlightenment is usually characterized as the period in which reason came to dominate the intellectual firmament.

The Enlightenment notwithstanding, classical moments remained in vogue in the nineteenth century. Economics was a discipline for preachers and historians trying to figure out how economic processes evolve and what their moral implications are. Darwin had stimulated the historical way of thinking with his story about evolution. Many an economist looked at economic behavior in terms of a struggle for survival.

In the first few decades of the twentieth century all this was about to change. A different imagination made its appearance, one that in many ways called to mind the imagination of Descartes and the Enlightenment. Physics had made a deep impression with its stories about atoms, energetic forces, the first and second laws of thermodynamics, and so on. Impressionists wanted to paint reality not as it seemed but as we actually see it. Looking back, we now discern the advent of modernism in the first decades of the twentieth century. The signs became apparent in a wide variety of disciplines. Russell and Whitehead tried to reduce mathematics to a form of logic; Mies van der Rohe designed stout, straight buildings with all their elementary horizontal and vertical lines clearly visible; Picasso, Mondrian, and Kandinsky turned abstract; cubism appeared on the scene; Schoenberg, Webern, and Berg came out with atonal music; Woolf, Proust, and Joyce explored the subconscious. This was also the time of John Maynard Keynes and his Bloomsbury group, whose members did everything they could to liberate themselves from Victorian morality and cluttered drawing rooms.

It was indeed a time of liberation for these intellectuals (Keynes was involved in a passionate homosexual relationship) and a time for new ideas, new movements, the future – and progress. The latter was clearly felt: modern art and modern science would serve the emancipation of the individual and the betterment of society. Forget about the church and other such traditional institutions. Artists and scientists alike saw for themselves a critical role in societal changes for the better. Architects such as Le Corbusier envisioned the eradication of old neighborhoods in order to build in a modern way to serve a new dynamic world. The city developer Moses implemented his ideas in New York with a network of highways and other major infrastructural projects all in the name of progress. Modern Russian artists such as Malevich imagined that they would be the pioneers leading the Russian people to a new and better world under communism. (They did not, however, persuade Stalin, who preferred classical figurative art; they ended up in exile.)

Economists followed suit. Keynes did not just want to understand how the economy worked; he wanted to improve it. Conversations of economists turned more and more to policy issues. To that end, economists worked on accounting to come up with a system of national accounts. They began experimenting with large-scale mathematical models with the intention of using them as instruments for economic policy.

Probably lured by its reasoning in analogy with physics, many new recruits came with a background in physics and engineering. From engineering, they took an instrumental look at economics as a science: the theory had to produce the instruments that politicians could use to combat unemployment, abate the impact of business cycles, control inflation, and diminish poverty and income inequality. Before that economists had strong opinions on matters such as free trade, but now they wanted to make economic policy a scientific enterprise. "You, the politician, tell us where you want to go and we, the modern economists, will tell you how to get closest to it." That was the message of people like Tinbergen and Koopmans (who came from physics). Some economists went as far as propagating scientific planning of the entire economy, as was done by communist regimes in the Soviet Union, China, and Cuba.

In the meantime the economic conversation became more and more abstract. I used to assign a 1939 article by Samuelson entitled "Interactions Between the Multiplier Analysis and the Principle of Acceleration" to my class on business cycles as it provided a concise exposition of a business cycle model based on the multiplier and the accelerator. When I began to think about the modernist moments in economics, I suddenly saw the article in a different light and realized I had been missing its major message. Here is how the article begins: "Few economists would deny the 'multiplier' analysis of the effect of governmental spending has thrown some light upon this important problem." This was 1939, when most economists were still struggling with the economics of Keynes and his multiplier analysis, and here was this young economist, still a PhD student, suggesting consensus. It is a move he learned from practices in physics: claim agreement and then show that something else is going on. He continues as follows (with commentaries in brackets): "Nevertheless, there would seem to be some ground for the fear that this extremely simplified mechanism [so he says – it was not for most economists at the time] is in danger of hardening into a dogma, hindering progress [God forbid] and obscuring important subsidiary relations [note that here he suggests that something is hidden and needs to be brought out]." So Samuelson is going to show how progress is to be made.

The story goes that he wrote this article after a class with his professor, Alvin Hansen. The latter got stuck in his analysis and this was his student's response. The article cites Hansen. After having laid out Hansen's problem, he continues as follows: "In order to remedy the situation in some measure [note the "some"], Professor Hansen has developed a new model sequence which ingeniously combines [ingeniously!] the multiplier analysis with that of the *acceleration* principle or *relation* [his emphasis]." Ever seen a graduate student flattering his professor so much before showing how obvious the solution was?

He subsequently does something odd, at least for us now. After describing the multiplier and accelerator effects (no equations yet), he does a few exercises with different numbers for both. That gets him tables with sequences for national income for different combinations of values for both effects. One sequence produces a neat business cycle, another explodes, and another again shows steady growth. "By this time the investigator is inclined to feel somewhat disorganized." The reader who is used to working with numbers is knocked out, hanging on the ropes, desperate for a way out. Samuelson offers it. His solution is "comparatively simple algebraic analysis" that "enables us to unify the results." The reader is willing to accept anything by now. And then the model appears that we now would have expected right away. At that time Samuelson felt he had to sway his readers first. He ends up with a differential equation that he solves in a footnote, apparently to coddle his non-mathematically inclined readers. A neat diagram follows that shows which values of the multiplier and the accelerator produce a regular business cycle. In the final paragraph Samuelson admits to some limitations of his model, which remains simplistic according to him, but spurs the reader to follow his lead and recognize mathematical methods as "a liberating device."

Accordingly, the article presents a methodological argument, that is, an argument as to what constitutes scientific economics. Forget about descriptive analysis, endless statistics, historical and institutional studies; the argument both admonishes and embraces abductive reasoning by way of mathematical models as the way to the truth. In this way we, the economists, can establish the invariant structure and, armed with that knowledge, can tell policy-makers what to do to meet their objectives. And that is not all. The article not only deletes references to the actual economy, it also precludes identification with economic actors such as investors and consumers. Nowhere in the analysis is the reader asked to imagine how a consumer or an investor would act. The analysis is highly abstract; all attention goes to the bare structure of the model. No distractions here, no clutter of things realistic. Parsimony prevails, just as in a Mondrian painting.

At first I thought that the article does away with narrative. After all, there are no characters like consumers and investors in it, and what to make of a plot? Yet, there is a story in the article, a story about us, the economists. The article begins right away with the identification of us. Remember that few of us would disagree? Then we are taken for a ride. First we are reminded that we do not want an analysis to harden "into a dogma hindering progress" for we want progress, don't we? Then we are told that we are having a problem that even Professor Hansen, one of us, could not solve. We want to solve that problem, don't we? Then we are made to do what we are used to – crunching numbers – to end up feeling "somewhat disorganized." Then the solution comes in the form of a "relatively simple algebraic analysis." How could we resist? If some of still were to have any doubts, the apotheosis comes in the form of a flaming ending promising us liberation with math as the liberating device. Liberation from what? You still dare to ask? In short, this very brief article tells the big story about us, about our discipline, about what we as serious scientist are supposed to do.

I discuss this little article at length to impress on you how remarkable the moves were that Samuelson made at the time, how modernist they were. Now they seem so common, but they were not then. Sense its persuasive powers, the force of, in particular, its methodological argument. And note its narrative with us, economists, as the only character. You can trace this narrative in any modernist article: Whatever its economic theme, it is an excuse to tell about us, the academic economists, over and over again. It is always about us who have a problem and it is about us who have to do something about it. The ending comes in the form of a solution or a result – although recently the conclusion might be that there is no solution. This is what is called the reflexivity in modernism, the look inwards. It is the same move that painters made. First they stepped away from their subjects (humans, the still life, landscapes), then they turned around to focus all their attention to the canvas and began painting about painting, about what preoccupied them as artists. Just as modernist economics is first all about economics and economists, modernist painting is about painting and painters.

The modernist moment prevailed but other moments were kept alive, making for lively scenery and enduring differences

In line with the earlier warning, I should point out that this modernist way of doing economics was not all there was. While Samuelson and others like him may have set the stage for a hard-nosed science of economics, many other prominent economists were telling different stories. Keynes, for one, insisted that uncertainty was a critical factor in economic processes and therefore resisted the strict modeling strategy of Samuelson and the strict reliance on econometric techniques as propagated by Tinbergen. Hicks held out for an economics that factored in time, just as Keynes, Shackle, and Knight stressed the importance of uncertainty and Hayek wrote about information and knowledge. Other conversations continued, including conversations on economic history and institutions. Even so, blackboard economics, as McCloskey calls Samuelson's modernist economics, quickly ascended; it came to dominate the teaching of economics and became the standard for journal articles. Just see what Hicks and Hansen did with Keynes's elaborate analysis. Keynes needed an entire book to get his point across. Hicks and Hansen needed only a few pages and got it all in one diagram (Figure 7.2).

Need I say more?

The square and the circle

Although this account of modernism in economics at first made a great deal of sense, to me at least, I was missing a dimension. I got stuck, for example, in the story of Keynes. He seemed a modernist all right by the way he turned from tradition and crafted a new science of economics. Yet, whence his attention to uncertainty? And how to account for his fascination with things personal? Keynes did not appear to be as hard-nosed as we associate with the modernist scientist. I got into further problems when I tried to make the connections with the arts. Mondrian was formal and reductionist enough, but how about a Rothko or a Pollock? Their abstract paintings seemed to be motivated more by emotion than by reason. That is how I came up with the contrast between the square and the circle as one of the main characteristics of modernism (Figure 7.3).

Accordingly, modernism asks for thinking in dualities, for thinking in two worlds and even living in two worlds. As a scientist you are to inhabit the square,

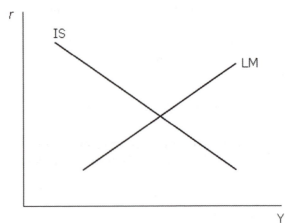

Figure 7.2 The IS/LM model

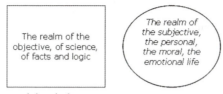

Figure 7.3 The square and the circle

that is, you are restricted to thinking in square terms. In the scientific realm you are to be objective, and thus to keep your emotions, your values, and whatever else pertains to the realm of the circle to yourself. In your personal life, however, the circle would be drawn large. There you would do better giving in your emotions ("Don't be so logical! Tell me what you *feel* about our marriage!")

The dualities of modernism pop up everywhere. Consider the list (drawn from a similar list that Deirdre McCloskey likes to make) in Table 7.1.

Turn to the modernist practice of economics and you will notice the modernist strategy to try to fit things in the square. Whatever can fit the square of economic analysis passes. Preferences are subjective and therefore pertain to the circle. They are allowed into the square only as exogenous variables, that is, variables that are left unexplained. Recently, Gary Becker and others have tried to square preferences by subsuming them in an economic framework of rational choice and investment. (A preference for art, for example, can be accounted for by previous investments in the consumption of art.) Cognitive processes – learning, creativity, and the like – stay in the circle until they are made endogenous in a square analysis.

Also square is the modernist conception of science, which equals the positivist stance described in Chapter 5. Square is the science that proceeds according to strict scientific standards. Logic and facts are square. Ideologies, values, passions, and something vague like conversations must belong to the realm of the circle.

Accordingly, in modernist science, the square overrules and dominates the circle. The modernist scientist tries to expunge the circle from his or her thinking. The modernist artist, on the other hand, may make a big deal of the circle. Abstract expressionism is all about giving expression to experiences in the realm of the circle, but in an abstract manner. To go back to the life of Keynes, while being pretty square as a scientist, he lived an exuberant life in the realm of the

Table 7.1 The dualities of modernism

The square	The circle
Science	Everyday life
Logic	Metaphor
Deduction	Abduction
Scientist	Therapist
Hard	Soft
Masculine	Feminine
Public sphere	Personal sphere
Manager	Leader

circle, consorting with artists and sharing intimate feelings with fellow members of the Bloomsbury group. Such a life appeals to the modernist imagination as long as the two separate lives remain just that: separate.

The problem with the timing of modernism

The alert reader will have noticed the fudging concerning the timing of the advent of modernism. And rightly so. Did it all start in the nineteenth century when economists like Leon Walras began to cast their theory in the abstract form of mathematical models and try to model their economics after the physics of their time, as Mirowski pointed out in *More Heat than Light* (1989)? This timing might make sense, as it was then that the Industrial Revolution had taken place and machines had made their entry in Western life. Modernity had begun, so why not modernism?

Most accounts, however, locate the advent of modernism in the first two decades of the twentieth century. Virginia Woolf, also a member of the Bloomsbury group, is often cited for having observed, "On or about December 1910 human character changed" (Woolf 1967). You note the tongue in her cheek, but the observation stands. Indeed, it was around then that dance became modern (Woolf referred to the ballet of Diaghilev and Nijinsky), that Kandinsky painted his first abstract painting (at the end of 1910), and that Picasso showed his *Les Mademoiselles d'Avignon* (which he had painted in 1907). Also, Mondrian turned abstract around the same time.

Sure, we can go farther back and see the advent of modernism in the planning of cities like Chicago and Vienna in the late nineteenth century, point to Walras's 1874 *Elements of Pure Economics*. As a matter of fact (heeding the warning of Amariglio), we can discern modernist moments throughout history. Even so, the first few decades of the twentieth century were particularly dense with modernist manifestations. Frederic W. Taylor published his immensely influential book *The Principles of Scientific Management* in 1911 and Ford introduced the first assembly line in 1913. Life was changing. As Mondrian observed in 1919, "The cultivated man of today is gradually turning away from things, and life is becoming more and more abstract."

Economists took a little longer, the work of early modernists notwithstanding. Statistical, historical, and institutional studies continued to dominate their conversations. Only in the 1930s did the shift occur, when a new generation – mostly Americans and European immigrants – emerged. They woke up to the modernist Zeitgeist, embraced mathematics, began to write brief, mainly theoretical articles, developed the scientific statistical methods that would continue under the banner of econometrics, and claimed the economic conversation to be theirs. As Samuelson reminisced later: "Yes, 1932 was a great time to be born as an economist. The sleeping beauty of political economy was waiting for the enlivening kiss of new methods, new paradigms, new hired hands, and new problems" (Samuelson 1985).

Wrapping up modernism

Having read, studied, and thought a great deal about modernism inside and out-side the conversation of economists, I have drawn up the list of characteristics in Box 7.2.

Then the phase of late modernism sets in

The excitement would last for a while. When I was born into economics in the early 1970s, it was still palpable. Economics appeared to matter a great deal. The fate of the world depended on who was right, the Keynesians or the monetarists. Or did the Marxists have a claim to the ultimate truth with their critical analysis of capitalism? And what about the criticisms of the post-Keynesians? We were still enacting the great meta-narrative of the Enlightenment, imagining ourselves the incoming saviors of the world. It was understood that in order to do so we had to master *the* scientific methods. Modeling was the way to get to the truth. At least, that is how I experienced the atmosphere at the time.

Slowly but surely, the optimism left the profession. It is hard to say when and why it happened. Maybe it was the experiences of the 1970s and 1980s – the Viet-nam War, stagflation, the loss of faith in planning and subsequently in Keynesian remedies. Maybe it had to do with the increasing uncertainties that the phase of late modernity brought with the closure of factories, the increasing importance of information, the emergence of digital technology, and therewith the computer. Maybe it was a sense that the scientific method failed us. People read Kuhn and got the message that science, too, was subject to revolutions; they began to real-ize that scientific knowledge could be responsible for bad things as well, such as atom bombs and environmental destruction. Maybe it was the awareness that all the utopian and activist fervor had come to nothing. Disillusionment had set in. Those following my generation appeared to give up on politics, to settle down to the science without the ambition and illusion that they were going to change the world.

Again, economists were mimicking what went on elsewhere. In his little book, *What is Post-Modernism?*, Charles Jencks (1986) proposes that we label pop art, minimalism, and buildings such as the Centre de Pompidou "Late Modern." In all this artwork, the utopian fervor of the early modernists had dissipated. Andy Warhol's portrayal of Campbell soup highlighted the everyday and seemingly dispensed with any political or aesthetic message. Minimalist art, like the boxes of Donald Judd, was austere to the point of standing on its own. Gone was the meta-narrative in which modernist art was cast. Yet the methodological commit-ment to modernist strategies remained. As Jencks describes late modernist art, "in architecture it is pragmatic and technocratic in its social ideology and from 1960 takes many of the stylistic ideas and values of Modernism to an extreme in order to resuscitate a dull (or clichéd) language" (Jencks 1986: 35). Late mod-erns, according to Jencks, may have lost the original faith of moderns, but still practice much of what the moderns preached. Some, like Warhol, have tried to popularize their discourse, but many late moderns, especially the minimalist and conceptual artists, continue to operate for a select, well-informed audience. These artists construct "strange objects," fill a gallery with sand, throw a heap of cloth in the corner of a museum, that is, they do things that an amateur will find hard to understand. "The morality of Late Modernism consists in . . . integrity of invention and usage; like Clement Greenberg's defense of Modernist morality the work has to be judged as a hermetic, internally related world where the meanings are self-referential" (Jencks 1986: 39).

Jencks looked at the arts and at architecture. Look at economics and you see something similar. Lucas, Barro, and numerous other mathematically inclined economists adopted the scientific heuristics of Samuelson, Solow, and other Keynesians, and turned them against the Keynesian conclusions. Their economics would be more rigorous, more consistent, more principled than Keynesian economics; it would also stop being instrumental in terms of policy-making. All the fudging of Keynesians with assumptions about efficiency wages, sticky prices, and the like – necessary to account for consistent macroeconomic disequilibria – was banned by these renegades. To speak with Lyotard, they took "the stylistic ideas and values of Modernism to an extreme in order to resuscitate a dull (or clichéd) language."

Most critically, the late moderns among economists have given up on the grand meta-narrative. They do not practice science to change the world, or to improve it. If anything, they are ironic to the point of becoming cynics. They are adamant about their scientific approach while at the same time denying its practical relevance. There is the irony – strongly asserting something and at the same time denying its import. A late modern economist such as Lucas prefers to stay out of political discussions. Late moderns scoff at the idea of a planned economy, and distrust fellow economists who advise governments to intervene in the economy, arguing that economists do not know enough to know what to do. They become cynics when they say they do science "for the fun of it," "for the income," "because I'm good at it," or "because there's nothing better to do."

Late moderns also tend to be agnostic concerning the truth-value of their theories. Not that they say so openly. It shows in the jocular remarks that they make. In a seminar I attended some time ago, it was pointed out to the presenter that a crucial assumption appeared to be unrealistic. The presenter responded, "You're probably right, but who cares, it's all 'as if' anyway, and the model is fun," at which everyone laughed. Frank Hahn was exceptionally honest when he wrote, "On the final truth of economics I am completely agnostic. Until such truth is unequivocally revealed I hold all coherent theorizing as worthy of attention and respect" (Hahn 1984: 18). When I spoke with him a few years later, he advised me to do serious economics, like the economics he was doing. Is that irony?

Disappearing acts

In other fields, there is much talk of the implosion of modernism. Post-modernists especially like to make that claim. They mean to say that modernist structures do not explode by means of an outside force but implode by destruction from within. They can refer to the efforts of late moderns. It could be argued, for example, that Andy Warhol erased the distinction between high art and popular art, a distinction that the modernists were so keen on. Minimalists took the modernist strategies to such austerity that they alienated the public. In economics something similar seemed to happen. At the hands of the late moderns it would become more austere, more bare, more hard-core, and, as some critics charged, more autistic. All kinds of characteristics of the (early) modernist conversations disappeared, such as the following.

Box 7.2 Eight characteristics of modernism

- *Problematization of representation.* Appearances deceive: reality is not what it seems to be or as it presents itself. When appearances deceive, the representation of reality becomes a problem (cf. physics, Marx, Freud).

- *Exploration of the invariant structure of reality while recognizing its ephemeral appearance.* To highlight the problem of representation, some modernists want to express "the transient, the fleeting, the contingent." Others are intent on exploring and determining the fundamental, invariant structure that underlies the appearances.

- *Predilection for formal, reductionistic, and axiomatic representations.* For those looking for the invariant, the preferred languages are logic, geometry, and mathematics; the dominant heuristic prescribes the development of formal systems from a minimal set of axioms, at least some of which concern the characteristics of the most basic units of the system (particles, individual decision-makers).

- *The machine as a dominant root metaphor.* The machine suggests the possibility of perfection and control. As such, it answers the ideal of a better life.

- *A break with history.* Commitment to the new calls for liberation from tradition. The future, not the past, should determine the present (cf. the avant-garde, the shock of the new, the bulldozer).

- *The turn inwards.* The medium becomes the issue. The significant audience comprises the initiated, the insiders, that is, colleagues and knowledgeable critics. Much of modernist work is self-referential and reflexive. One implication is the

> distinction between highbrow and lowbrow, that is, the
> distinction between academic art (economics) and popular
> art (economics). Another implication is the professionalization
> of the arts and sciences, and the departmentalization of their
> instruction in universities.
>
> - *The square versus the circle*. Modernism operates in both
>   the square and the circle. The square is the domain of the
>   scientific, the circle of the therapeutic. The sharp distinction of
>   the square and the circle in modernist consciousness accounts
>   for a basic tension within modernism. It is responsible for the
>   gulf that separates the humanities and the sciences in modern
>   academia, as well as professional and personal life in general.
> - *Endorsement of the Enlightenment meta-narrative*. Modernists
>   seek to overcome historical and cultural barriers in the search
>   for universal truth, peace, or a better world, or all three.
>
> You can do with this list whatever you please. You may consider it a
> modernist ploy to nail down what modernism is all about, or take it for
> what it is – a list. Criticize it and make a better list; use it to reflect on what
> you have experienced yourself and make up your own mind, or ignore
> it. But whatever you do, please note how preoccupied modernists are
> with the problem of representation, how much store they put in square
> reasoning, how attached they are to machine-like metaphors (as in
> transmission and price mechanism, calculated behavior), how hard-
> nosed they are when it comes to their methodology, and how idealistic
> they are in the end, imagining how their scientific efforts will contribute
> to a better world. Question: How much of a modernist are you? Your
> teachers? Your colleagues?

The human subject

Even though economists like to tell outsiders (students included) that their science is about humans making choices, there are no humans in modernist and late
modernist models, nor is there choice. The neoclassical account portrays Max U,
a genderless, silent, asocial, unemotional calculator intent on solving constrained
maximization problems with algorithms that are mathematically demanding.
Early modernists like Hicks and Samuelson began to eliminate the psychological content of economic agents (to reduce the circle); now the portrayal of the
economic agent is entirely abstract and looks nothing like any human you or I
know. Economic agents have become mathematical entities. They do not choose,

either, unless the choice of a suboptimal outcome is considered an option. Max U does not fret between plausible alternatives as we all so often do; it does not face existential choices, it merely solves constrained maximization problems.

Macroeconomics as a subject

The early modernists installed macroeconomics as a separate subject from microeconomics. The idea was that the study of the economy as a whole required special methods, like the multiplier analysis and the Phillips curve. New classical economists used the modernist techniques to show that macroeconomics was nothing but microeconomics writ large. We still teach macroeconomics as a separate subject, but that will end if it is up to the late moderns.

Prediction as a goal

Modernists saw predictive accuracy as the test of serious scientific theories. Late moderns have given up on that. They simulate, do time-series analyses, and estimate parameters but, in doing so, do not test theories.

Theory in empirical work

This follows from the previous disappearing act. By abandoning the attempts to test theories, lots of empirical work dispenses with economic theory. You can analyze time-series of the money supply and national income, for example, without modeling their interaction. Likewise, you can do experiments with only vague reference to the theory of economics. The number crunching will do.

Empirical backing in theoretical work

A majority of articles dispense with empirical work altogether. They present a competitive-equilibrium model or a new iteration of a non-cooperative game without even bothering about references to the real world or to economic data.

The disappearance of history

Whereas modernists were interested in the history of their discipline as well as economic history, that interest is waning. The teaching of either history of economic thought or economic history has all but disappeared from the graduate curriculum. History has gone.

The disappearance of conventional economic subjects like markets and government policies

More and more articles discuss non-economic topics such as the relationship between abortion and crime, addiction, marriage. The outsider will wonder where the economy is in all those topics. Is economics dissolving itself as a separate discipline to become a social science?

The disappearance of political ambitions

A modernist article typically ended with a declaration of the political implications of its analysis. That habit is disappearing. Economics is increasingly done for its own sake.

So where is contemporary economics?

David Ruccio and Jack Amariglio see, in their book entitled *Postmodern Moments in Modern Economics* (2003), postmodern moments in modern economics. They see them in the disappearing acts, in particular the decentering of the subject (as they prefer to call the disappearance of the human subject), the loss of the credulity of the meta-narrative of progress and emancipation, and the plurality of economic approaches that make up contemporary economics. So have economic conversations entered the postmodernist phase or, better put, have postmodern moments come to dominate them? I beg to differ from the assessment of Ruccio and Amariglio. To show why, we need to look at what postmodernism stands for.

Have you ever come to believe that movies are more real than real life? Have you ever considered Bruce Willis, Sean Connery, or Harrison Ford actual heroes? Have you lost faith in a better world, in the possibility of eradicating poverty and hunger and cleaning up the environment? Do you believe in a borderless world, the end of the nation-state, the multicultural society, the end of politics, the end of history, the end of ideologies, the fakeness of life? If any of these apply, you may attribute to yourself postmodern sensibilities.

Postmodern architects, for example, try to upset the standards of modernist architecture. They like to mix styles, say combining modern constructions with classical facades or adding pillars and superfluous decorations. They delight in weird buildings, especially when they are temporary or when one of their roofs (what bliss!) caves in. Postmodern artists deny art its special status and do performances in public spaces with no traceable signs, copy old masters and present the result as if it were authentic, post their ideas on the Internet, and make installations that self-destruct. Postmodern expressions make boundaries disappear, like those between art and non-art, science and non-science, nations and ethnic groups. Postmodernism makes you think of fragmentation, pluralism, deconstruction, pastiche, simulations, and simulacra (imitations that are presented for real; see, for example, Baudrillard 1988). Postmodernism is also anti-humanist by denying the "I" its central place in the universe and with that its autonomy and integrity; it stresses context and flux – everything depends on everything else, everything has only meaning in context, everything is always changing. In science, you recognize postmodern moments in the denial of a fixed truth. Remember the postmodernist umpire of Chapter 5: "They ain't nothin' 'til I calls 'em." All knowledge is a social construction; facts are artifacts, too. Scientific knowledge has no firm foundations and therefore no privileged status. You see, if you have any modernist fibers left in your body, the postmodernist world looks chaotic, undisciplined, weird, disturbing, and offensive.

So how dominant are the postmodernist moments in contemporary economics? I recognize them in the various disappearing acts, in the fascination for theories with little or no application, in the theoretical exercises for theory's sake. I recognize them in the theorizing of chaos and of complex systems insofar as such theorizing leaves practical people clueless about what to do and what to make of this world, this economy. I recognize them in the loosening of neoclassical norms, the idea of multiple selves, and the playfulness of some articles (ever wonder what the deadweight loss of Christmas shopping is?). Amariglio and Ruccio also stress the theorizing of the uncertainties of economic life as in Keynes and Shackle. Also postmodern is the game-theoretic model that does not have a solution, or the assertion that the economy is too complex to know how to influence its course. There are quite a few postmodern moments to be discerned in contemporary economics.

Yet I doubt that the postmodern moments are so dominant that we can speak of a postmodern phase in economics. Notice for example the hermetic force of what heterodox economists call orthodox economics. Still dominant is the emphasis on mathematical modeling; contemporary economics is more than ever about technique, about axioms and lemmas. Hard-nosed attitudes prevail. The *Journal of Economic Perspectives* notwithstanding, there are no plural perspectives in economics, at least not according to the economic establishment. Never before have heterodox economists been so marginalized. If you do history, political economy, radical economics, institutional economics, interpretative economics (as in interpreting what economic subjects say and think), you stand no chance of getting a job in standard economic departments. So much for plurality and the postmodern credo, "Let a thousand flowers bloom."

When orthodox economists maintain that their way of doing economics is scientific and all the other ways are not, I hear modernists or late modernists (depending on whether they believe in the contribution of their science to human progress or not). And when they are not explicit, they show the (late) modern spirit by keeping out all the "softies" and hiring only hard-nosed people with even better mathematical skills than they have themselves.

So where does that leave the economic conversations?

Frankly, the current state is worrisome. Although I doubt that an outburst of postmodern sensibilities will be beneficial (I am already dreading the deconstructivist performances that have come to dominate literary and philosophical scholarship), late modernist economics is aloof from interested in finding out about and making sense of economic processes. To students' big questions – "Where is society heading?," "The effects of globalization?," "The digital revolution?," "The gap between rich and poor parts of the world?," "Economic institutions?" – economic courses remain mute. The running conversation is not equipped to deal with them, at least not in its axiomatic terms. When given a chance, students opt for something practical such as business economics, or something fashionable such as communication or media studies. At European universities, business faculties are crowding out economics faculties. At American universities, economic faculties still hold out because many do not allow undergraduates to major in business, so they have to take general economics as the next best alternative. Foreigners who do not loathe the math take a rapidly increasing share of graduate school slots. Late modernist conversation appears to be pricing itself out of the market.

My postmodern sensibility is sufficiently developed to refrain from predictions. What do I know? I know only that the current situation will not last and that changes are imminent. That is easy to say, for no current situation lasts. That much this chapter has made clear. Who knows, the future may be with theories of complexity and chaos. Maybe econometrics will turn obsolete as advanced computer programs do the empirical work for us. Maybe behavioral economics will take over to kill off Max U and its obsession with constrained maximization. Maybe history will make a reappearance. Who knows?

I myself hold out for the reemergence of classical moments in the economic conversation. That would mean a reassessment of the importance of values and virtues, of traditions, and of interpretative approaches. This neo-Aristotelian or neotraditionalist approach, as I like to call it, harks back to Aristotle, Adam Smith, and classical institutionalists like Commons. You may note a few neo-Aristotelian moments in this text if you look for them, but this is not the place to propagate another economics. That requires another book. If you realize how modernism and its later variants have manifested in the conversations of economists, and how relative each approach really is, I have succeeded in making my point.

Further reading

When you want to know more about the changes of the economic conversation, numerous sources exist in the rich literature on the history of economic thought. Robert Heilbroner's *The Worldly Philosophers* (Touchstone, 1953) continues to be a classic primer. Should you want to delve deeper, a comprehensive survey such as Blaug's *Economic Theory in Retrospect* (Cambridge University Press, 1997) is a good start. Nothing replaces the reading of the originals. Read Adam Smith's *The Wealth of Nations* (Norton, 1987 [1776]) and you realize how differently that text reads from what is written now. Read Hicks's *Value and Capital* (Oxford University Press, 1975 [1939]) and Samuelson's *Foundations of Economic Analysis* (Harvard University Press, 1947) and you will watch the making of modern economics. *The General Theory of Employment, Interest and Money* by Keynes (Macmillan, 1936) will tell you why he is not really a modernist economist as Samuelson is.

The writings of Phil Mirowski, in particular *More Heat than Light* (Cambridge University Press, 1989) and *Machine Dreams* (Cambridge University Press, 2001), and E. Roy Weintraub's *How Economics Became a Mathematical Science*

(Duke University Press, 2002) take you to the roots of modern economics. They make for difficult reading but the work is worth it.

For a general introduction into the themes of modernism and late postmodernism, I recommend:

- Jean-François Lyotard's *The Postmodern Condition: A Report on Knowledge* (University of Minnesota Press, 1984);
- David Harvey's *The Condition of Postmodernity* (Basil Blackwell, 1990);
- Charles Jencks's *Modern Movements in Architecture* (Anchor Press, 1973);
- Charles Jencks's *What is Post-Modernism?* (St. Martin's Press, 1986);
- Stephen Kern's *The Culture of Time and Space* (Cambridge University Press, 1983);
- Anson Rabinbach's *The Human Motor* (Basic Books, 1990);
- Carl E. Schorske's *Fin-de-Siècle Vienna* (Vintage Press, 1981);
- Steven Connor's *Postmodernist Culture* (Basil Blackwell, 1989).

There is a great deal more but these books are good for a start.

Ruccio and Amariglio provide the most exhaustive accounts of modernist and postmodernist moments in economics in their book *Postmodern Moments in Modern Economics* (Princeton University Press, 2003). They will tell you in what respect my account differs from theirs. Deirdre McCloskey addresses and tackles modernist economics in her *Rhetoric of Economics* (University of Wisconsin Press, 1998 [1985]).

8 How and why everyday conversations differ from academic ones and how and why academic conversations clash with political ones

Introducing gaps

What good does all the modernist and late modernist writing in economics do? And why should you, a non-economist, care? I sympathize with such questions – especially when economists themselves have become ironic and cynical about the relevance of their science. When the belief that economic models matter for policy-making has been displaced by the belief that economists do better keeping their discipline to themselves, all the money spent on economics benefits . . . whom?

The questions and confusion arise because practicing economists face two more gaps in addition to the epistemological gap with reality and the rhetorical gap with other minds. The one between academic economics and everyday life is more like a canyon. Non-economists are too easily frustrated with economists and economists are too easily upset about the denseness of non-economists. The emotions that this gap brings about signal that it is not well understood. It makes economists vulnerable to questions about their relevance and meaning. The other (related) gap concerns the divide between academic economics and the political world. Here, too, emotions on both sides get intense.

A common way of dealing with these gaps is to ignore them; academicians are especially fond of this. But that doesn't bridge anything or eliminate mutual frustration. Another approach is to get indignant about the other side and call it stupid. It is not a very convincing strategy, as we shall see. Another – the one I will pursue – is to face them, to try to understand why they occur and realize that they are inevitable. Then, perhaps, figure out how to cope with them.

The stupidity problem

Get indignant about the gap and you step into the "stupidity trap" (with thanks to McCloskey for the name). Everyday people standing on the other side of the everyday gap will charge that academic economists are stupid for their inability to predict, their disagreements, and their incomprehensible econospeak. To them economists are *weltfremd* – not of this world, aloof. One consequence of this popular view is that journalists shun academic economists when they need commentary on economic news. They prefer to speak to "economists" working for an investment bank or the White House because they deliver plainspoken messages about the economy, such as "It's going up [down]."

On the other side stand economists eager to return the compliment. They scoff at unscientific economists who, in addressing the press, "dumb down" economics. Paul Krugman, an academic who actually does well in the popular press, speaks disparagingly of "up-and-down" economists. He does not use those words but obviously thinks them rather stupid, certainly unscientific, and, for that matter, dishonest. Deirdre McCloskey gets indignant about what she calls "ersatz economics," the everyday economics that non-economists (sometimes handsomely) get by with (McCloskey 1990). She particularly targets brokers and business economists for claiming they can "read" the economy when they know they cannot. "They're selling snake-oil," she charges. You hear her wondering why sensible people fall for it. Are they that stupid?

The frustration on the side of academic economists comes especially to the surface after a government stint. They complain about the economic illiteracy of congress, the irrationality of government programs, the superficiality of the decision-making process, the dominance of lawyers (who seem to get a far better hearing), and a chronic lack of attention to economic arguments. Krugman cannot lash out enough at the inclination of politicians to believe soothsayers and go for the latest hype, such as supply-side economics, which promises reduced deficits after major tax cuts, or strategic trading, which calls for a (hopeless) interventionist trade policy. Similarly, when businesspeople show exasperation with academic economists for the vagueness and ambiguity of their pronouncements, academic economists turn around and declare them ignorant, irrational, devoid of economic sense, and clueless about basic economic principles.

Now and then economists or economic journalists conduct surveys to test the economic knowledge of politicians, businesspeople, and people on the street. The results invariably show that they all know little about economic matters. They do not know how money is created, how large the government deficit is, or how it differs from the government debt. They cannot distinguish a government deficit from a foreign deficit, have no notion of opportunity costs, and confuse productivity with production. They believe that someone has to lose in a trade, that international trade is a war or a competition between nations, that big business is getting ever bigger, and that the sucking sound coming out of Asian countries is the sound of domestic jobs disappearing. Much more economic nonsense thrives among them.

The remedy is, of course, more economic teaching at school, more economics students in colleges, and more economics in the news – in short, more work for economists. If only people would listen more to economists.

Then again, economists must admit, the teaching does not go over easily. Even after taking students through the four semesters of macro and micro (and assorted other econ courses), teachers find that many of them simply do not get it. How stupid can they be? In the meantime some students wonder what all these models are good for as they surely do not help to make sense of their lives. Most give up on economics because, really now, could it be more stupid?

The gaps – need I emphasize? – are real.

Box 8.1 A story

Caroline went into the store to buy laundry detergent. Coming out, she was confronted by a lean man whom she knew vaguely from some social occasion.

"Do you want to know what you just did?"

"I'm not sure but it looks like you're going to tell me anyway."

"You engaged in a market transaction; you operated in a market for – let's see what you have there – laundry detergent. You furthermore maximized your preferences under certain constraints."

" I didn't maximize anything and I don't think I'm constrained. I bought detergent."

"That's not what I mean. Think of it this way – you have certain preferences. You like some things more than others, don't you?"

"Sure," said Caroline, wondering now how to end this useless conversation. "Well, think of it," the man said patiently, "given those preferences, understanding what you just did requires thinking about your income and looking at the price of what you bought."

"Hmm, I never thought of it that way," replied Caroline, focusing on a leather-jacketed guy in the background who was fiddling with his grocery cart so he could eavesdrop. Recognizing his opportunity, he called out, "Hey, I'm an economist, too. Why are you listening to him? We're victims of this consumer society – just look around this hideous shopping plaza," he cried, waving his arms all around. "What do you think goes on here? We're being manipulated by the people who own it."

As the lean economist was bestowing a disdainful look of irritation upon him, another bystander offered, "Well, how about her social background – shouldn't we take into account her environment, which made her what she is now? Assuming constant preferences, we ignore that altogether." "Right," a woman added, "and then think of her psychological state. There's a cognitive issue here. Tell me," she turned to Caroline, "why did you buy the large box?" "Because bigger is cheaper, isn't it?" she replied sheepishly, embarrassed now by the melee that had broken out around her. "But you see," the woman continued, "we've found that most people can't or don't calculate the best price. Dividing numbers is too great a problem and therefore they operate by rules of thumb." She looked defiantly at the lean one. Shouting (politely) to overcome the noise of the crowd, he shot back, "But that's an information problem! People learn soon enough." Leather-jacket yelled, "That's so naive!"

People started to talk through each other. Caroline slowly edged out of the crowd. "I don't belong with these people," she said to no one in particular, "and I don't want to."

Epilogue

"Nice story but irrelevant," said the economist. "We don't intend to explain Caroline's behavior. The utility-maximizing model is – to speak with McCloskey – just a metaphor. We use it because it gives good results."

"What about the psychologist, the sociologist?"

"I don't know and I don't particularly care. I don't keep up with what they do. We do our thing, let them do theirs."

"But don't you see that what you're saying doesn't make sense? You're not getting your point across."

"It's a matter of translation. If I talk in plain English, people will understand."

"And did they?"

"Maybe I should speak more slowly."

The gap with everyday economics

Economists operate on the tenth floor

To clear up the stupidity problem and see what the gap with everyday economics stands for, we go back to the "conversation" metaphor and its sister "rhetoric." All you need to see is that economists are involved in a conversation that differs from the conversations others are involved in. The differences do not make mutual understanding impossible, but nearly so.

The differences escape the solution of a simple translation. "People buy less when the price goes up" is quite different from writing "$\delta q/\delta p < 0$". To appreciate the latter expression a mathematical mindset helps. And that makes for an immeasurable difference. (Some economists would prefer that this book came in equations for easier reading.) The gaps are rhetorical, and separate the two worlds – socially as well. It is not a matter of translation – of transposing a piece of information to the other side in a digestible form – because that piece of information will be taken out of context and stripped of meanings that made it so meaningful in the original conversation. When economists talk about markets they have a different, more complex, understanding of what that concept means (associating it with general equilibrium, elasticities, *ceteris paribus* conditions, Pareto optimum, stability conditions, and so on) from everyday people. The latter will think of profit, freedom, greed, big business, and the like. Accordingly, it is the conversation that matters, and that entity is not easily transposed.

To understand the academic position and make it seem less stupid, it helps to imagine academic economics high up in a building. There the world looks different; the perspective changes and the talk adjusts accordingly. Judging economists from the ground floor up is pointless. To judge that conversation high up you need to enter it and that takes a while, a few years at least, and preferably graduate study. Figure 8.1 makes the point.

We all live out on the street where we are busy getting from A to B. There we live our everyday lives. Most of the time we do pretty well going from A to B and get along fine just talking with others who are more or less doing the same

---

Box 8.2 The embarrassment of the Nobel Prize for economics (a.k.a. direct translation distortion)

A highly embarrassing moment usually follows a new Nobel Prize-winning economist being asked, "What for?" I remember Franco Modigliani on the morning news. He was in his dressing gown because in the US the news comes through very early. When asked what he had invented, he said something like: "Well . . . uhm . . . I had this idea that people save for the future." James Tobin told the reporter of public radio that *his* great idea was that people, when investing their money, "do not put all their eggs in one basket." You could hear the reporter's gasp. "Is that it?" "Yes, more or less, that's it," Tobin responded. When James Buchanan explained that he got the prize for the insight that politicians pursue their own interests just like everyone else, Mike Royko, a columnist, claimed half the prize because it had been his insight, too.

Bob Solow anticipated the risk of directly translating his Nobel Prize-winning idea. He explained on public radio that he had the idea that technological development was responsible for a great part of economic growth but, he continued, the challenge was to put that in the form of an economic model. He told the story of how he was playing with some formula while in a doctor's waiting room, and right there and then, it struck him how to do it.

Direct translations of Nobel Prize-winning ideas sound silly. They need context to make them meaningful – the context of the academic conversation, as Solow tried to make clear with his story.

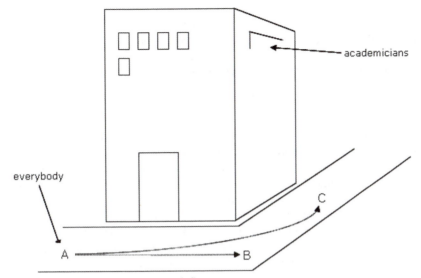

Figure 8.1 Economists live on the tenth floor

thing. Academics also operate on the street since they, like everybody else, live an everyday life. But when they do their academic thing, they go up to the tenth floor, far away from the hustle and bustle of everyday life, to have another conversation, an academic conversation, wondering how and why street life is the way it is.

Because of the distance, the academic conversation is of no immediate use for the street life. Our Caroline in the story has no need to be bothered with what is discussed up there on the tenth floor. Only when people in their everyday life start wondering "Why?" and "How so?" may they develop an interest in what academics have to say. From the tenth floor the perspective is different. Who knows, people may realize looking down that they could just as well traverse to C instead of B, or stay at A. The academic conversation is, in that case, a source that life on the street can draw from. It is not that the academics will tell them how to get to B. Even though physicists may know how we keep our balance on a bike – not by balancing but by turning to make a large circle and causing centrifugal force to push us upright – they have no idea how to actually ride a bike unless they learn it themselves out on the street.

The street requires *phronesis*, practical knowledge; the tenth floor provides *theoria*, abstract and usually general knowledge. *Sophia*, wisdom, is reserved for those who are able to combine theoria and phronesis.

The point is that economists are not stupid for not knowing how to get from A to B, or for being unable to predict what people will find in C. Their conversation is not about how to make money, how to manage a business or an economy, or about predicting the future of interest and exchange rates. Nor is the conversation privileged in the sense that they have a unique claim on the truth, one that they and only they, the scientists, know. They may have ideas about "why" but are more than likely unable to show "how," impractical as most academics tend to be.

The picture with the tenth floor helps to defuse mistaken expectations of my audience when I give a lecture with academic content. I do not want them to think that I will have the answers for them, the practitioners. They may know much better than I how to get from A to B but maybe I have an insight for them, a concept or an idea that compels them to reevaluate what they are doing.

Nor are non-economists stupid

On the ground, on the other side of the everyday gap, the world looks different. It is the lifeworld, the world as experienced by everyday people living everyday lives. They have to get from A to B and, although they may do so routinely and habitually, now and then they pause or are asked to reflect on what they are doing. And this reflection will show that everybody has a theory about the economy.

Everyone is a practitioner of everyday economics, including economists. Those who have not studied economics (roughly 99.99999 percent of humankind) may have the delusion that they do not know any economics. True enough, their everyday economics may be simple, implicit, barely articulated, and fickle, but it exists. No one can live without beliefs about the economy.

Ask, for example, for the reaction of your companions to the beggar who awaits you after you have enjoyed dinner at a good restaurant and they reveal their economics. If the reaction is an irritated mutter ("Why doesn't he do something instead of bothering me?"), the implied economics is one of faith in the economic system: "Markets work. There are opportunities for anyone interested in grabbing them." A reaction of guilt and embarrassment betrays the liberal or Keynesian belief that the system is flawed: "Markets work, but not always. We should do something about poverty." A radical reaction is directed at the (capitalist) system for bringing about such "obscene inequalities." The conservative reaction, too, could be directed against the system, but with the government as the target "for creating programs that dull incentive." Each of these responses resonates with perspectives that are held among academic economists. The latter will have more to offer in terms of arguments, empirical tests, and numbers but the core beliefs are the same. (Incidentally, how do *you* react to the beggar?)

Everyday economics shows up everywhere. When parking fees at work go up, people deliberate the causes. Is it a power play by the employer? The reflection of rising prices everywhere? Or a socially motivated move to encourage public transportation? When people lose a job, they need to understand why. Is the problem with them, the management, the president, or foreign competition? When a female employee is passed up for promotion in favor of a less qualified male and then sues the company, she recognizes that the problem is bigger than she is, and market competition is not going to solve it (as some academic economists would have her believe). In each case the final reading tells about everyday economics.

Everyday economics shows up most expressly in markets. Buying and selling involves an assessment of market conditions. That requires the application of some economic model or another. People entering the housing market form expectations of interest rates and housing prices months (or years) hence. Whether they are serious economists or not, they have to ponder economic issues such as demand and supply, the economic strength of the area ("When foreign competition kills the regional industry, unemployment will go up, demand for houses will go down and down goes the value of my house"), actions of the monetary authorities ("Will they continue to drive down short-term interest rates and, if so, will long-term rates be affected?"), developments in the foreign exchange market ("high foreign rates may drive up domestic rates") and so on. Buyers of frozen orange juice apply economics when they figure that freezing weather in Florida will increase its price. When people assess the remuneration for a job they have to "read" the market ("Thirty-seven thousand is the best I can offer," or "Ten dollars an hour should be enough for housecleaning"). "Reading" markets is the livelihood of traders in financial markets. Much activity is the result of a different reading of the market condition, or a different everyday economics.

Everyday economics makes for good business. Brokers sell their readings of markets ("Ameritech will be a winner with the Japanese slacking off"), as do economic consultants and economic advisors. Sales clerks make a living because they have a story to tell. So do entrepreneurs who persuade partners, venture capitalists, bankers, government officials, and workers that there is a market with great opportunity for profit. Apparently, people need some coherent story to justify their expensive houses, their exorbitant salaries, and the Ameritech stock in their portfolios – and thus they are willing to pay those who sell them a version of everyday economics. Caroline (of our story) undoubtedly has a rationale for what she did in the store; it simply is not the one that the economist tried to sell her. People do make sense of their lives and do so in ways that help them cope.

Even economists do not use their scientific accounts to cope with everyday life. Robert Lucas, a distinguished economist and a purist in his theorizing, concedes that the econospeak stops at the threshold of his house:

> In my house we don't use words like "marginal" everyday. I don't find the language of economics to be useful to think about individual decision problems. I also don't use economic principles at home. I never pay my children to do their jobs. I try to use family loyalty or an exchange system; you help me, I'll help you.
>
> (Klamer 1983: 48)

This becomes understandable when we recognize the differences between academic and everyday economics better.

Everyday economics is different

The metaphors and models are different

When economists ask students (who are still wedded to everyday economics) to study the problem of unemployment, their first inclination is to search newspapers for what seem to be relevant articles. When asked to do independent research they are likely to collect numbers or look into the history of unemployment. Academic economists, on the other hand, will first try to find an aspect of the problem that the academic literature has not considered and then construct a model or design an empirical test around it.

The difference here is metaphorical. Where everyday economists tend to "constitute" the economy *as if* it were a historical process, academic economists are wont to think of the economy *as if* it were a mechanical or stochastic system that can be captured in diagrams and mathematical equations.

Everyday economic rhetoric, although crowded with metaphors, is without explicitly articulated models. Economic journalists use metaphors primarily to embellish and clarify the exposition. "Time is money," one of many popular metaphors, is not a model and, as economists know, is too imprecise to be expanded into one. Models are deemed intolerable in everyday discourse. When journalists get a chance, they say so, apparently perceiving that they should disavow this (crucial) element of academic rhetoric to demonstrate affinity with their readers.

This is not to say that everyday discussions of economics are without models entirely. Boynton and Deissenberg (1987) have shown that the model is implicit in journalist reporting to be distilled from the endless "stories." They conclude that "the 'implicit' model is one most economists would recognize as falling within the 'canon'" (ibid: 135). What they mean is that the implicit model of journalists roughly resembles the bastard Keynesian model, with disposable income as the prime mover of consumption and investment mainly explained by interest rates and current production. Although this model may resemble the canon of introductory economic textbooks, it is far from the macroeconomic models that grace the pages of today's academic journals. The journalistic model does not make explicit, for example, the rationality of agents, and ignores altogether the rational expectations hypothesis (which is standard in academic models), not to speak of complex systems and Nash equilibria. Journalistic accounts are also imprecise in causal relationships. Their theory is usually presented in a blanket statement such as "because of the projection of an increased federal deficit, interest rates are expected to rise." Conditionals are scarce. We might say that their theory is sketchy or impressionistic.

Reporting has its fashions and theoretical biases. I distinguish various distinct perspectives in the way journalist report the economic news. (A nice assignment for class: take any newspaper article on an economic issue and determine which perspective it represents. Please motivate.)

In a serious study of a series of newspapers for their reporting of the economic news, I found a dominance of the *Keynesian perspective*, with emphasis on expenditures (consumption, investment, government spending, and net exports) and the belief that government intervention affects macroeconomic trends. (And this was after the surge of interest in conservative, free market economics.) A strict Keynesian perspective is often expanded with a psychological component, in which case consumer confidence, the mood of purchasing agents, or the feelings of CEOs – factors absent in most academic models – are highlighted. Psychology also prevails in the reporting of financial markets, which can be "frantic," "jittery," "bullish," "nervous," or "calm." Even if academic rhetoric relegates psychology to the realm of non-science, everyday rhetoric appears to be full of it. And that makes for a significant difference.

A *monetarist perspective* stresses financial factors, in particular the money supply. It was dominant in the late 1970s and early 1980s – reporters would wait outside the Federal Reserve each Friday afternoon to snatch the latest money supply figures just before Wall Street closed. The perspective that draws the financial sector into the foreground is related. In that case financial figures dominate the news, the lead being the latest news about the stock markets, interest rates, and exchange rates. This perspective gets little credit in academic circles as few economists see the financial sector as critical (a fall on Wall Street may have little effect on the real economy), but it does make for good stories with lots of drama and excitement.

During the 1980s the *Wall Street Journal perspective* became dominant. Inspired by the stuff of the *Journal*'s editorial pages, it focuses on the supply side of the economy, that is, on entrepreneurial efforts (or the curtailing thereof), incentives to work and save, technology, and the importance of tax and budget cuts. This is also the perspective that celebrates markets and depicts government as the villain with the black hat, the antagonist in stories of abuse and excess – $500 toilet seats and all that. The pervasiveness of this shows in the generous attention awarded to CEOs, venture capitalists, and other business leaders. The presumption is that, as apparent movers and shakers of the economic process, knowing about their feelings and motivations tells us something about where the economy is heading.

Quite prominent in everyday economics is the *Aristotelian perspective*. I call it so because, like Aristotle, everyday economists tend to perceive the economy as a moral order in which people are selfish or caring, salaries are right or wrong (i.e., deserved or not), and nations do good or bad. But morals may change. In the 1980s, journalists saw CEOs' fantastic salaries as signs of success and reason for admiration. At the turn of this century, they use the same story to tell about greed and abuse. Sometimes newspapers tell how good free trade is, how wonderful it is that the EU eliminated barriers, that NAFTA was implemented, and that countries like China are become important trading partners. But, possibly under pressure of the various pro and con globalists, disapproving stories referencing such things as the power of big business and the fate of farmers in Poland appear more frequently. The media contribute to deliberations about the good and bad in contemporary economy. Economists may dismiss these deliberations but everyday people, needing to make sense of their world, buy into them wholeheartedly.

Everyday economics has more – and a more dramatic – narrative

The good and bad is best discussed and shown in the form of stories. And journalists write them because everyday economics revolves around stories rather than metaphors. Everyday economists prefer to think in terms of "what happened, who did what, and why," and that is what journal articles try to tell. According to

William Blundell of the *Wall Street Journal*, the common demand of readers everywhere is: "For Pete's sake, make it interesting. Tell me a *story*" (Blundell 1988: xii). He lists the following ingredients that make a good story, in order of importance: "(a) dogs, followed by other cute animals and well-behaved small children, (b) people/actors, (c) facts, (d) people/observers, (e) numbers." He warns that observers (academic and expert economists) should be used sparingly; the story characters make far better copy. The point is to create the sense that something dramatic is happening.

How undramatic academic stories are by comparison. They lack characters that people can relate to. They bore outsiders. Their characters are academic economists who, troubled by some anomaly or another, go through some complicated technical analysis and end happily with a result. But consider the plots and characters of everyday narratives: markets take nosedives, presidents mess up, bankers cheat the public, entrepreneurs are driven by animal spirits, rich magnates commit suicide, world-changing power brokers get caught, consumers lose confidence, union officials are angry, inflation is destroying the economy, Chinese toes are stepping on American heels in the economic race, and the Europeans take on the Americans in another round of their trade war. In such descriptions the economy emerges as a human drama, complete with villains and heroes. The actors in this action drama affect the course of events and it thus makes sense to blame presidents (bankers, unions, managers, foreigners) for economic woes. In contrast, academic accounts lack villains and heroes; they are about market imperfections and other systemic failures.

Everyday economics is anthropomorphic when it presents the economy as growing in strength, suffering, or recovering. It often visualizes the economy as a very large household, as Aristotle did. Adam Smith liked to make the comparison as well, noting, for example, "What is prudence in the conduct of every private family can hardly be folly in that of a great kingdom" (Smith 1987 [1776]: 478). Smith and other classical economists made the analogy explicit by speaking of "political economy" when considering it as a whole, reading "economy" in its original meaning as *nomos* (rule) of the *oikos* (house). Marshall, in an attempt to make economics a scientific subject, dropped the adjective "political."

The bias toward story in everyday economics entails a moral bias and feeds the Aristotelian perspective. When students are asked to comment on the differential between the salaries for doctors and nurses they will invariably compare responsibilities and hours spent on the job. In other words, they assess the salary differential based on what people deserve. Academic economics, on the contrary, "demoralizes" the phenomenon of the salary difference by discussing it in terms of demand and supply, investment in human capital, and possibly the monopoly of the medical profession.

Because of its predilection for drama, everyday economics is filled with terms such as conflict, power, war, exploitation. In everyday economics foreign trade becomes war; the Japanese and the Americans are engaged in an economic conflict; minorities are exploited; business is about power. Academic language expunges these terms or disarms them. The term "conflict," for example, could not until recently be used in any meaningful way in neoclassical economics. That has changed with the emergence of game theory, which analyzes the rational responses to conflictual situations. The difference, however, is that the mention of conflict in everyday economics is intended to get the audience angry, whereas in academic economics it poses an intriguing theoretical problem.

The academic version of everyday economics, having been stripped of its drama, makes everyday life uninteresting. And perhaps unlivable. People need stories to give coherence to their actions. Even economists need stories to make sense of what they do themselves. Accordingly, everyday economics serves a different purpose from the one of academic economics. If we leave for a moment the purpose of the latter, the purpose of everyday economics is to make sense of what people do every day and to motivate them to do things one way rather than another way. In his *Collected Writings*, Keynes points out:

> To avoid being in the position of Buridan's ass, we fall back, therefore, and necessarily do so, on motives of another kind, which are not "rational," in the sense of being concerned with the evaluation of consequences, but are decided by habit, instinct, preference, desire, will, etc.
>
> (Keynes 1978: 294)

And where habit, instinct, preference, desire, and will rule, everyday economics is the conversation to have. It represents not stupidity but the sound way to act. This will not prevent people from saying and thinking silly things, but the decision to do so comes from the context of everyday economics.

Ye who are without sin, throw the first stone

When others are operating in a different world and are in a different conversation, it is senseless to call them stupid. Would I call Italians stupid for failing to make sense in their Italian language and Italian ways? I am not that stupid. I am sure that Italians say stupid things, abuse their own language, and don't do as the Romans do, but I should know Italy and its culture a great deal better to be confident in exposing such stupidities. If I find a problem in Windows, am I justified to call the programmers of Microsoft stupid? Of course not. I know nothing about its complexities or its programmers' levels of competence. And when a game theorist presents a complicated game that I do not understand, I may have questions about its relevance, but I will be unable to judge how this particular game fits into the conversation about games. To call it stupid would say more about my own ignorance.

Yes, maybe arguments heard on the ground level seem stupid. But they may in fact be effective. My sister, in our youth, refused to argue with me when I wanted to get something from her. How stupid, I thought, could she be? But now I realize how clever she was – she knew she only stood to lose if she acquiesced to my demand for arguments. By remaining silent, she left me powerless and stood her ground. Now when I come to the family table with strong arguments based on my knowledge of economics, I will be easily disarmed with seemingly irrational arguments such as "my friends get even more money." "How arrogant you can be with your stupid economic arguments." "Who cares about economics anyway?" The only chance left is to abandon economic reason and get emotional myself. Is that stupid? Suppose it works?

Of course, people do and say stupid things in everyday life all the time. But to know what is stupid and what is not, we have to go to their level and figure it out in their context. Maintaining a lofty position may just lead to getting it all wrong. And before calling others stupid, we should think of the Chinese proverb: anyone pointing a finger at someone else points three fingers at himself.

The gap with the world of politics

Like the previous gap, this one stands for two entirely different, incommensurate conversations. (That at least is my claim.) In the political arena different interests are at stake, different metaphors and stories apply, and different values rule. Like the everyday gap, crossing it is not a matter of better translation or more education. Political economics is simply too different a conversation in too different a world.

Economists are not accustomed to looking at the gap this way. One reason is that many of us grew up believing that the gap had to be crossed *scientifically*. The mechanical metaphor, the one that came with the modernist picture of science, led us astray. Accordingly, the economic cohort was taught to think of science as instrumental to make things better. Scientists were to research the underlying structure of reality to get humans to the moon, or find a cure for cancer. Economists were to be like engineers, whose goal was to rationalize otherwise whimsical and ill-founded economic policies. Thanks to this objective outlook, politicians could fend off special interests and opportunism. This characterization fed the meta-narrative of scientists working for the sake of progress and emancipation. It was how Jan Tinbergen, among others, made it look, how the textbooks presented it, and how articles were written. Politicians presumably made their preferences known and economists or econometricians would show them which instruments they could use to achieve their targets. The implicit assumption was that rational politicians would do just that. And that meant that if they did not, they had to be stupid. What a wonderful and conceited representation that was!

A warning should have been that research demonstrating the effectiveness of economists in the policy arena was (now conspicuously) absent. There were plenty of studies on the impact of fiscal and monetary policies, of course, but not of how effective economists were in crossing the divide between academic and political economics. How productive is the work of economists, really? How rational and efficient has their research been? Does the investment of an additional dollar or euro weigh up against its marginal benefits? What are those benefits? Economists do not know, nor have they given it serious thought. An exception was when Clinton appointed Laura Tyson, an academic outsider, as chair of the Council of Economic Advisors. Robert Barro then ran a regression between economic performance and the quality of economic advisors to the president. He found an inverse relationship and concluded that Tyson's appointment augured well for the American economy (a prediction that turned out well for a change). The need for serious research remains. (Even the recent interest in the economics of economics leaves out the critical issue of the effects of economic research on society at large and organizations in particular.) When economists want to claim that their knowledge makes a difference, they should be able to show that with good economics and economists in the production function, economic performance improves. Curiously, economists and their theories are nowhere to be seen in their own models. And when they are, as in rational expectations models, they are a given. Apparently the amount that a country invests in the science of economics has no bearing on its economic performance. It is strange that economists would allow such a conclusion. How do they justify their efforts?

A matter of misguided metaphors?

The problem lies with the metaphors that economists customarily use. The standard metaphor equates knowledge with information and conceives decision-making as a constrained maximization problem with information as one of the constraints. Such a metaphor does not alert us to the problems of communication, or the problem of knowledge coming in ambiguous forms that are hard to interpret. It does not acknowledge that political discourse may have its own codes, rhetoric, values, and institutions that are quite different from the academic ones. Economists may then be actually quite sensible not to entertain the metaphor when it comes to their own activity.

Now and then economists do have to justify what they do. In textbooks, for example, or in conversation. Interestingly, they will in that case usually take recourse to everyday tactics telling anecdotes. They will refer to the application of Black's equation in the financial markets or the importance of game theory in the design of auctions. Those with a sense of history will point to the repeal of the British Corn Laws at the suggestion of Smith, Ricardo, and McCulloch, among others. Most famous, of course, is Keynes, who is said to have provided the solution to the Great Depression of the 1930s in the form of public work and other government spending. Walter Heller likes to claim that the effective tax cut during the Kennedy administration originated at his desk, and Milton Friedman may lay claim to the monetarist policy that Paul Volcker, the chairman of the Federal Reserve in the US, adopted in 1979. But all these are anecdotes and most likely do not stand up to scientific scrutiny.

As George Stigler of Chicago admitted, the Corn Laws probably would have been repealed without the economists as the economic tide was changing and the laws' effectiveness had greatly diminished. Public works were already a commonly accepted public policy when Keynes came along to give it an economic justification. Keyserling, an active economist at the time, relates how "senators like Wagner, Costigan, and LaFolette repeatedly were introducing bills on public works although they did not get accepted until 1933, long before there was any popular appraisal of Keynes" (and three years before his *General Theory* came out, I might add). Keyserling himself read *The General Theory* but did not consider it new, as "we were *doing* these things," adding that college professors had no impact on policy anyway. They were not even witnesses in hearings on economics issues. When Keynes met Franklin Roosevelt, the American President, "he came away feeling that Roosevelt didn't understand anything he was saying." Earlier Keynes had failed to influence the economics of the peace agreement after World War I (as he so magnificently describes in *The Economic Consequences of the Peace* (1988), a book still worth reading). And later, at the pinnacle of his career, his plan for a new international currency system lost to the plan of a minor American economist, Harry Dexter White. So much for the direct influence of one of greatest economists of the twentieth century.

The Black–Scholes formula lost some of its luster when Black's own financial operation faltered (he had to quit academia to cash in on his success). Auctions are really too complicated for us to believe that economists will ever be in sole control of them. Walter Heller may be quite right in his claim, but he leaves many questions open: How and why did he get to that desk and not someone else? Why did the President act upon his proposal and not another economist's? How did he succeed in making his case where so many other economists failed? How important were the personalities of Kennedy and Johnson in this? What role did the political constellation play at the time? The problem is causation. You may think that you changed your mind because of reading this book, but then why, I ask you, didn't everyone else? Might the causes lie further back, so deep in your consciousness that you are unaware of them? My writing may be an immediate cause, but not the real cause of your action. It is the same for the causes of political actions. The effect of the intervention of one or more economists is probably more accidental than systematic, in the sense that it would be the same in another situation.

Another ploy to shore up the reputation and self-confidence of economists is to refer to institutions and people. Of course, by doing so, economists deviate once again from their scientific rhetoric as they step away from their otherwise abstract representations and turn to real-life institutions and accounts of economists in important political positions. The fact that economists become ministers of finance (Larry Summers), foreign secretaries (George Schultz), or even prime ministers (Salinas in Mexico, Andreas Papandreou in Greece) is considered proof of their effectiveness. But scientific these studies are not. And, as they will admit, being in a political position does not allow for the application of a great deal of their economic knowledge, saying, in effect, that they are in a different conversation. Many remark that all the economic knowledge they needed was that taught to first-year students (although Otto Eckstein added that that level is really understood only with a PhD in economics). They all will say that, because so many non-economic issues and interests are at stake, versatile lawyers are better equipped than economists to negotiate the corridors of power. I once asked Rick van der Ploeg – an academically successful economist who served a stint as secretary of culture in the Dutch cabinet – whether he pushed for the application of economic tools such as contingent valuation. The answer was no, nothing like it. In answer to "What weight of influence, on a scale of one to ten, have economists enjoyed in drafting the original tax program of the Reagan administration's tax cuts?" Murray Weidenbaum, an economist who served as economic advisor to President Reagan, answered, "Zilch." Accordingly, having economists in high positions is no guarantee that scientific economic knowledge will make its way into the political discussions. Far from it.

William Allen interviewed many economists about their role in government and concludes as follows:

> In speaking with economists who are or have been in government, one obtains a picture and gains an impression which is sobering. The government economist typically is not a highly independent researcher and analyst, . . . commonly devoting the bulk of his time specified from on high . . . conscious of a prevailing orientation and purpose on the part of these administrative superiors who constitute his main audience . . . bringing to his task . . . an arsenal of techniques which for all their elegance, refinement, and academic glamour are often too time-consuming for purposes of shooting from the hip and too esoteric for the data, the colleagues and the audience, and having little reason to suppose that his work has significant impact in the making of policy.
>
> (Allen 1977: 86–7)

Robert Nelson, who cites Allen in an article about economists as policy analysts, was a policy analyst himself. When he later became an academic – a highly unusual move in the US – he became generous with sobering advice such as: economics PhDs who accept a job with a government agency had better check their intellectual baggage at the entrance; learn how the bureaucracy works; know how to cast arguments that they be noticed. It is another game there. The few times I sat down with politicians I learned that a solid, responsible, economic argument is generally followed by this scenario: While I am being content with myself for having been so thorough, I hear a polite "thank you" from the chairperson and notice that the discussion proceeds as if I had said nothing. Later, the minutes read something like, "Klamer made an interesting contribution, after which blah, blah, blah." The content of what I said is lost totally. I might just as well not have been there.

Admittedly, academic economists are famously inept in the policy arena. They do not have the right ethos; they are often considered tedious, arrogant, abstract, and indirect. Economists who do well usually have dubious PhDs and no academic standing. Their knowledge of economics can be easily exposed as limited (if not faulty) in an academic seminar, but in the corridors of power it does wonderfully. Often drafted from think-tanks, they know how to approach politicians and their staff, what people need to hear and in what form, and how to tinge it with just the right emotion. They are quick to respond to the press and know what a soundbite is. (In the early 1980s, I was writing an article on Larry Summers for the *New*

York Times. When I called Lester Thurow to get his opinion, he was not in. I said I was calling for the *Times* – within five or six seconds, he was on the phone, most willing to answer any question. The editors rejected the article as they found the story of Summers below their threshold of "interesting." Summers went on to become Secretary of the Treasury and president of Harvard University.) Paul Krugman calls these economists "policy entrepreneurs" and sees them as "peddlers of prosperity." He has nothing good to say about them. But they appear to play an important role anyway. If politicians are so rational as to listen to these peddlers of prosperity, shouldn't economists be able to model that? After all, consistent irrational behavior has no place in economic models.

But economists do not yield easily. They will advance more anecdotal evidence of the policy relevance of economic research. They may point to institutions such as the International Monetary Fund (IMF), the World Bank, and the World Trade Organization, all of which are stuffed with economists, and all of which undoubtedly influence world affairs. The questions remain: how does their influence work in fact, and what is the role of academic research? Perhaps they merely apply basic accounting when they advise countries, not advanced economic theory. And when reputable academicians such as Jeffrey Sachs and Joe Stiglitz take the IMF and the World Bank to task for being ill-guided and mistaken in their policies, the apologists have reason to pause, to reconsider submitting such institutions as evidence. In the Netherlands, the Centraal Planbureau (CPB), the brainchild of Tinbergen, continues to have major influence on political proceedings. No political party submits its economic plans and no government implements its plans without a mark of approval from the CPB. The irrelevance of economics, then, is a hard case to make in the Netherlands. Yet the CPB works with large-scale econometric models that today's academic economists would not touch. Furthermore, the CPB is often overruled, especially when cautioning against large infrastructure projects. So, even in the Netherlands, economists have reason to be puzzled now and then, and wonder what they are good for.

When it comes to more technical issues – constructing dams, building railways, implementing environmental regulations, and such – we would expect a bigger role for economists and, indeed, we find just that. But they are still not sure how influential they are. It is possible that politicians consider them when pointing to the desired outcome and ignore them otherwise. In major economic events, economists have been noticeably absent. No economist was involved in the breaking down of the Soviet Union and few had anticipated it. After the fall of communism, Western economists offered their services to the transitioning societies but quickly found themselves replaced by lawyers, who, apparently, had concrete contributions. And the EU decided on the euro before academic economists had given it serious thought. Before 1992, when the Maastricht Treaty stipulated the introduction of the euro, the academic literature was silent on the issue with the exception of a few articles on optimal currency area (all of which were biased against the euro). Only after the fact did an avalanche of academic articles on the subject break loose. And then there was the North American Free Trade Agreement (NAFTA) . . .

Crowding out academic economists: the case of NAFTA

The quest to create, develop, and implement NAFTA began officially on June 10, 1990, when US President George Bush and Mexican President Carlos Salinas (the Harvard economist) issued a joint statement supporting the general principles of a trade agreement between the US and Mexico. Canada quickly joined the effort. Economists seemed perfectly positioned here. After all, they had been making the case for free trade since Adam Smith, and had amassed an impressive library of scholarly literature on the issue. In August 1991, the US government asked the International Trade Committee (ITC) to investigate the findings of recent economic research into the effects of a potential NAFTA. The ITC commissioned twelve academic papers and reviewed them in a report dated May 1992.

All but one of the twelve papers presented so-called computable general equilibrium models. And, although they all found positive gains for all three countries (with Mexico at the top), there were quite a few provisosm such as the static character of the models, and assumptions such as homogeneous and perfectly mobile labor. Moreover, the effects were small.

In 1992, the ITC heard the testimony of 150 organizations and conducted a study to assess the effects on different sectors. Its subsequent report referenced the earlier academic studies – but that would be the last time they would factor in the discussion. The think-tanks took over, as did special interest cohorts such as labor unions and environmental groups (all of which were opposed to NAFTA). The Brookings Institution organized a conference on NAFTA at which economists critical of NAFTA spoke. The level of analysis ceased to be academic, turning impressionistic and anecdotal.

A report issued by the Institute for International Economics had arguably the most impact on the subsequent debate. It appeared in large print (easier for members of congress to read?) and calculated that with NAFTA the US would gain 171,000 jobs. In any academic seminar this result would have been (at the least) shredded. But politicians ran with it. Clinton rounded it up to 200,000 for the remainder of the debate. Academic economists still tried to influence things by means of a letter signed by 300 of them, including every living Nobel laureate. Paul Krugman went on record as asserting that NAFTA would be economically trivial.

None of it mattered much. The debate was taken over by special interests. The public sentiment originally in favor of NAFTA was moving strongly against it. In September 1992, 57 percent of those polled were against and only 33 percent in favor. By March 1993, 63 percent were opposed. Clinton was fighting an uphill battle. And he was doing so without economists on his side. Although journalists and politicians would now and then cite the letter of the laureates, the academic studies were long forgotten. Some politicians even made a point of questioning the integrity of economists who pushed for the treaty with the argument that "they don't stand to lose their jobs."

The turning point came in a televised debate between then Vice President Al Gore and Ross Perot, an ardent opponent of NAFTA. Gore, who otherwise made a stiff impression, proved to be agile in the debate and most effective with *ad hominem* attacks, questioning the interests that businessman Perot had in defeating NAFTA. The sucking sound from the South lost volume. Clinton and Republican senate leader Bob Dole immediately shifted the rhetoric from economic topoi to the topoi of the American identity. "Who are we?" became the question. "What kind of nation are we to vote against a free trade agreement?" General interest took over from special interest. And although the outcome remained in doubt until the last moment, emotional pleas won the debate. Accordingly, political, not economic, arguments proved to be decisive. Academic economists celebrated while licking their political wounds. They had been crowded out of the debate.

Economists have a place in the council of politics

A bleak picture emerges from these accounts. But it becomes so only when you look at it through the spectacles that economists usually wear. Yes, when they look for immediate impact, for a case where scientific findings directed the design and implementation of policy, for people who listen when economists speak, economists tend to become frustrated and even cynical. But things human simply do not work that neatly – not in science, not in everyday life, and certainly not in the policy arena.

Decision-making is a complicated process in everyday life. Few, if any, economists go through an elaborate cost–benefit analysis when they decide on a new job, a new car, a partner, or another child. Just like everyone else they will listen to what others have to say, seek the advice of "experts," consider alternatives, get a little worked up, and in the end do what habit dictates. Politicians are no different. Like economists, they do not like to be told what to do; they do not want to be cornered by a report and are skeptical of whatever number is thrown at them. When they have to decide, they deliberate, allow a variety of factors, preferences, interests, and values in the stew, and then decide to vote for, say, NAFTA, anyway, despite the concerns of their constituency. Even if they claim that a remark of an economist clinched the decision for them, other factors may have made them receptive.

Economists undoubtedly have a role in politics. As Stigler notes, they are important to be present as advocates of prudence and efficiency. Dutch engineers insist on making the dikes so strong that there is only one chance in 16 million of a lost life over the course of a year. Economists should point out how costly that strategy is and how arbitrary such a target is. When politicians are eager to go for a prestigious project such as a new harbor, economists have the responsibility to point to the economic costs and benefits. And when politicians want to continue the project even if the costs are getting out of hand, the incumbent economist brings in the concept of sunk costs.

Accordingly, I advance the metaphor of a council to account for what happens in political processes. The quality of the process is determined by whether – and how well – the relevant voices are heard at the council. When a government has to make an important political decision, it does well holding a council and hearing what various stakeholders have to say. For many subjects – budget decisions, major infrastructure projects, trade agreements and so on – it calls for the voices of economists, and there it does better hearing a variety of them. But in no case should the government expect the various economists to speak with one voice, give clear-cut answers, or present solid evidence, for the science of economics does not have that in the offing. The government should then allow the council to deliberate (while observing the policy entrepreneurs as they fend off the academicians), weigh in special interests, and come to its decision. A messy process, but what decision-making process is not? The important point is to hear a variety of economic voices.

Economics is too important to be left to economists

Arguing the irrelevance of economics is silly anyway, unless you live under a rock. The chatter in newspapers, on television, in politics, and at home is filled with economics. People judge political leaders for their economic performance, and refer to GNP growth and the unemployment, and inflation rates. Politicians (at least in the years before this writing) talk about the blessings of the market, and like nothing better than to privatize public companies and liberalize international trade. People at home discuss demand and supply, and wonder whether to put money aside should their pensions be cut. They know about markets, costs and benefits, and sometimes may do a rough cost–benefit analysis themselves. Businesses keep account of their expenses and managers think of sunk and opportunity costs. The air vibrates with concepts, ideas, and facts that emanate from the conversations of economists.

In the Netherlands, almost all students learn economics in high school; this is increasingly the case also in the US. They learn about GNP, marginal cost and benefit, elasticity, opportunity costs, and other gems of economic conversations. That they do not get psychology lessons – despite the fact that they might be more practical in their subsequent lives than economics – is something to reflect on. Making money, after all, is quite a bit easier than sustaining a marriage, attending to teenagers, and figuring yourself out. Even so, economics is on the agenda of teachers. Economics has its own section in the newspaper and is a fixed item on the news. Economists are getting their way, so it seems.

But the impact is not immediate. It is not that economists feed information, data, and evidence to the populace so they can act upon it. It is not that economists are telling people what to do. The influences are indirect and hard to trace. It's like with computers. Computer scientists constitute a world of their own. They have complicated conversations about class, objects, inheritance, delegation, assertion – but in a context such that it would escape those of us who are outside that world. Nor do many of us have use for their technical and abstract ways of thinking. But how influential the computer is. If we do not work with one, we start thinking like one. The computer has become a metaphor to understand our brains and even to understand the economy, an example of how influence – by means of metaphors – is not direct, but indirect. People borrow economic metaphors from the conversations of economists to make sense of their lives, to help make decisions. But they will not adopt the metaphor exactly as it functioned in the (academic) economic conversation. In the transition, they will change some of its meanings and place it in a narrative that may affront an academic economist but make the concept work in the everyday context.

Economists influence public opinion in other ways as well. When Keynes wrote *The Economic Consequences of the Peace* (Keynes 1988), it was too late to redo a treaty that was disastrous in an economic sense because it extracted more from the loser, Germany, than it sensibly could without jeopardizing its economic recovery and that of the European continent. It took an economist to make that point, and he did so in a powerful and poetic way. Thus, he ended his book:

> We have been moved already beyond endurance, and need rest. Never in a lifetime of men now living has the universal element in the soul of man burnt so dimly.
> For these reasons the true voice of the new generation has not yet spoken, and silent opinion is not yet formed. To his formation of the general opinion of the future I dedicate this book.
>
> (Keynes 1988 [1919]: 297–8)

We know now better, possibly thanks to Keynes. Someone interested in the causes of World War II may turn to this book because it helps to make sense of what happened in the interbellum period. The lessons that Keynes drew may also have moved the Allied forces to be less exacting on the German economy the second time around (after immeasurably more gruesome deeds) and even proceeded to stimulate and support its recovery. Of course, Keynes could not have foreseen such consequences in his none-too-academic polemic. Nowadays the writings of economists like Paul Krugman, John Kenneth Galbraith, and Robert Reich (although a lawyer by training) can be picked up at the local bookstore. People buy them to understand their world a little better. That is influence in a way. And what to say of the influence of Karl Marx? Although his status as economist is disputed, his economic writings kept a few billion people preoccupied for more than half a century – a feat accomplished by no one, in my guess, but Adam Smith.

Smith, Marx, and Keynes succeeded in influencing everyday thinking. Milton Friedman, another effective advocate for economic ideas in the public realm, is convinced that trying to persuade politicians directly is a waste of time; the best strategy is to direct efforts at public opinion. If economists keep hammering on about the benefits of free trade, floating exchange rates, or the flaws of the euro in the media, popular writings, and public speeches, the ideas circulate and politicians begin to pay attention. Such strategy is different from what Tinbergen and his contemporaries taught, but now that I know more about how conversations work, including those in everyday life and the political arena, it makes sense.

Accordingly, the divide between everyday and political conversations is crossed, but not in the way that the engineers and instrumentalists among economists would wish. Thinking in terms of conversation allows us to understand that influences across conversations are hard to trace and difficult to predict. When one conversation borrows a metaphor from another, the meanings of that metaphor will most likely change and its function will differ from the one in which it took form. That is human life.

Further reading

The stock of writings on the contrast between academic and everyday economics is slim. For a typically economistic way of looking at daily economic life, read Landsburg, *The Armchair Economist: Economics and Everyday Life* (The Free Press, 1993). The writings of Paul Krugman lend insights on the contrast between academic and political economics; see especially *Peddling Prosperity* (Norton, 1994). Other good sources are Robert Garnett's *What Do Economists Know? New Economics of Knowledge* (Routledge, 1999), which contains the study of the NAFTA debate by Jennifer Meehan and me, and several books by David Colander, such as *Educating Economists* (University of Michigan Press, 1992).

   To gain insight into the (limited) role of economists in the corridors of power, I recommend the writings of Bob Coats, such as those in his *The Sociology and Professionalization of Economics: British and American Economic Essays*, Vol. II (Routledge, 1993); see especially "The Economics Profession and the Role of Economists in Government" in part III. Read also Robert Nelson's 1987 article titled "The Economics Profession and the Making of Public Policy" in the *Journal of Economic Literature*, 25: 42–84. It contains many other useful references.

Peroratio

Why the science of economics is not all that strange

Let us return to those hotels filled with 6,000 economists. A disaster of colossal proportions strikes the conference. All that economic brainpower evaporates. Just like that. For a few days the news is about nothing else. And then . . . Is the world different? Will those economists be missed? Would universities (after a decent period of mourning and the installation of a first-rate commemorative plaque) seize the opportunity to close their economics departments, or surrender them to business economists? Would governmental agencies and the like contentedly fill the empty slots with more practical-minded people?

If what economists do is of such little significance as some readers are inclined to think, we would expect as much. If the conversations of economists had so little to contribute to other conversations, the evaporation of those 6,000 economists would be forgotten as quickly as the Americas forgot about the Incas. But it wouldn't happen. Economists are too important. Their conversations, as a source for others, would not be left unattended and uncared for.

❖ ❖ ❖

A conversation is a source. When people like soccer, they benefit from a world of soccer out there, including all the talk that surrounds the game. When people like novels, they benefit from the rich literature of people who know about them, review them, and teach them. When people are interested in economic issues, they benefit similarly. Imagine such a person alone in Mali (where, I gather, good economists are scarce and economics books are impossible to find) – he or she would lack the source of a good economic conversation. Even when not making use of it, Mali is better off having it there. To use an economic term, the conversation has option value. It is good to know that there are interesting books to read, that people are seriously studying and discussing the themes that you might get interested in, someday, even if you do not have the time or patience right now to get into their conversation. It also has bequest value as our children can go back to the economic literature to see how current economists made sense of their world.

So, although the predictive power of the science of economics is limited, although economists disagree, although the scientific quality of their work is less than optimal, and although econospeak is hard to understand, the science is not so strange *if you see it as a conversation*. Seeing it that way makes sense of all kinds of otherwise strange features.

It is a practical perspective, that of conversations. Instead of having to work out an abstract system with simplifying assumptions, complicated conditionals, and universalizing theses, the metaphor highlights the here and now. The danger of dwelling on the tenth floor is that the urge for universalizing ideas overtakes practical sense. But even the construction of abstract competitive equilibrium models involves practice and a great deal of conversation. The metaphor of conversations has meaning insofar as it can make sense of daily practice, especially if we go beyond the mere chatter and allow for the institutions, values, rhetoric, and culture that bolster and sustain a conversation.

But, some people object, economists are close to autistic when it comes to their interactions. They talk about their universities, salaries, grants, and so on – but rarely about their economics. And when they talk about economics they do so in abstract and technical monologues. So how can we speak of conversations? These critics discovered how a metaphor works, at least in one way: it generates meanings that do not connect, but there are also meanings that do connect. Their experience is about bad communications, conference sessions with no exchange, faculty members who have stopped talking to each other, or an econospeak that renders a sensible communication senseless to the rest of world. Yes, this happens, but the metaphor does not have to mean literally that economists are talking all the time. Economists are in the conversation while reading articles and writing models even if they are not saying anything to anyone. Further, truly autistic economists – those who do not publish or present their work – do not survive very long.

To get these points, it may help to recall the four gaps that practicing economists face. One is between their minds and the reality out there. They have to cross that epistemological gap somehow or suggest that they have done so. This is about truth. More treacherous is the gap that separates their minds from others'. Covering this rhetorical gap requires a rhetorical astuteness, know-how, good judgment, and ethos. It is about meanings, about being interesting. Then there is the gap from everyday life. Some may be more bothered by this gap than others. It is a rhetorical gap of sorts but now one that separates the scientists from the conversations of everyday. If they do want to make sense in everyday life – and quite a few economists do – they have to know how to cope with this gap, a capability beyond straightforward translations and slow speaking. Finally, there is the gap from politics. This is serious because so much economics is intended to affect politics directly. The last two gaps are about the interested character of economics, of the desire to have an impact on the outside worlds.

In all cases it helps to realize that conversations are at stake. It is by means of conversations that scientists negotiate the gap from reality and the rhetorical gap from each other. In the gaps from everyday and political life, it is the problem of different conversations that confronts them.

To be meaningful, the metaphor of conversation should make practical sense. It should make sense of what it takes to get into economics. Students will realize that it takes more than being good at problems sets and exams to qualify as an economist. A lot of work and a great deal of adjustment are needed to get into the conversation.

Practicing economists will acknowledge the efforts that are required to stay in the conversation. Even if they disavow the pursuit of attention – modest scientists as they might be – they will recognize how critical a role the giving and receiving of attention plays in scientific conversations and how unequal its distribution is. They will also know that the conversation has a peculiar culture of collegiality in the face of competitive pressures, the sharing of knowledge and the contributions of participants in the form of generous comments on the work of others, free refereeing, and academic entrepreneurship. And that for economists who have their conversations revolve around the notion of self-interested behavior.

When the metaphor leads us to think of economics as a bunch of conversations, the going may get a little trickier. After all, quite a few economists insist that there is only one conversation, the scientific one: the conversation that relies on the use of mathematics, models, and heavy-duty statistics. They hold the hard-nosed TINA (There Is No Alternative) position. Do as we do, they imply, and you are in; otherwise you are neither an economist nor, for that matter, a scientist. By insisting on "a bunch of conversations," I would like to suggest that economics has always known a variety of conversations going on at the same time, and that the conversations change over time. That was the point of Chapter 7. My request to the TINA fellows, therefore, is to leave the tenth floor for a moment, get in a helicopter, and look at what is going on. Let them tell how they have the privilege of knowing what constitutes science when others – who have spent their life figuring that out – do not quite know. I ask them to look (and read earlier chapters) to see the feebleness of the epistemological foundations on which they want to rest their science. I also invite them to review their field. If mathematical astuteness is a criterion, does that disqualify Smith, Marshall, Schumpeter, Becker, Buchanan, and Friedman as serious economists? This is, therefore, a gentle invitation to let the hard-nosed attitude go – it can get so mean-spirited at times – and face up to a reality that is diverse and complex.

So let a thousand flowers bloom? No, reality is too tough for that. Resources are scarce and the space for attention is limited. A department cannot accommodate all possible conversations. Some will be deemed more critical, more prestigious, or more interesting than others. So the Marxist will be denied a position and the model-builder-turned-Austrian will be denied tenure. Whether a faculty goes for the historian of thought or the game theorist depends on where it stands, who has the power.

A conversation's dynamics cannot be changed at will. Maybe a crisis will occur when students stop taking economics classes because they are too mathematical, too abstract, and cover too little history. The inflow of graduate students dries up. Such developments may influence the dynamics. Or things may change because young economists are trying something different, something less esoteric, like those who started the postautistic movement in France. It happened in the 1930s with Samuelson, Tobin, and Solow as the young rebels who changed the conversation around. Maybe outside forces will gather to force a change. Economists may realize that, when they continue to fail to bridge the gaps between them and everyday and political reality, they have to change their tune and possibly their questions and subjects of inquiry. The world wants to know what is going on: Will a greater Europe work? Is globalization about to change the world? Will the digital revolution revolutionize science and the way it is organized (such that universities become virtual)? Will China be the great economic power? Does culture matter? Does privatization work? . . . The new Keynes, the next Hayek, Friedman, Marx, or Smith, please stand up.

A few readers have come away disappointed. They were expecting criteria to judge conversations and failed to find any in the preceding pages. I am sorry to have to disappoint them but it is better to be realistic and fair to the reality of the conversation. As I discussed in Chapter 6, there are no criteria that can be firmly established outside a conversation. Truthfulness, for one, fails as a criterion, as do all the other norms and rules that methodologists and practicing scientists have suggested. There is no absolute way to say that one theory or conversation is right and another is wrong.

Because there are no absolute criteria that students can learn by heart, participants in a conversation have to develop their judgment and taste. They will learn by doing what assumption is a good one, what model will be appreciated, and which technique gets by the referees. Partaking in a conversation requires one judgment after another. Good economists have good judgment; excellent economists have excellent judgment. That is a good reason to study with them. Doing economics is a true art. As Aristotle would say, it combines the virtues of poiesis (knowing how to make things well, things like models and tests) and of phronesis (practical judgment).

As truth is too elusive an ideal, scientists do better if they realize that, in reality, they settle for something less: soundness (as Dewey would suggest), or a reasonable argument that stands the test of all kinds of criticisms (as Toulmin and Janik put it). A contribution to the conversation will never be perfect or ideal. The model can always be improved, the testing can always be extended to include more data and use ever more sophisticated techniques. But we settle for something that is good enough. Then we move on.

Other readers will have wondered whether this gentle way of viewing the practice of economics undercuts and neutralizes criticism. You did not give me much, they say, on how to tell that certain theories are mistaken. But no, reading the preceding chapters in this way does not do them justice, or I have failed to make the point clear. Once we consider conversations rather than propositions, and once we recognize that conversations should not only pursue the truth but also be meaningful and interesting, it becomes clear that conversations are vulnerable when they fail to be meaningful and are judged interesting in the wrong way. Let me elaborate.

Quite a few economists are drawn, for example, into the conversation surrounding game theory and make a living out of it. But who says that everybody has to do the same? Forget about its truth, or its scientific claims and pretenses.

Those criteria do not commit anyone. People may judge the conversation uninteresting, lacking in meaning because it is too mathematical, too abstract, or because it uses assumptions that do not make sense to them. Or they may question the interests that the conversation serves. Maybe they consider it too self-serving, too poor in insights that will matter for other conversations such as political ones. Accordingly, with the metaphor of conversations, space opens up for serious criticism. And remember, economics is a bunch of conversations. Maybe other conversations are more suitable, more meaningful, and more appealing to them. Go for those, I'd say.

In a similar fashion people can resist the dictate of how economics needs to be done, what conversation is the norm. Not all economists have to be theorists. If the theoretical conversation is not their cup of tea, there are other possibilities. Joining a conversation is an existential decision, mind you; do not take it lightly. Being in one conversation rather than another can make all the difference. Too often I hear from colleagues how frustrated they are about the conversation they are in. They would like to switch but do not have the courage. I know how difficult switching conversations is, and how costly – that is what the metaphor of conversation reveals – but why work yourself senseless, why risking getting dispirited? Life is short.

> It makes all the difference in the world whether a thinker stands in personal relation to his problems, in which he sees his destiny, his need, and even highest happiness, or can only feel and grasp them impersonally with the tentacles of cold, prying thought.
>
> (Nietzsche 1999)

Nietzsche also wrote, "The will to systematize shows a lack of intellectual integrity."

Whose applause are you seeking?

Whether people consider joining the conversations of neoclassical economists, game theorists, experimental economists, behavioralists, Austrians, pomo Marxists, feminists, economic historians, they still have a series of other options, each of which makes for a different life. To see what suits them best, apart from considering their talents, preferences, and values, they may ask themselves whose applause they are seeking. The answer matters.

The conversation of pure theory

People will enjoy this conversation when they like thinking abstractly, get drawn to the exploration of systems, appreciate the esthetics of arguments, and like perfecting techniques without having to bother about practical applications. They do not mind that their mothers and partners have no clue as to what they are doing and that they can share their insights only with a small group of like-minded people. Maybe they are attracted to the status that nowadays is awarded to this conversation. The applause they are seeking? They may have the Nobel Prize in mind, or the judgment of history, but otherwise they are satisfied getting the appreciation from others who are in the conversation. (They do not mind being the academic dogs of Chapter 3.)

The conversation of economic teaching

Instead of focusing their energy on research, participants in this conversation prefer to teach undergraduates. They enjoy discussing economic ideas with students, and get pleasure from watching them develop into economists. It is their applause they are seeking.

The conversation of applied research

Rather than teaching or doing high-minded and abstract theorizing, these people prefer getting down to real things, developments, events. They are motivated by practical and topical questions and like doing the research, working with data, and using whatever theory or model appears suitable. They are probably more comfortable in the research department of a central bank, a government agency, a think-tank, or even a commercial organization, as long as they are free to do research. It is not the applause of their academic colleagues that they are seeking; the Nobel is out of their sight. The appreciation of their colleagues is good enough for them, although the recognition of their superiors would not hurt.

The intellectual conversation

The quest for knowledge takes precedence over disciplinary constraints. Those who strive to be in this conversation will have an economics PhD but look beyond the disciplinary boundaries to be in conversation with other disciplinarians doing the same. Their shelves display a wide range of books and their writings have interdisciplinary characteristics. They may seek the applause of the great intellectual minds or simply be content with the pleasures and stimulation that the intellectual conversation brings. Some will seek appreciation in the intellectual forum and have their moment when they see their book displayed in a good bookstore.

The conversation of policy advisers

What these people want most is influence on the policy-making process, thus they want to be as close to that process as possible. They are willing to give up academic standards and do the quick and dirty work that harried political reality often asks for, and they will adjust their rhetoric just to get through to the politicians they are serving. They get their kick when they find their contribution in a political speech, an amendment or a new law. It is the applause of the politicians that they are seeking. It's just too bad that their former academic colleagues are not able to appreciate the creative work that they are doing

The conversation of policy entrepreneurs

These people do not only want the ears of politicians, they also want to be publicly known. Ignoring academic judgments that they learned at graduate school they write reports that members of Congress and their staff can grasp, with smooth prose, crude but strong numbers, pointed arguments, and politically prudent summaries. If some arguments have to be left out and some nuances have to be sacrificed, so be it. They like to be in the thick of public discussion, love to give speeches to trade associations and press clubs, and, if they have the opportunity and the talent, will write books with ringing titles such as *The Work of Nations*, *Peddling Prosperity*, and *The Economic Lies of the President*. They are seeking public applause – the louder, the better. Who cares about those academics anyway? And who cares about the Nobel Prize? And before history is ready to judge our contributions, we are already dead.

The conversation of consultants

Consultants are willing to give up their academic standing in order to supply their skills to the highest bidder. Their most important skill is to know what their clients want and to show them what their problem is. Their reports aim at immediate effect. The applause they are seeking comes in the form of big contracts from satisfied clients and the recognition from other consultants.

Other conversations

People with an economics degree may leave academia, give up their status as economists, and join other conversations. They may become lawyers, journalists, executives, theologians, politicians, or full-time parents. They can do so for positive reasons because they seek the applause of people outside the world of economists, or because they are frustrated with academic life and the economic conversation, or because they reckon that the applause they stand to receive as economists will be too meager.

These do not exhaust all possible conversations. There are all kinds of intermediate forms. Think of specialized conversations, e.g., about urban economics or cultural economics, which tend to be less theoretical than the purely theoretical conversation but more theoretical than the applied research conversation. If they are content with the applause of such a subgroup of economists, they grab their chance.

When I started this book I wanted to make sense of this strange science of economists and the people that make it up. It all is making more sense now. If going through the preceding pages has produced an *Aha Erlebnis* now and then, or moments of recognition and identification, or the feeling that one's experience is quite different from the one described here, the argument has been successful. Whether the metaphor of the conversation and all the argument that goes with it will fly remains to be seen. That will depend upon the readers. Conversations are strange things.

Notes

1 The strangeness of the discipline

1 I am not talking about predicting the economy, which economists admittedly can't do; economics in government is about thinking of ways to better the human condition in terms of labor, poverty, taxes, etc.

2 A group of French students have begun a protest movement against mainstream economic curricula, which they claim to be autistic (www.paecon.net). They object to the absence of economic history, the lack of attention to the history of economic thought, and the neglect of the integration of economic institutions in their studies. They complain that they learn a prodigious amount about modeling, the solving of equations, and the running of regressions but virtually nothing about how the economy actually works. They advocate a post-autistic economics, that is, an economics that reflects the economy in a way that non-economists would recognize.

3 This study compelled the profession to take a critical look at its graduate curriculum. The consequence, so it seems, was that graduate programs began to stress mathematical skills in their selection of students.

4 There have been studies of the role of economists in political life and public institutions (see Coats 1993). Their main weakness is the dubious assumption that the presence of an economist signifies the impact of economic knowledge. Economic PhDs, such as Mexican president Carlos Salinas and the Greek premier Andreas Papandreou, may very well put their academic knowledge on the backburner and begin to think like politicians. Research suggests that they cannot avoid switching modes, and that there is a rhetorical gap between the academic and political.

2 Economics is a converstation or, better, a bunch of conversations

1 This was while she was still in Iowa. In Chicago, the books were rearranged somewhat, with even more prominent display of poetry and other non-economic books.

2 See, for example, the introductory essay in Klamer et al. (1988).

3 See, for example, Latour and Woolgar (1979), Latour (1987).

4 See, for example, Knorr Cetina (1981).

5 The mirror is Rorty's characterization.

6 See Popper (1959, 1962), Klant (1985), and Blaug (1990 [1982]).

7 To witness the disappointments it has generated, read Hands's *Reflection without Rules* (2001).

8 See Maddock (1983) and Fisher (1986).

9 There will be more on this later.

10 The literature in which this metaphor figures is very much in the Marxist tradition. I first got into it by means of a little book by Joan Robinson, *Economic Philosophy* (1962).

11 At most European universities, tenure is immediate; at American universities, it is granted after six years, given the required demonstration of skills and fit.

3 What it takes to be an academic dog, or the culture of the academic conversation

1 The author was Jan Pen. He is witty and erudite, writes well, plays jazz, and paints. (One of his paintings was on the cover of the program of an AEA conference.) I owe him not only for this first experience with an excellent book on economics but also for his support in getting me my current job.

2 The distinction is from Pickering (1992).

3 From sociologist Pierre Bourdieu, who speaks of the habitus of academic life, meaning what we are disposed to do in the setting of academia.

4 I found the first reference to this phenomenon in Hagstrom (1965).

5 The phrase is from Jake Ryan and Charles Sackrey, two working-class academics who collected a series of essays by fellow travelers and made a book of them under that title (Ryan and Sackrey 1984).

4 It's the attention, stupid!

1 This chapter owes a great deal to the research done with Harry van Dalen (Klamer and van Dalen 2002, 2005). If you like this chapter, please give him the credit as well.

2 See Berlyne (1960) and Kahneman (1973).

3 Studies done by the utility industry demonstrate power surges during the commercials of, say, an attention-grabbing Superbowl. Only then do people attend to hunger (opening the fridge, using the microwave) and various impulses involving water.

4 See Kahneman (1973).

5 These figures and those that appear later are for the year 1999. An important source is the Institute for Scientific Information, Philadelphia, Journal Citation Reports, 2000.

6 See Durden and Ellis (1993).

7 This relationship is not tight. Especially classics get cited in articles without a serious discussion of their content.

8 With thanks to Barend van Heusden, who made this suggestion in jest in his dissertation (1994).

9 See Frey (1997).

5 A good scientific conversation, or contribution thereto, is truthful and meaningful and serves certain interests

1 This is what Frank Hahn gave as advice after a long discussion about the state of economics during which we had gone on about the fallacies and silliness of the discipline.

2 The three-by-five card methodology is Deirdre McCloskey's favorite expression.

3 After John Maynard Keynes.

4 Author's emphasis.

5 See Davis and Hersh (1987).

6 See Klamer and Colander (1990).

7 See Mirowski and Sent (2002).

6 The art of economic persuasion: about rhetoric and all that

1   The text can be found at http://www.textkit.com/files/gorgias.PDF.
2   I am referring to George Akerlof's article titled "The Market for 'Lemons'" (Akerlof 1970). He had great difficulty in getting it published; editors found its discussion trivial. It would end up earning him the Nobel Prize in 2001. The title has undoubtedly been a factor in the continuing attention the article has received. I too have found it a good title for a course syllabus; it intrigues the students.
3   W. H. Auden, "Stop All the Clocks."

Bibliography

Akerlof, G.A. (1970) "The Market for 'Lemons': Quality Uncertainty and the Market Mechanism," *Quarterly Journal of Economics*, 84: 488–500.

Allen, W. (1977) "Economics, Economists, and Economic Policy: Modern American Experiences," *History of Political Economy*, 9: 48–88.

Auerbach, A.J. (1992) "Taxes and Spending in the Age of Deficits: A View from Washington and Academe," *National Tax Journal*, 45: 239–42.

Baudrillard, J. (1988) "Simulacra and Simulations," in M. Poster (ed.) *Jean Baudrillard, Selected Writings*, Stanford: Stanford University Press, pp. 166–84.

Becker, G.A. (1965) "Theory of the Allocation of Time," *The Economic Journal*, 75(299): 493–517.

Berlyne, D.E. (1960) *Conflict, Arousal, and Curiosity*, New York: McGraw-Hill.

Blaug, M. (1990 [1982]) *The Methodology of Economics*, Cambridge, Cambridge University Press.

Blundell, W.E. (1988) *The Art and Craft of Feature Writing*, New York: Plume.

Booth, W. (1988) *The Company We Keep: The Ethics of Fiction*, Berkeley, CA: University of California Press.

Boynton, G.R., and C. Deissenberg (1987) "Models of the Economy Implicit in the Public Discourse," *Policy Sciences*, 20: 129–51.

Coats, A.W. (1993) *The Sociology and Professionalization of Economics: British and American Economic Essays*, Vol. II, London: Routledge.

Collins, R. (1998) *The Sociology of Philosophies: A Global Theory of Intellectual Change*, Cambridge, MA: Harvard University Press.

Coupé, T. (2000) *Statistics 101 for (Wannabee) Economists*, Brussels: Université Libre de Bruxelles.

Crane, D. (1972) *Invisible Colleges: Diffusion of Knowledge in Scientific Communities*, Chicago, IL: University of Chicago Press.

Davis, P.J. and Hersh, R. (1987) "Rhetoric and Mathematics," in John S. Nelson, Allan Megill, and Donald N. McCloskey (eds) *The Rhetoric of the Human Sciences*, Madison, WI: University of Wisconsin Press, pp. 53–68.

Defoe, D. (1994) *Robinson Crusoe*, London: Penguin Books.

Descartes, R. (1968 [1621]) *Discourse on Method and the Meditations*, Harmondsworth: Penguin Books.

Durden, G.C. and Ellis, L.V. (1993) "A Method for Identifying the Most Influential Articles in an Academic Discipline," *Atlantic Economic Journal*, 21(4): 1–10.

Eizenstat, S.E. (1992) "Economists and White House Decisions," *Journal of Economic Perspectives*, 6(3): 65–71.

Feyerabend, P. (1975) *Against Method: Outline of an Anarchistic Theory of Knowledge*, London: NLB.

Fisher, R.M. (1986) *The Logic of Economic Discovery: Neoclassical Economics and the Marginal Revolution*, Brighton: Wheatsheaf.

Franck, G. (1999) "Scientific Communication: A Vanity Fair?," *Science*, 286: 53–5.

—— (2000) "In Search of Attention," unpublished paper, Vienna.

Frey, B.S. (1997) *Not Just for the Money: An Economic Theory of Personal Motivation*, Cheltenham: Edward Elgar.

Friedman, M. (1953) *Essays in Positive Economics*, Chicago, IL: University of Chicago Press.

—— (1963) *A Monetary History of the United States, 1867–1960*, Princeton, NJ: Princeton University Press.

Frost, R. (1923) *New Hampshire*, New York: Henry Holt.

Garfield, E. (1990) "The Most Cited Papers of All Time, SCI 1945–1988," *Current Comments*, 7: 3–14.

Geertz, C. (1973) *The Interpretation of Cultures: Selected Essays*, New York: Basic Books.

Hacking, I. (1983) *Representing and Intervening: Introductory Topics in the Philosophy of Natural Science*, Cambridge: Cambridge University Press.

Hagstrom, W.O. (1965) *The Scientific Community*, New York: Basic Books.

Hahn, F. (1984) *Equilibrium and Macroeconomics*, Oxford: Blackwell.

Hands, D.W. (2001) *Reflection without Rules: Economic Methodology and Contemporary Science Theory*, Cambridge: Cambridge University Press.

Harré, R. (1983) *Personal Being: A Theory for Individual Psychology*, Oxford: Blackwell.

van Heusden, B.P. (1994) *Why Literature? An Inquiry into the Nature of Literary Semiosis*, Groningen: RUG.

Jencks, C.A. (1986) *What is Post-Modernism?*, New York: St. Martin's Press.

Jevons, W.S. (1958 [1874]) *The Principles of Science: A Treatise on Logic and Scientific Method*, New York: Dover Publications.

Kahneman, D. (1973) *Attention and Effort*, Englewood Cliffs, NJ: Prentice Hall.

Keynes, J.M. (1936) *The General Theory of Employment, Interest and Money*, London: Macmillan.

—— (1978) *The Collected Writings*, Vol. 39, London: Macmillan.

—— (1988 [1919]) *The Economic Consequences of the Peace*, London: Macmillan.

Klamer, A. (1983) *Conversations with Economists*, Totowa, NJ: Rowman & Allanheld.

—— (1989) "An Accountant Among Economists: Conversation with Sir John R. Hicks," *Journal of Economic Perspectives*, 3: 167–80.

Klamer, A., and Colander, D.C. (1987) "The Making of an Economist," *Journal of Economic Perspectives*, 1(2): 95–111.

—— (1990) *The Making of an Economist: Studies in the History, Methods, and Boundaries of Economics*, Boulder, CO: Westview Press.

Klamer, A., and van Dalen, H.P. (2002) "Attention and the Art of Scientific Publishing," *Journal of Economic Methodology*, 9: 289–315.

—— (2005) "Is There Such a Thing called Scientific Waste?," unpublished discussion paper, Tinbergen Institute, the Netherlands.

Klamer, A., and McCloskey, D.N. (1992) "Accounting as the Master Metaphor of Economics," *The European Accounting Review*, 1(1): 145–60.

Klamer, A., McCloskey, D.N., and Solow, R.M. (1988) *The Consequences of Economic Rhetoric*, Cambridge: Cambridge University Press.

Klant, J. (1985) *The Rules of the Game: The Logical Structure of Economic Theories*, Cambridge: Cambridge University Press.

Knorr Cetina, K. (1981) *The Manufacture of Knowledge: An Essay on the Constructivist and Contextual Nature of Science*, New York: Pergamon.

Krugman, P.R. (1994) *Peddling Prosperity: Economic Sense and Nonsense in the Age of Diminished Expectations*, New York: Norton.

Kuhn, T. (1970 [1962]) *The Structure of Scientific Revolutions*, Chicago, IL: University of Chicago Press.

Lakatos, I. (1970) "Falsification and the Methodology of Scientific Research Programmes," in I. Lakatos and A. Musgrave (eds) *Criticism and the Growth of Knowledge*, Cambridge University Press: Cambridge, pp. 91–196.

——— (1976) *Proofs and Refutations: The Logic of Mathematical Discovery*, Cambridge: Cambridge University Press.

Lakoff, G., and Johnson, M. (1980) *Metaphors We Live By*, Chicago, IL: University of Chicago Press.

Latour, B. (1987) *Science in Action, How to Follow Scientists and Engineers through Society*, Cambridge, MA: Harvard University Press.

Latour, B., and Woolgar, S. (1979) *Laboratory Life: The Social Construction of Scientific Facts*, London: Sage Publications.

Leamer, E. (1981) "The Hit Parade of Economic Articles," *Comparative Economic Systems*, 14: 3–54.

Lucas, R.E. (1987) *Models of Business Cycles*, Malden, MA: Blackwell Publishers.

McCloskey, D.N. (1983) "The Rhetoric of Economics," *Journal of Economic Literature*, 21: 481–517.

——— (1990) *If You're so Smart: The Narrative of Economic Expertise*, Chicago, IL: University of Chicago Press.

——— (1998 [1985]) *The Rhetoric of Economics*, Madison, WI: University of Wisconsin Press.

——— (2000) *Crossing: A Memoir*, Chicago, IL: University of Chicago Press.

McCloskey, D.N., and Ziliak, S.T. (1996) "The Standard Error of Regression," *Journal of Economic Literature*, 34(1): 97–114.

——— (2004) "Size Matters: The Standard Error of Regressions in the *American Economic Review*," *Journal of Socio-Economics*, 33: 527–46.

MacIntyre, A. (1981) *After Virtue: A Study in Moral Theory*, London: Duckworth.

Maddock, R. (1983) "Rational Expectations Macrotheory: A Lakatosian Reconstruction," working paper for *Economic History*, Canberra: Australian National University.

Maki, U. (1995) "Diagnosing McCloskey," *Journal of Economic Literature*, 33: 1300–18.

Marshall, A. (1920) *Principles of Economics: An Introductory Volume*, London: Macmillan.

Merton, R.K. (1968) "The Matthew Effect in Science," *Science*, 159: 56–63.

Mirowski, P. (1989) *More Heat than Light: Economics as Social Physics; Physics as Nature's Economics*, Cambridge: Cambridge University Press.

Mirowski, P., and Sent, E.M. (2002) *Science Bought and Sold: Essays in the Economics of Science*, Chicago, IL: University of Chicago Press.

Nietzsche, F. (1999) *Philosophy and Truth – Selections from Nietzsche's Notebooks of the Early 1870's* (edited by D. Breazeale), Amherst, MA: Humanity Books.

Odlyzko, A. (1997) "The Economics of Electronic Journals," *First Monday* (http://www.firstmonday.org/issues/issue2_8/odlyzko/index.html), 2(8).

Peirce, C.S. (1966 [1878]) "How to Make Our Ideas Clear," in P.P. Weiner (ed.) *Charles S. Peirce, Selected Writings*, New York: Dover Publications.

Perelman, C., and L. Olbrechts-Tyteca (1969) *The New Rhetoric: A Treatise on Argumentation*, Notre Dame, IN: University of Notre Dame Press.

Pickering, A. (ed.) (1992) *Science as Practice and Culture*, Chicago, IL: University of Chicago Press.

Polanyi, M. (1962 [1958]) *Personal Knowledge: Towards a Post-Critical Philosophy*, Chicago, IL: University of Chicago Press.

Popper, K. (1959) *The Logic of Scientific Discovery*, London: Hutchinson & Co.

—— (1962) *Conjectures and Refutations: The Growth of Scientific Knowledge*, New York: Basic Books.

Robinson, J. (1962) *Economic Philosophy: The New Thinker's Library*, London: Watts.

Rorty, R. (1979) *Philosophy and the Mirror of Nature*, Princeton, NJ: Princeton University Press.

Ruccio, D.F., and Amariglio, J. (2003) *Postmodern Moments in Modern Economics*, Princeton, NJ: Princeton University Press.

Ryan, J., and Sackrey, C. (eds) (1984) *Strangers in Paradise: Academics from the Working Class*, Boston, MA: South End Press.

Samuelson, P.A. (1939) "Interaction Between the Multiplier Analysis and the Principle of Acceleration," *Review of Economic Statistics*, 21: 75–8.

—— (1947) *Foundations of Economic Analysis*, Cambridge, MA: Harvard University Press.

—— (1963) *The Collected Scientific Papers of Paul A. Samuelson*, Vol. 1, Cambridge, MA: MIT Press.

—— (1964) *The Collected Scientific Papers of Paul A. Samuelson*, Vol. 2, Cambridge, MA: MIT Press.

—— (1985) Lecture at Trinity University (http://www.trinity.edu/nobel/Samuelson_files/Samuelson%20web%20quotes.htm).

—— (1992) "My Life Philosophy: Policy Credos and Working Ways," in M. Szenberg (ed.) *Eminent Economists: Their Life Philosophies*, Cambridge: Cambridge University Press, pp. 236–47.

Simon, H.A. (1971) "Designing Organizations for an Information-Rich World," in M. Greenberger (ed.) *Computers, Communications, and the Public Interest*, Baltimore, MD: Johns Hopkins University Press, pp. 37–53.

Simonton, D.K. (1984) *Genius, Creativity, and Leadership: Historiometric Inquiries*, Cambridge, MA: Harvard University Press, 1984.

—— (1988) *Scientific Genius: A Psychology of Science*, Cambridge: Cambridge University Press.

Smith, A. (1987 [1776]) "The Wealth of Nations," in R. Heilbroner (ed.) *The Essential Adam Smith*, New York: W.W. Norton.

Taylor, F.W. (1911) *The Principles of Scientific Management*, New York: Harper.

Thomson, W. (2001) *A Guide for the Young Economist: Writing and Speaking Effectively about Economics*, Cambridge, MA: MIT Press.

Velthuis, O. (2005) *Talking Prices: Symbolic Meanings of Prices on the Market for Contemporary Art*, Princeton, NJ: Princeton University Press.

Walras, L. (1954) *Elements of Pure Economics*, London: Allen & Unwin.

Woolf, V. (1967) "Mr. Bennett and Mrs. Brown," in *Collected Essays*, Vol. I, New York: Harcourt, Brace and World.

Index

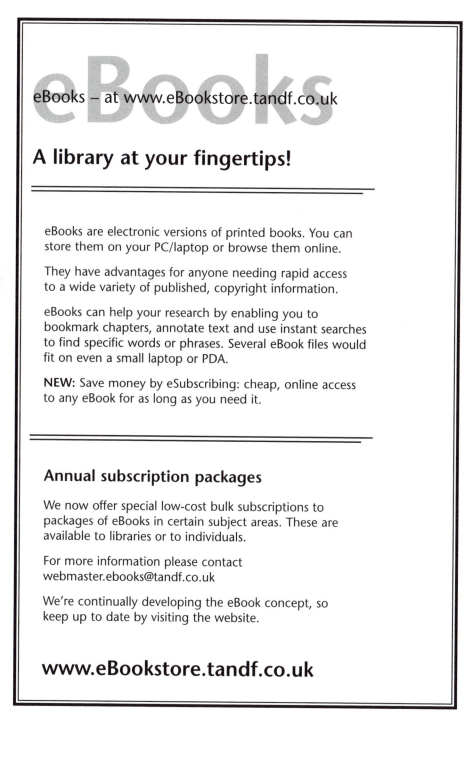